TALES OF TEXAS:
A
COLLECTION
OF
TRUE
SHORT STORIES
~BOOK I~

BY: LYNN HOBBS

Tales of Texas

BOOK I

A COLLECTION
OF TRUE SHORT
STORIES

LYNN HOBBS

Acknowledgements

Special thanks to my son, Jeff Brannon, for not only his encouragement; but his work in creating my book cover, editing, formatting, and publishing my book. Yehovah's blessings to you!

I want to thank my family and friends for their encouragement as well. Blessings to each of you for your support.

It was exciting to watch the word count grow as I continued writing the book!

When it all comes together and falls in place, it is a blessing indeed! I can't say it enough; to Yehovah be the glory!

Dedication

I dedicate this book to Yehovah. I could never make it without Him! I continue learning Torah (that is the first five books of the Bible that are His laws; not man's). His Word is the same yesterday, today, and tomorrow. I praise Yehovah for opening my eyes to man's pagan laws that I no longer practise.

All scripture quoted is either from the Kings James Version or the New Living Translation of the Holy Bible.

Any reference to Yehovah is the Hebrew name for the God of Abraham, Isaac, and Jacob.

Any reference to Yeshua is the Hebrew name for Jesus Christ.

Prologue

Tales of Texas: A Collection of True, Short Stories

I wrote this collection of stories for your reading pleasure. As a Christian daily learning Yehovah's Word, I welcome you to my latest book. Names have been changed in each story unless I state otherwise at the beginning of each.

Some of these stories are tender, and some are tough. They happened to real people. Life isn't always fair. These stories are part of life. Each is followed by an inspiring scripture and the moral of the story.

There is no profanity in any of the stories. I have included a section of fiction stories I wrote at the back of the book as a bonus.

It's easy to reflect on a situation and decide what you should have done. Sometimes bad choices are made, and we suffer the consequences. In living it as it happens, you try to do the best you possibly can without knowing the result. Pray for guidance and Yehovah's's will. If it lines up with Yehovah's Word in the Bible, then it's His will. If not, then it's your will. None of us are perfect. I am certainly not, but I try daily. And I believe in the power of prayer.

You may notice that I use the names *Yeshua* and *Yehovah* instead of *Jesus* and *the LORD*. I do this out of love and reverence for the original Hebrew names. *Yeshua* means "Yehovah saves," and *Yehovah* is the personal name of our Heavenly Father revealed in Scripture. Using these names reminds me of His covenant faithfulness and draws me closer to the roots of my faith.

Are you struggling with something? Is it what you want or what you need? Are you helping or needing help? Inspiring or needing encouragement? These stories are true. I hope you can learn from what others have experienced. Sometimes we are too naïve to see what is happening until it's over. I try to read my Bible daily. It is uplifting to read a scripture that helps with whatever situation you are currently in. I mentioned the word currently as we do not need to stay in the valleys. They are for reaching the top of a mountain, or goal. My faith sees me through! I could not make it without my Heavenly Father!

Some might say, "You're judging by writing these stories." I'm not. Yeshua said in John 7:24, "Look beneath the surface so you can judge correctly." These stories weren't written to condemn anyone. As you read, ask yourself whether this was a blessing or a lesson. My hope is that you find meaning and enjoyment in each one.

Table Of Contents

Chapter Title	Page

One

The Elevator

Longview, Texas was busy and bustling when we arrived. Tires screeched as cars barely stopped from running red lights. It resembled lunch-time traffic with long lines of cars bumper to bumper traveling just over the speed limit.

I'd fixed breakfast, dressed Mom and I, and placed her in her wheelchair earlier. She had Alzheimer's and Dementia, I was her 24/7 caretaker, and this was Doctor Day.

I turned onto Fourth Street to the Towers Medical Center. Her doctor's office was on the fifth floor.

Her eyes sparkled, and with a light, bubbly voice, she belted out the song, "Revive Us Again." I joined in with her.

Circling the packed parking lot I finally found a vacant space in the back lot.

No problem. We were early. I simply wheeled her through the parked cars and maneuvered to the building.

Going inside, we entered the long corridor leading to the two elevators.

You never knew which one would be working. One would always have a handmade sign haphazardly taped to its door stating it was Out of Order.

The two elevators were side by side of each other.

We approached and I glanced down at Mom. "Well, today there's no sign on either door. We have our choice."

We both grinned. I pushed the up button on the elevator on the right side and the doors opened. I backed Mom's wheelchair in, and the doors almost closed when a couple entered and smiled at us.

We smiled back.

They pushed the button for the 2nd floor, and I pushed the one for the fifth floor.

We were off.

It came to a stop on the 2nd floor, and the couple left. The doors shut again.

And nothing happened.

I pushed the button for the fifth floor and the elevator moved up a bit and then stopped.

I was standing behind Mom's wheelchair and holding onto the wheelchair's hand locks when she turned sideways and gazed at me.

"Wouldn't it be something if we were stuck in the elevator?" She chuckled, and I exchanged a brief smile with her. "Yes, it would." I agreed.

I punched the button for the fifth floor again and nothing happened.

I heard the elevator next to us go up the shaft to whatever floor it was going to. When it passed the elevator we were on, ours creaked and slightly shook.

Instantly alarming!

I knew I couldn't upset Mom with her high blood pressure and hypertension. I tried to keep a light conversation going between us as if this wasn't a major problem at all.

We discussed our preference for lunch later after the doctor's appointment. Taco's quickly won!

I pulled out my cellphone and discovered there was no way a signal could get through this metal box we were in. No use trying to call anyone.

I looked around and spotted the red alarm button on the call box of the elevator.

"Press Red Button for Emergency" was written in black letters around the button.

I sighed and pressed the red button.

We'll be out of here in no time, I thought.

I heard static, and then a recorded message came on.

"The number you have reached is no longer a working number. If you feel you have reached this message in error, please call again, or dial your operator."

I laughed out loud and knew we'd had it.

We were stuck indeed!

I stared at the back of my mother's frail body in the wheelchair, and said a silent prayer for Yehovah's help, and for our safety.

Faith over fear!

I could hear distant voices from the lobby below us and yelled at them. "Hey! We are stuck in here! We can't get out. Get someone to help us!"

It got quiet. Everyone in the lobby stopped talking.

I yelled again.

This time they heard me.

"We'll get help! Just hang on!" A man apparently yelled back, but his voice was muffled by the thick metal surrounding us, and the distance. I had to strain to hear him.

Soon, I heard another muffled voice; a woman was yelling that she was the manager and told me her name.

She began yelling questions, and distant conversations seemed to continue on and on. I kept praying to remain calm and trusting my Heavenly Father to help us.

"How many are in the elevator with you?"

"Just myself and my elderly mother."

A man introduced himself as part of the security for the building. He also asked questions.

"How is she doing?"

"She's sitting in her wheelchair, waiting to get out of here."

"How are you feeling?"

"Trying to remain calm, but it's hot in here."

"We'll get help on the way. It won't be long, and we'll get you out."

"Okay." I answered.

I kept glancing at my watch, and five minutes turned into a long, agonizing twenty minutes. It remained unbearably silent during that time. Yet, my relaxed hold onto the wheelchair handles... could have been a tight, white-knuckled grip while our elevator shook when the other one passed us going either up or down. I thanked Yehovah for giving me my newfound capabilities of remaining calm.

I heard people call out to each other, "Someone's stuck on the elevator, don't take the other one. Use the stairs." Then we'd hear them racing out of the lobby.

It grew hotter.

"How are you doing now?" The woman shouted.

"It's getting hard to breathe."

"It won't take much longer. They just arrived in the parking lot."

Startled at this announcement I pleaded, "Who? Who just arrived?"

4

"The fire department." She bellowed.

Oh, my goodness! The fire department! Visions of rescues I'd seen on television flooded my mind. I immediately pictured Mom and I being lifted with ropes and cables through the ceiling of our elevator and felt butterflies in my stomach!

I critically studied each panel of the ceiling, and it was solid. No escape hatch.

Now what?

I prayed again.

I knew I had to trust the Lord and not let doubt creep into my thoughts.

Time marched on, and I did wonder why it took 25 minutes for someone to decide to call the Fire department for help...and then stopped. I didn't know the details of their plan to get us out, but Yehovah did. I was part of His plan. Again, I refused to be negative.

I thought of the song we'd sang earlier; "Revive Us Again." Mom's own mother had taught it to her before she had passed away. Mom was seven years old then. My Grandmother had been ill and had called her sixteen children to come into her bedroom. They surrounded her bed as they sang it with her. She had them promise to remember it and to sing it often. What an incredible woman to think first of her children's spiritualty. She later died, but the song lives on. And it's amazing with Mom's 97 years of jumbled memories that she can still remember the words to her favorite gospel songs.

Such a blessing, I thought.

I assured Mom we would be out soon, and she gave me her sweet little smile.

Relieved she hadn't been nervous and had a heart attack or stroke, and that I had kept her calm; I said another silent prayer of thanks.

Moments later, I heard metal clanging against our elevator doors and voices that seemed to be talking to each other.

Someone repeated, "It won't be much longer, and you'll be out."

I had stopped looking at my watch. Nothing positive could come of it. I'd look at it again when this was over.

It grew eerily quiet for several minutes again.

Suddenly, the doors of the elevator barely opened. I saw just the tips of someone's fingers trying to pry the doors apart. More fingertips appeared at the seam of the two heavy, metal doors.

Then, slowly whole fingers appeared …and finally hands emerged painstakingly pulling the doors apart! They had opened the doors manually!

I yelled "Hallelujah! Thank you, Yeshua!"

The firemen helped us out, and the manager and security officer stood next to them. Big smiles were across all of our faces! I hugged each one, and thanked them for their help, also thanking the manager and the security officer for their encouragement.

We were fine! And no, I didn't sue anyone.

And yes, it took everything I had, but I wheeled Mom to the other elevator and went to her doctor's appointment. We were late. I told them what had happened. They had heard someone was stuck in the elevator, but they sure didn't know it was us.

We later left his office, and yes, I was anxious returning to the ground floor from the fifth floor in the elevator. I also dreaded her next appointment in three months, and it took a lot of prayer, or I'd never have been able to ride in another elevator again.

I reported this to the CEO and told them to update the RED Emergency Button inside the elevator.

Within a few months, Mom's doctor retired, and I found one with a single-story building that even had an awning to unload passengers in wheelchairs during rainy weather! And the doctor is very knowledgeable and caring.

I give Yehovah the glory! And I am so thankful to Him that it all worked out fine!

† † †

Isaiah 41:10 New Living Translation:" Don't be afraid, for I am with you. Don't be discouraged, for I am your God. I will strengthen you and help you. I will hold you up with my victorious right hand."

Psalms 34: 4 New Living Translation: "I prayed to the Lord, and he answered me. He freed me from all my fears."

Philippians 4: 6-7 New Living Translation: "Don't worry about anything; instead, pray about everything. Tell God what you need, and thank Him for all He has done. Then you will experience God's peace, which exceeds anything we can understand. His peace will guard your hearts and minds as you live in Christ Jesus."

Moral of the story: We never know what situation we can suddenly be in. Fear and doubt will make it agonizing with "What If" scenarios. Pray and trust Yehovah. Turn it over to Him, and don't take the problem back!

The End

Chapter Two

The Feisty Woman

We got off to a bad start. I heard a loud noise pounding on my front door and hurried to it. "Must be an emergency," I thought, "for someone to make that much of a commotion." I flung the door open without looking through the peep hole first. Squinting her eyes at me, the strange woman held her hand in mid-air ready to knock again. I looked down at her short frame. She stood rigidly with a deep frown.

"I need to rent your house."

I shook my head in a negative manner. "I'm sorry, it's not for rent. I have it for sale." I pulled the door toward me to close it, and she sputtered.

"You don't understand. I need to move right away. I need to live closer to my daughter."

I thought how I always did a background check on anyone when I did rent the small house out, waited for references to respond, and drove by the potential new renter's old house to see if it and the yard looked to be in a favorable condition, or if it was trashed.

She must have taken my silence as promising to her dilemma. Her frown disappeared. She glanced at the house blessing wall plaque near the front door on my house.

"No, I am sorry," I told her, "But it's no longer for rent. It needs repairs and is not livable."

"Wait!" She cried as I closed the door. "Maybe we can work something out."

"No ma'am, unless you want to buy it." I closed the door and watched her through the peep hole as she walked across the street to the small house. The "For Sale" sign on the tree in the front lawn boldly stated my phone number.

She calmly retrieved her smartphone from her purse and clearly took a snapshot of the sign.

"Oh, great," I thought, "Now she has my phone number. I hope she doesn't harass me with phone calls."

She drove off and I mumbled to myself for opening the door to a stranger in the first place.

Returning to the kitchen, I looked at my son in amazement. "Did you hear that?"

"Yes," he answered in a surprised tone, "I can't imagine anyone wanting to 'work something out' to stay in a house that's unlivable."

"I know. I can't either."

"It's unheard of." My daughter-in-law Miranda added.

We finished our visit. It was a long drive home for them as he and his wife lived out of state. They packed their luggage into the car, and we hugged goodbye. Excited waves were exchanged as they left. I prayed for their safety and went back inside.

Pouring myself another cup of coffee, I was about to enjoy my first sip when something caught my eye from the kitchen window. Some kind of movement, brief, but I saw it. I walked closer to the window, and gasped. It was the short, older woman again.

I marched outside. She and a younger woman were peeping in the windows of the house across the street. An older model Buick was parked near the carport. The chipping white paint on the vehicle displayed small areas with rust. Gray duct tape covered an entire passenger window by the rear door on the left side. "Texas license plate. Good tread on the tires." I said under my breath.

"Hello" I yelled and continued marching towards them.

They turned and greeted me with big smiles across their faces.

"Can I help you?" I gave them my full attention.

The older woman had to walk around a tree to approach me, and I noticed her one, long, gray braided pigtail hanging halfway down her back. She wore blue jeans and a short-sleeved shirt. I would guess she was about 67 years old. She was clean. They both were. The younger woman appeared to be about 35 years old. She wore cut off shorts and a tight tank top.

"Yes ma'am. I'm Sallie Mae Jones and this is my daughter, Kat. This place looks okay to us, and I really need to rent it right away. I've been praying for a place to live," her voice rose in pitch, and she instantly had tears in her eyes. "This is an answer to prayer!"

I looked at her wrinkled face and could see the desperation in her eyes. I felt her response tugging at my Christian values.

"I told you earlier, it's not livable. It's in the middle of being remodeled, and the gas is shut off."

"Kat's husband builds houses. We can do the work here, whatever it needs. We could take it off the rent and…"

"No, I am sorry. It has a water leak under the house and under the kitchen sink. It is not livable now."

"But I need to live closer to my daughter." She moaned.

Kat spoke with a strong southern accent. "My mama was taking care of my Granny for the last three years and Granny passed away last week. Mama has nowhere to go and can't stay there anymore. Granny was renting, she didn't own her house."

"Why can't your Mama stay with you?" I questioned.

They both laughed.

10

"Kat and her husband have a two-bedroom home and their son, his wife and their two grandchildren live with them. They don't have room to turn around in." Sallie Mae laughed again.

"We did put Mama's boxes and her furniture in our barn, along with Granny's belongings. That's all we could do. I only live ten miles from here, so if she rented this house, we could visit often. We'd help her get everything in order here. It would be no problem." Kat sounded sincere.

They looked so pitiful, but I had been lied to before. I'd had strangers more convincing with lies spewing from their lips sweeter than any honey a bee could ever produce. And could trash a rent house faster than you could eat a hamburger.

"I'll have to think about it."

"Oh, thank you." They blurted and climbed into the car. "God bless you. We'll call you later."

I nodded and crossed the street without waving bye. I smelt heavy cigarette smoke on both, and I didn't rent to smokers. Everything inside the house would smell of smoke after they left.

She did see my Christian wall plaque near my front door earlier. "Is she playing off that, or is she for real?" I pondered out loud. As a Christian I'd help someone I thought was sincere until they did something to break my trust. Lately, all I'd encountered were conniving liars.

"Dear Lord, should I help these people?" I prayed. "I can't see their heart. Only You know if it's pure. And only You are the Savior. I'm not. There is only so much I can do. So many good people do need help, maybe I should let them earn my trust first. Maybe I've been too fast to swim across the river instead of treading water first…to test it out. Is it too cold, too warm, or about to be caught up in a storm? Lord, I pray for Your guidance, and Your Will to be done. In Yeshua's name I pray, Amen."

I glanced at the house the woman wanted to rent. It was vacant. I didn't have anyone wanting to buy it. There was a possibility Sallie Mae, Kat, and her husband could do some repairs on the house instead of me spending money and hiring someone. I wouldn't be out anything. What

11

could possibly go wrong? I tried being objective but decided it seemed like a workable solution for all of us. Was I jumping into this too fast again? Time would tell.

Yes, against my better judgement, I decided to rent to Sallie Mae Jones.

She called within an hour. Apparently, she had me on speakerphone. When I told her I agreed to renting it on a trial basis, she and her daughter both hollered in excitement.

"Okay, ladies; we'll try the arrangement for thirty days. If it doesn't work out to my satisfaction, you must leave. The rent is six hundred a month, and you pay the utilities to me. They are in my name. The gas will remain turned off. You are expected to take your trash off. No pets, and no smoking. I have a written contract for renting or leasing. Of course, we'll have to make more detailed arrangements with this situation as it is."

They verbally agreed and began moving her belongings into the house within the hour. Of course, we walked through the house while I showed them what worked and what didn't work. The stove was not working. She instantly insisted on cooking outside on her bar-b-q pit. I agreed. New doors I'd bought were leaning in doorways to be installed. She announced she'd place all of them inside the large walk-in closet in the second bathroom. The new vent-a hood I'd bought was sitting on the floor near the island stove. Again, she said she'd put it in the large closet with the doors. She signed the 30-day contract. I added that any repairs she did would be brought to my attention first so we could agree on how much money would be deducted from the rent for her work. No problem.

After moving her in, both women mowed the lawn, edged around the concrete walkway, and even dug and transplanted flower bulbs that were appearing at random in the front lawn. Kat took some to her home. No one asked about that, but it was okay with me. They proceeded to remove the Hosta plants behind the house and place all of them in a row in the front flower bed. Again, no one asked, but I didn't care about moving the plants.

After the lawn had been given a new landscape, Kat left. I watched as Sallie Mae took a ladder and washed all the outside windows of the house. Washed and rinsed each one, by herself.

"Where does she get this energy, and how can she stay constantly busy?" I wondered.

Later. it took three men to unload her bar-b-q pit. It was on wheels, massive, and heavy. Black, with a grill and smoker pit attached, they placed it under the front covered porch near the kitchen's entry of glass double doors.

Kat would help her mom for hours each day, then return to her own home. I soon learned that her husband had been injured on the job and couldn't work. He was taking pain pills that were expensive, and this kept her from buying groceries like she was previously used to buying. She cooked for four adults and two children. Sallie Mae was now cooking for herself. Kat complained to me about the price of bread going up to four dollars a loaf and how difficult it was to even fix sandwiches for her family.

I thought of my brand-new bread maker machine I'd only used once. I didn't like it and preferred making my bread by hand.

"I have a bread-maker machine I no longer use, if you'd like it." I offered.

She opened her eyes wide and her mouth fell open. "What? Are you kidding? Yes, I want it!" She gushed. "Years ago, I worked in a bakery. I loved it and always loved making bread. I could never afford to buy one, but I know how to make all kinds of bread. God bless you!"

"Well great, I'll give it to you. If anyone deserves it, you do." I smiled and went home, returning with the machine. I brought all the attachments, measuring cups, etc. and put them in the back seat as she swung the car's back door open. Her grin widened across her face, and she jumped up and down with excitement.

The bread maker had found a good home.

A few days went by, and I overheard someone cursing as I walked to the mailbox near the street. The neighbors weren't at home. Surely, it wasn't Sallie Mae…

It was.

I followed the ranting of foul language to the back of the rent house and gasped.

There she was, removing the metal underpinning from the length of the mobile home, displaying everything underneath it. Water pipes, insulation, air conditioner/ heater ducts, all were now exposed a few feet off the ground; but still attached to the bottom of the home. So far, that is.

I was speechless. I marched toward her. She was like a tiny ant running from section to section of the side of the house jerking at the metal material.

"Feisty, that's the word my late father-in-law would use for a description of her at this moment." I thought with irony.

"What are you doing?"

She flinched. Slowly, she turned to face me and let out an exaggerated deep breath. "I'm going to fix the water leak under the kitchen sink, dear. I must remove this so I can see what I'm doing. It's too dark under there."

"We agreed to discuss a repair before it's done." I replied.

Laughing, she shook her head. "I guess I got carried away. I'm tired now, so I'll get under there tomorrow and look for the leak. If I find it, I'll let you know. Don't worry, I'll put it all back."

I nodded and left.

Within an hour, I smelt the aroma coming from her bar-b-q pit and decided it was nice to have someone living across the street after all. No one is perfect, and her cursing may have been a bad moment for her; not her usual daily language. After all, she was doing hard labor for a woman her age. She did look frail.

14

Later that day, I had to make a quick trip to the grocery store and walked to her front door first.

"Do you need anything from the store? I am going into town and can pick something up for you." I inquired.

She wiped her brow with a hand towel. "No, but thank you."

"Alright then, I'll be right back."

I walked across her front yard when she silently caught up with me and motioned to be quiet.

Frowning, I followed where she was pointing and saw it.

A snake. And not just any snake, a water moccasin, or cotton-mouth as the locals called it. They are venomous, aggressive, and will chase you.

"I'll go get my gun." I whispered to her.

"No, stand by the bar-b-q pit. I'll go get my machete. It's closer."

My mind whirled. "A machete? She's going to kill that big snake with a long knife. She's only going to be an arm's length away from it…and it strikes at you from a farther distance than that," I thought. I turned to get my pistol, but she arrived instantly brandishing that machete in the air like a sword.

The snake was under the lattice that held the climbing roses in the front flower bed. She and Kat had transplanted the row of Hosta plants in front of it days earlier.

There was no stopping her.

The snake drew its curved body together tighter and raised its head as she approached. Long fangs appeared as the mouth instantly opened about to strike and bite her when the machete came down upon it in one mighty blow. Her one long, gray, braid of hair swung across her back as she continued one blow after another on the snake.

She did it. She cut it in half.

15

I was appalled at what this frail, elderly woman did.

"Stand back." She yelled. "It can still bite." She finished cutting the head off the snake and pitched the whole thing into the street.

That was a common practice here in the country. It warned others to be careful as a snake was in the area. They usually travel in pairs.

"That was incredible." I told her. I honestly can't believe she had the gumption to do that!

"Oh, that's nothing. Years ago, when we lived on the river, and my husband took off and left me and our three kids, I had to kill snakes. No one else was around to do it. You learn fast." She laughed and did a little happy dance. "That one's gone now."

I left to drive to the store not knowing if she meant the husband or the snake. It was comforting to know she could take care of herself, but at the same time sad to imagine what she had endured all those years ago.

The following day, she knocked on my door.

"I hate to bother you, but I need help with the wires. I didn't know wires would be there and they are in the way."[i] She addressed me solemnly.

"What are you talking about?" I blurted.

"That vent-a-hood over the stove. I took it out of the ceiling, and wires are hanging out of the hole." Calm as she could be, she stood in front of me as if this were a simple request for help like borrowing a cup of sugar or using your telephone. Just a simple task. Just a little help.

"Oh, no!" I groaned. I knew she was used to taking care of herself, and had taken care of her own mother, but this was too much independence.

And she had gone against our agreement again. It was supposed to be no work until we discussed it first.

I ran across the street to the house and slid the glass sliding doors open to the kitchen. There it was. Or there it used to be. The vent-a hood lay on top of the gas burner stove, and yes, wires were hanging down from the hole in the ceiling where it had been. The new vent-a-hood lay on the floor untouched.

"I can't believe you did this." I moaned.

"Well, the new one was laying there on the floor and I thought I'd install it for you."

"Sallie Mae, I told you not to do anything until we talked about it first."

"You are being too picky." She huffed and walked outside.

I followed her and instead of sitting on the front porch chairs where she was, I went to the back yard.

"Uh huh!" My gut feeling was right, she had never put the underpinning back on the mobile home. I pivoted and returned to the front porch. She sat smoking a cigarette.

"Sallie Mae, it looks like you won't be here for the whole thirty days. You have one week left in our contract. I suggest you read it again and do what we agreed. All I'm seeing is one mess after another."

"And you have everything that works over there, so don't yell at me." She raised her voice defiantly.

"I have never yelled at you, and you are wrong. Two of my kitchen wall plugs went out and must be rewired."

"Well, you're no better off than I am." She smirked and went back into the house, slamming the glass doors shut.

I saw her dial someone on her phone and I left as she began a conversation.

Her loud voice penetrated the walls, and I could distinctly hear cursing again.

"Where did she get that attitude?" I thought in amazement as she changed right before my eyes. I sure wasn't hearing any of the "God bless you" sweet phrases like I had heard from her earlier. But that's it!

17

That's all it was …just a phrase to say at the right moment; no meaning of true blessings behind it.

That's when I realized it was not Yehovah's Will for her to be here or for me to help her. I rushed into the arrangement way too fast. I should have become more acquainted with her to recognize she wasn't what she showed to be. Certainty not a Christian…a true Christian would not destroy your property. She had acted like a poor helpless elderly woman and used that act to move in.

It was getting dark outside, so I went in and fixed supper. I could not get her off my mind. I prayed about the whole situation and asked for guidance in the matter. I washed the dishes and noticed her car leaving. She left the porch light out though. That was odd. She would need that light to walk up the steps and get back into the house. Strange indeed.

I put a load of clothes in the washing machine and set the timer to go off when it finished. Next, I poured myself a cup of coffee, adding a teaspoon of the thick liquid from a can of Eagle Brand Condensed milk. Sprinkled a bit of ground ginger in the cup, along with a few sprinkles of ground Ceylon cinnamon. Placed it in the microwave for a minute, stirred it and yum! So good! And no chemicals!

I'd been in my recliner for a few minutes with my coffee when I heard her car door slam. I jumped up and peeped out the window. It looked like she was bringing clothes either in or out of the house, and I thought I saw something move on the ground near her.

"She must have dropped something." I thought. "Leave her alone, what she does is none of my business." I put her out of my mind then, reheated my coffee, and enjoyed the rest of it.

The next day I thought I heard a dog bark. A large dog.

"Hmm, maybe one of my neighbors' dogs got loose." I dismissed it and went on with my day. I was in the kitchen baking when I heard her door slam again. I glanced out the kitchen window and noticed Sallie Mae with an armful of clothes on coat hangers laying across her arm.

18

"Wonder if she is moving out?" I thought and watched for a while longer. She had another bundle of clothes on coat hangers and placed them in the back seat of her car again.

"Hmm, could be."

At that moment I heard the same deep bark of a large dog I'd heard earlier, and this time he appeared. There it was. The dog was a white pit bull with an extremely large head. It was white faced with pinkish blotches. It was huge and well-muscled. And it came out of my rent house.

I was furious! Enough was enough! Time to go. I called her daughter and told her to come and get her. It wasn't working out, and she had to leave.

She was so sorry and so soft-spoken. But she came within the hour and helped her mother pack her belongings.

I went inside to inspect the house, and Sallie Mae was very quiet. I noticed the lower cabinet doors open under the stove in the kitchen island.
"I'm sorry, but I thought the dog would sleep there and you'd never know it was here, but it ate through both shelves."

"It did what?" I spun around and went to the kitchen and saw what remained of the jagged edged pieces of shelving still in place. I shook my head in disbelief. "Why did you even bring the dog in here? You knew no pets allowed."

"I was scared at night. Someone in the woods was shining a red light into the living room, you know the kind of tiny light a cat will play with in the air and try to catch? "

"I don't know why anyone would do that." I answered. "What a complete mess. This is ruined." I shook my head again and spotted a lot of gray duct tape in a kitchen window. I walked over to it. "What in the world is this?" I exclaimed and walked closer.

My two-ton air conditioner unit was gone from the window, and in its place was a small air conditioner. It was sitting in the large hole made by

19

the larger AC unit and had duct tape across the top and bottom of the window holding it together so it would not fall out.

Kat spoke first. "I was going to tell you it quit working, so we put it in the carport. We bought a new one at Lowes. Here's the remote to it." She handed me the device, and I just sat it down on the counter.

"How did you ever remove that heavy AC unit from that window?"

"It took us awhile, but we did it. I got a dolly to take it to the carport." Kat answered.

"And I thought she was moving out the other day, I saw a lot of clothes coming and going from her car."

"Oh, I've been drying their clothes. Kat washes them but their dryer went out, so I go get them and dry them for her." Sallie Mae proudly informed me. "But your dryer went out last night." She added.

"I've heard enough. I'm giving you until tomorrow night to move out." I said and drew my mouth together to keep anything else from coming out that I might regret.

I walked out and Kat yelled, "Wait."

I turned and faced her as she ran after me.

"I called a Senior Living Center in Louisiana, and they have room for her. We used my Granny's Louisiana address as she can't have a Texas address. I put your name as a reference, and they will call you. If you give a good reference she can live there. I have to think of her future. She is my elderly mother."

"Kat, you already figured she'd be leaving. And you want a good reference from me? So, it is all up to me?" I felt my blood pressure rise and tried to control my anger.

 I turned and faced Sallie Mae. "You should be the one responsible for your actions."

Before I could say anything else, Sallie Mae grinned. "You tell them you saw me washing windows, they'll like that," she said.

Kat was busy moving her belongings back into their cars.

Yes, the manager of the Senior Living Center called, and yes, I said I watched her washing windows.

The next day and her last one here, her two brothers arrived in a dented, old truck to move her bar-b-q- pit. Sallie Mae came outside, grinned and put her hands on her hips.

"Since you were nice to me, I'll be nice to you. I'll take all my garbage to the dump. I won't leave it for you to haul off." I was shocked as they removed 11 large trash bags from the utility building and put them into the truck. She had hidden all that trash when I thought she was taking it off each week!

Later that day, she was completely moved out.

I was to learn the following week while I was mowing grass in that backyard that she had buried a large metal bucket in the ground. It was full of sand and her cigarette butts. It had been rained on and stunk badly.

And that's the moral of this true story. Sin stinks. It makes a mess and grows into a larger mess.

And how did I know having her as a renter was not Yehovah's will? His Word lines up with the Bible, hers did not.

† † †

 Psalm 41:1 Blessed is he who considers the poor: the LORD will deliver him in time of trouble.

Psalm 39:1 I said, I will take heed to My ways, that I sin not with My tongue: I will keep My mouth with a bridle, while the wicked is before Me.

John 8:7 So when they continued asking Him, He lifted up Himself, and said unto them, He who is without sin among you, let him first cast a stone at her.

"Sin will take you farther than you want to go, keep you longer than you want to stay, and cost you more than you want to pay." - R. G. Lee.

Second moral of the story: You cannot help everyone. You are not someone's Savior. Sometimes they must help themselves and seek Yehovah's guidance through prayer.

The End

Chapter Three

Walter and Wilma

I have met many people in my life, but none stand out as much as Walter and Wilma. Of course, their names have been changed, but many will recognize them regardless.

For many years, they owned a popular catfish restaurant in rural N. E. Texas on a river that also had the best, juiciest, tenderest steaks you could ever enjoy anywhere.

Mrs. Wilma would visit customers at each table and knew everyone by their names. This is an incredible feat in itself as they would have hundreds of customers daily during the summer. Other times of the year they had steady business but not two or three hundred from the time they opened until they closed late that night. She not only asked how they were doing but asked about their extended family too.

Mrs. Wilma was genuine. With a warm smile, her customers became long-time friends. You could watch her face light up as she saw someone come in that she hadn't seen in a while. That smile would spread across her face and her eyebrows shot up with excitement. You felt her gladness at that moment.

And the catfish dinners? Nothing could compare. The fish were crisp fried in corn meal; the hush puppies were with or without chopped jalapeno peppers in the batter. Cole slaw was fresh; hand stirred in a number three washtub. Relish tray provided with the meal, and French fries that were not greasy. The menu offered much more but those were the specialties.

Walter personally grilled the steaks. He always loved visiting with the customers and would strike up a conversation with all of them. The restaurant had a wonderful family atmosphere.

23

Did it get loud inside the restaurant? Oh, yes!

I honestly don't think anyone would have considered themselves to have been part of a rowdy group. It was just joyously loud on weekends. You would experience the same feeling as if you walked in at a reunion and saw an old friend across the room and happily yelled a greeting to them, and they stood from their table and yelled back waving at you to come over.

Informal? Yes, and it couldn't have been any better! Chatter from all the tables full of customers would drown out the music from the jukebox.

Yet when someone at a table prayed over the food, it got quiet, and there was respect for their right to pray. You often saw many stopping to bless and give thanks for the food before they ate.

Even waiting outside, standing in line to enter was not a problem. It was well worth it. People would nod at each other often striking up conversations with total strangers, as they viewed the river and the smell of freshly fried fish wafted through the air.

Then the unthinkable happened.

They were robbed late one night while the restaurant was packed with customers.

The robbers came by boat, each wearing a mask.

They were never caught.

It did prompt Walter to obtain a license to buy and sell guns and ammunition in the restaurant. He was a former law officer from a larger city and was determined not to be a target for crooks again.

And no one robbed Walter and Wilma, or their customers, after that.

Through the years of operating their business, many employes became like family to the childless couple as well. Waitresses, busboys, cooks, kitchen helpers, and wait staff.

They cared for one older man in particular, Brother Chico Perez. Well known in the community, he carried off the many metal barrels of trash from the kitchen each night...and talked constantly while doing his work. He would chuckle and laugh at his own stories and was a delight to be around. Everyone loved him, especially Walter and Wilma.

Very few people knew that Brother Chico was stealing from them.

I lived in the area and never heard about it until many years later.

He would remove a fourth of the trash from the top of the trash barrels and place a layer of heavy paper there. Then, he'd put entire plastic packages of rib-eye steaks, T-bone steaks, and fileted fish in their own plastic bags inside with crumpled paper on top to conceal the meat. The barrels lid would be placed on top of the barrel, and he'd load everything into his truck.

He sold meat for years without getting caught.

And no, I never knew anyone he sold to.

At that time, my young husband was hunting and fishing on weekends when he was off of work. He'd come home with a feral hog. It was so ugly with the coarse hair sticking up sparsely from its skin...and that nasty snout! I refused to eat it, but he would clean and process it. The meat was beautiful. He'd package it in white, butcher paper and either give it or sell it to friends. I never knew what he did with it. He would trap catfish in wire baskets for our freezer, and he also went frog gigging. I learned how to pull the leaders apart in the legs to prevent the legs from jumping in the hot grease while I fried them. The last time I ate one was when I opened the frog and found a dead fly inside. I gagged.

I no longer eat pork, frog legs, shrimp, or catfish. They are all bottom feeders and eat poop. Besides, the Bible states they are unclean. It would be the same thing as you sitting down to eat a buzzard. They are natures garbage can. And yes, they do have parasites.

Anyway, the point is that at that time, in my area, it was not unusual for anyone to sell or trade for food. This was about fifty years ago. My husband often bought an entire dressed and quartered deer for twenty dollars. A local farmer with a rural garden, growing peas, would shoot the deer in his pea patch. He put the clean meat in a waxed, large chicken box that came from meat markets to the stores. His son would bring it to your house after dark.

So, with all of that going on, it's no wonder Brother Chico never got caught.

I heard that some of his customers asked their friends if they wanted to buy meat from Brother Chico and those people turned out to be friends of Walter and Wilma.

The couple found out about it, and the stealing and selling of meat came to a halt for Bro. Chico.

But he didn't get fired. He didn't go to jail.

Walter and Wilma talked to him, and he apologized.

Very few people even know this happened, much less that they forgave him.

Business went on as usual…only without meat leaving the restaurant being concealed.

Much later, Brother Chico became deathly ill.

Walter and Wilma visited him daily in the hospital.

They paid for whatever he needed.

And they gave him love.

The three were still as close as a family when he passed away.

And unlike today, it was not made known publicly what they did for him. There was no public pat on the back for helping him.

It was genuine, and it is still how Christians actions should speak for themselves.

† † †

Matther 19: 21-22 (New Living Translation)

Then Peter came to Him and asked, "Lord, how often should I forgive someone who sins against me? Seven times?"

"No, not seven times," Jesus replied, "but seventy times seven!"

Moral of the story: Don't be quick to ruin someone's life or reputation because of a mistake they made. Stealing is a temptation that can be overpowering to a person in poverty. Sincere repentance is genuine, and you can tell the difference if someone is truly sorry for their bad decision to steal. They will never do it again.

The End

Chapter Four

Molly

This name was not changed. Molly is her real name.

High stepping down the middle of our secluded, country road; the red Irish Setter held her head high. Clumps of matted hair flopped across bald splotches. Mange? Hot spots? I had never seen this animal before. I decided the dog must have been dumped into our neighborhood by its owner. My heart ached as I watched the dog glancing left and right. It appeared to search for something, or someone. The owner?

Four houses dotted the area surrounded by woods and overflowing creek beds. No longer in my line of vision, I could only guess which house the dog may have marched towards. Harsh voices yelled breaking the stillness of the evening. "Get out of here, go on, get." I peered out of my kitchen window in time to see the dog scramble back to the road and head straight into the woods.

I knew coyotes killed several of the area feral cats before and some of my neighbors' chickens. Not a good place to go, I mumbled aloud grabbing my jacket in the foyer and heading outside. I scanned the area and could no longer see the dog. Coyotes had become bold in rushing after prey in broad open daylight and hid just behind the tree line of the woods. I positioned myself in the exact spot the dog had been when it charged into the woods and focused on any movement among the bushes. Not even a leaf fell. Silence. I tried whistling. No response.

"Hey! Have you seen a dog running by?"

Startled, I turned in the direction of the voice. My neighbor, Bob, approached from near the end of the road.

"Yes, I saw a dog, I think someone dumped it here overnight."

He ran and caught up with me. "No, that's Molly. I adopted her. She escapes ever so often and tries to find her former owner. She was abandoned."

"How cruel! To abandon anything is cold-hearted!" I blurted.

"Her owner did not abandon the dog. It's a long story. The dog was left at the homesite by the owner's relatives."

"Really? What homesite?"

"See that 8 x 10 storage building on the lot near the end of the road?"

"Yes."

"Well, the daughter had her mother move into it."

"She lived in it?"

"Yes, ma'am. The daughter and her husband didn't work…they lived off the elderly woman's social security check. They lived in their own 8 x 10 storage building until the elderly woman demanded control of her finances. I talked to her when she'd walk her dog, Molly. She finally returned to her home in another state believing the couple would take care of her dog. That's when the couple sold their property and moved away leaving the dog to fend for itself. I brought Molly home that afternoon. The dog apparently remembers the elderly lady, and searches for her often. It will lay near the woman's 8 x 10 storage building and whine."

"How sad for the dog, and what horrible treatment for the woman."

"Yes, but that's drug addicts. All they care about is their drugs. At least they can't use the elderly woman anymore, and the dog's taken care of."

"It's like picking up pieces discarded from someone's life."

"I guess you could say that ma'am."

Cupping his hands over his mouth, he hollered, "Molly! Molly! Come on girl! Molly!"

I watched as the dog emerged from a pine thicket and galloped towards him. He bent and gently patted her back. Wagging her tail, she made eye contact with him, and quickly licked his hand. Their bond was clearly growing. He stood and nodded at me, and the two of them departed walking side by side down the middle of the road to his house.

Two weeks later, I noticed a well-groomed red Irish Setter with short stubs of hair growing all over its body. Yes, it was Molly. She trotted beside her new owner, and I smiled as she held her head high with the wind ruffling her new hair.

† † †

This was a true story, and like Bob literally being there to take care of Molly.

Proverbs 12:10 (NLT) The godly care for their animals, but the wicked are always cruel.

Moral of the story: Every dumped or stray animal deserves to be treated kindly. They cannot help the situation they are in. And just like humans, they have feelings and memories too.

The End

Chapter Five

Mr. Hollister

I sat in the car with my future ex-husband. He insisted I go into the grocery store and apply for a job. He was more ...in my face...than encouraging me for this endeavor.

It meant so much to him for me to get this job. He was almost desperate.

I thought of all I was doing, and while I enjoyed everything I did, I couldn't see how I could work in a full-time, 40-hour weekly job. I canned produce from our garden, worked the garden, drove our two sons to school and to band practice (they weren't old enough to drive), did the checkbook statements, mowed the yard, cleaned our home and cooked for us...along with cleaning his office and doing the bookwork there.

"I'll do it for him," I thought.

I sighed, exiting the car and walked across the parking lot.

Little did I know how working at this grocery store would forever change my life.

I went through the front door and asked for the manager, Mr. Hollister.

He was well known and well thought of in the community. He offered the Boy Scouts free use of the store's water for their many car wash fundraisers each summer. And the Girl Scouts often had their tables placed on the store's sidewalk to sell their cookies.

He was a Major in the U.S. Army having served in World War II, Korea, and Vietnam; before retiring and taking the job as manager at this store in a national grocery chain. Most in the town were aware that he received the Honored Medals of Bronze Star, Purple Heart, and Oak Leaf Cluster for his service.

I knew nothing about him at this time.

This was in the mid 1970's.

I climbed the stairs to his office and knocked on his door.

I heard his loud, "Come in" and pushed the door open.

He remained seated and raised his eyebrows at me.

Instantly, I made eye contact with him and held it. "Good morning, I am here to apply for a position with your store."

He stood then. "Have a seat." He motioned me to one of the two chairs in front of his desk.

"Tell me what you can do to help my store." He gazed at me intently. No smile. No nonsense.

"I give 100% of myself in anything I do. I am quick to learn, and I am a people person. I have always taken an interest in people, and I am just naturally friendly."

He said something under his breath I couldn't distinguish. But he pulled an application from his desk drawer and handed it to me.

"Take this with you, fill it out. Return it to me this afternoon."

"I will," I said, taking it from him. "Thank you."

I turned to leave, and he nodded at me returning to whatever he had been working on before I interrupted him.

No encouragement whatsoever.

I trekked down the stairs and noticed two other young women looking at all the shelves high on the walls of the back room full of inventory. The walls were over 20 feet high. It was impressive.

"We're looking for the manager's office. Do you know where it is?"

I smiled. "You're close. It's right up these stairs."

"Thanks. We're hoping to work here."

"So am I."

We grinned and I left.

Entering the car, my husband was ecstatic.

"You got the job! I knew you would."

"No. I just got an application. I will return it this afternoon. But thankfully I did get an application." I smiled.

He nodded and seemed to be happy with the proceedings of this potential job.

I did get the job, and I was the last full-time employee to be hired over the next decade.

I began training the following day.

The front-end supervisor was a woman who could easily be the future woman with a mega-phone at an LGBTQ rally in 2025.

But I didn't know this at the time.

Most men customers would enjoy discussing what homemade ingredients she used for her fish bait. She was relaxed with them and seemed like "one of the good o' boys." It was mind-boggling to me how she could be heard laughing with them versus how she treated employees.

She seemed to delight in finding the most deformed fruit to display on a table...with a number by each one...for checkers to name each one on a test paper.

No one ever passed the "name the fruit" test.

Then it was memorizing the code for each fruit and vegetable.

Another 'test' she enjoyed giving was to place items in a cart and send a "mystery shopper" through your check-out line. As the checker greeted the customer, checked the items on the bottom of the cart first, requested coupons from the customer, counted their money back to them out loud, thanked her /him for shopping with us, and handed them their receipt; the supervisor loudly announced, "you failed!"

Of course, every customer within hearing range would gasp and look at you surprised.

She would proudly grab a magazine that you checked and placed in a bag...hold it up by its spine and flip the pages apart. A package of gravy mix would fall out that she had wedged between the pages.

I learned to sort the customers items onto the conveyer belt in groups: cold items, canned items, soft items, etc. We were taught how to use the cash register and to turn it on and off after each customer...to speed up our hourly production rate. And in between all of this we were told to always be friendly to the customer.

 I did learn quickly. Later, when business was slow; I'd arrange the items on the conveyer belt to form a sentence on the receipt. Example: Little Debbie, lettuce, meat, Sloppy Joe. It was fun, and the customers enjoyed what I was doing. Soon it caught on, and other employees did it too.

I also learned how the store used psychology in placing items to sale at the end of each aisle on shelves called an end-cap. Women were targeted for impulse buying. It worked. To this day, I refuse to buy anything placed for sale on an end-cap. And they used mood music on the shoppers. It worked too.

The manager had one office in the back room where I had originally met him and another one upstairs overlooking the line of check out registers. He sat behind a two-way mirror and watched everyone; employees for making mistakes and customers for shoplifting.

Our store was more than a grocery store at that time.

It had a shoe department, a fabric department with a large table to cut material, clothes, a dressing room to try on clothes, a full meat market with butchers, glassware department, and towels, etc.

A few checkers were later placed in charge of these departments and checked groceries only when the store was busy with customers.

I was the manager of the shoe department. (One of my best friends was the manager of the fabric department.)

For example, I would set up summer displays of flip-flop shoes with a summer umbrella with sunscreen, picnic items, etc. to give customers ideas of how they'd enjoy buying these items. I ordered shoes for the whole family, placed them on shelves, and kept the area neat, clean, and visually appealing.

Sounds wonderful, right?

Wrong.

Whoever had the shoe department also had to climb the 20-foot ladder in the backroom and remove the heavy shoe boxes off the shelves. If you needed to add to one type of shoes that had nearly sold out, you often had to open several boxes to locate the same kind…as they were not marked by children, men, or women's shoes. It could be time consuming.

On one such occasion, I was at the top of the ladder and opened two boxes. All the shoe boxes were huge and extremely heavy.

Suddenly, Mr. Hollister burst through the double doors into the back room.

"They are calling you on the store intercom to come and check on the front end." He yelled.

"I'm sorry, sir, but there is no speaker back here. I couldn't hear it. I was about to bring some shoe boxes down."

"Get down from there." He demanded rudely.

I carefully climbed down the tall ladder.

He climbed up.

"You want shoes?" He hollered, "Well, catch these."

He moved box after box off the shelf and pitched them towards me. The first box landed on the concrete floor near me, burst apart, and men's tennis shoes bounced into the air striking me. I moved away as box after box hit the floor and burst open from a twenty-foot drop. Shoes were flying everywhere!

"Stop! You're hurting me!" I screamed as I covered my head and ran.

Two employees heard me and rushed into the back room.

Both took a long look at him standing at the top of the ladder and the busted boxes around me.

He suddenly remained still.

"All of you go on and get back to work. Now!" He ordered.

There was no one to report him to. We went back to work.

Incident after incident began mounting.

Alice was the older woman in charge of the fabric department. She had several rent houses and didn't need to work, but she loved her job. She too, loved people.

The first time I heard her crying, I decided it was none of my business. She was alone in the break room. Maybe something happened at her home, and she was remembering it. I gave her the privacy I thought she needed.

The next time I heard her crying; I saw Mr. Hollister racing from the cutting table and saw bolts of material unrolled on the floor.

I instantly thought of those busted, thrown boxes of shoes on the floor in the back room.

"Hey, are you okay?" I asked gently.

"No." She whimpered. "I can't believe he talked to me like that. I try so hard to do a good job and please him."

"Some people you cannot please."

"But to curse at you…"

"What happened?"

"I was folding a bolt of material that a woman wanted 3 yards from. She had left, and he walked by and looked at me and stopped.

"Is that all you've got to do? Stand there? I'm tired of having a high employee cost on my profit sheet! Get to work. Do something." He yelled.

She continued telling me that he started cursing and throwing material everywhere.

Cursing became his way of dealing with stressful situations. More and more often, employees experienced his wrath.

The employees of our store became like family. We watched out for each other. We visited each other's homes. We prayed for each other, and we prayed together.

It wasn't long and we voted to be a Union store. I was voted to be the Union Steward of Local 504 of the UFCW. (It was the United Food & Commercial Workers Union, but the local number is one I made up.)

Now, if someone were treated badly, we had an organization to report it to.

And we did.

Juanita was a very sweet, hardworking young woman. She had been an employee for two years and was happily married and eight months pregnant. Mr. Hollister seemed annoyed by her presence, and I overheard him tell the manager of the meat department that she should be at home and not working out in public with her condition.

Sometimes you could watch his eyes squint as he followed every movement she made at the checkout counter.

It wasn't that busy and he decided to have Juanita do other work.

That wasn't so unusual. Sometimes we would go into the walk-in freezer, load ice cream or frozen food onto a long metal cart and take it to restock the frozen food department. Other times, we'd restock the spices that were displayed on the shelves in alphabetical order, making it easy to work the product quickly.

But this time was different.

This time no one had been told to do this job.

Mr. Hollister told Juanita, at eight months pregnant, to work all night, Tuesday night, from 11pm until 7am scrubbing the public restrooms. He stated he would inspect them at 7am when he came to work on Wednesday morning, and she wasn't to leave that morning until he inspected them, and they had passed the inspection.

I reported it instantly to the Union representative.

I was told that yes, she had to do it.

He said if the manager wanted her to sweep the parking lot all night, she had to do it. Refusing any job would be giving him a right to fire her. As long as he paid her regular hourly wage, she had to do any work he assigned.

She did it.

I still don't see how she squeezed in between the stalls with her huge belly and got on her hands and knees and did it.

But she did and the restroom was spotless.

After that, all employees were cordial to him. No one was rude to him, but they were never friendly towards him again.

He never asked her or anyone else to clean the public restrooms after that episode. It had been the one and only time.

I reported him almost every week.

When the candy bars get slightly warm, they'd also get tiny, needle size holes in the wrappers from bugs or worms in the soft chocolate. He'd have the night stockers roll the racks into the walk-in freezers at night and freeze the bugs to kill them. The following morning, they'd roll the racks back to the checkout lanes to resale the product. The same with dog food bags when they got weevils.

38

He didn't keep the temperature cool enough inside the store during the hot summers…to keep his profits high and the stores operating loss low. It was all about his monthly report.

And health certificates?

We didn't know anything about those.

He would have rib-eyes and T-bone steaks to give the health inspector.

We all saw it and thought the man was buying them as Mr. Hollister always took the large, metal tray of meat to the last checkout line where no one could hear them. And it was always an empty checkout counter with him being the only one working it.

Many years later, my group would go to the local courthouse to follow the procedure to obtain our health certificates. The employees from other grocery stores (Winn-Dixie, Safeway, etc.) in our town were shocked that we had never had a health certificate. They had to get one each year and told us what to expect. Employees from all of the grocery stores waited in line together at the courthouse for their own turn. All were stunned at how Mr. Hollister had deceived the entire town.

Then, after all the checkers had been to the penny correct on their cash tills (cash register drawers that held the money), at the end of their shift; suddenly, within a three-week period, they were not. Five of them were coming up short on their money…and a lot short. Some were short by one hundred and twenty dollars, some seventy-five dollars. I knew the employees and knew they did not steal money from their cash register. During those three weeks, other employes experienced the same thing. One was two hundred and thirty dollars short, someone else was one hundred and seventy dollars short.

I knew something was wrong but could not prove anything. The tills were given to the employee at the service desk to count, and she'd usually have a stack of about four or five tills to count alone. She'd been doing this for years.

Was she stealing from the tills?

Of course, I reported it to the Union representative, and the store manager reported it to our security officer, Cecil Davis, and the stores division manager, Milton Douglas.

We all began watching as much as possible while still waiting on customers.

Then I was told my till came up short one evening. Mine was short ninety dollars and twenty-three cents.

I became angry. I told the front-end supervisor that it was impossible for my till to even be short by a penny, much less ninety dollars and twenty-three cents. My routine was to look at the display on the register to see how much cash the customer received back. Then I counted it out to myself as I got it from the register and counted it out loud as I placed it into the customer's hand. I knew my till had been stolen from.

I was so upset that I wrote about it. It was a poem, but I sang it as a slow ballad. The employees loved it, but store management did not. They did not want attention brought to our store in a negative manner.

Eventually the thief was caught, but it took two years. It was the Supervisor at the service desk who counted the tills. She was escorted out of the service desk in hand cuffs with a blank stare on her face.

We later learned that she was placing her child in beauty pageants and was using the stolen money for registration and glamourous pageant clothing.

So sad, and no one's till was short again, as long as I worked there. The District Store Management apologized to those of us who had been falsely accused.

We prayed for the employee who was guilty and felt sorry for her.

She was living beyond her means, and that lifestyle demanded money she didn't have. It finally caught up with her.

It was a relief though, for working conditions to resume to normal, at least for a while.

I discovered both of Mr. Hollister's girlfriend's quite by accident.

I was told by the service desk manager to take a large, yellow envelope to Mr. Hollister's upstairs office in the back room and put it on his desk.

It was almost time for me to clock out, and my shift would be over for the day.

I rushed through the store and hurried up the stairs to his office. Shoving the door open, I gasped at what I saw.

They did too.

Robin was sitting on Mr. Hollister's lap with her blouse open. He sat in his chair behind the desk with complete horror etched on his face. She was wide eyed.

I pitched the envelope to them and ran out.

I assume they didn't want me to talk about what I saw. He was the pillar of the community and she...well...she was Robin. The one who programmed new weekly sale prices on all store products into the computer. She was accurate, and no one else could do her job. We would scan the item knowing it had the new price that was entered into the computer. Robin could do nothing wrong.

At the end of that week, I was given a new work schedule.

I would now work all night every weekend; 11pm to 7am. Then continue my 40-hour week with late nights and one day shift. I would get drowsy driving home from work in the mornings as the sun came up.

And I did it because I was making $14.10 an hour in the 1970's with all insurance paid by the company for myself, my husband, and our two sons. Of course, I did get future pay raises for having seniority, but in the 1970's receiving $14.10 an hour was not common anywhere.

And so, the night shift began.

I was still the only one who cooked, and cleaned etc., at home. I still drove my sons to school. I was still married all those 12 and a half years I worked

41

there, but my divorce would take two years. Later, my youngest son would come to the store after school and play in the toy department. My oldest son would go to his dad's business after school and either do homework or work there. And the young man who straightened the toy department invited my son to his interdenominational church called "Love Has No Color." It had multi races attending and not only did my son and I begin attending, but my mother, sister and her son as well. And my son ended up preaching there.

This was also the same grocery store where my estranged husband raced around the store parking lot in his car trying to run over my youngest son and myself. He had kept us out of court for two years without paying child support and had just given me a hundred-dollar bill and he wanted it back. We dodged his car by running in-between parked cars while we screamed at him to stop. Red faced, he circled round and round from the adjoining strip mall into the store's parking lot. Finally, we ran into the store while customers stood on the sidewalk staring at him. He left then.

Just some of my memories of that store. Later, my estranged husband and his wealthy girlfriend would stroll hand in hand into the store and laugh at me as I worked. It was a public place, and they did it on purpose. But enough of that. This story is about Mr. Hollister!

I have pictures of me wearing my store uniform then, showing off the wide, red ribbon attached to the front of my uniform. It was covered in small, embroidered roses that were part of the Friendliness Program. The only way you could receive a rose was by customers turning your name into the store for some act of kindness you did. My ribbon was completely covered. In the picture I am smiling happily, but it was hard to miss that I was skin and bones. I had lost a lot of weight.

I could write an entire book on working the night shift.

But again, this is about Mr. Hollister…not everything I experienced there.

I worked all night with two older women, Audrey, and Virginia. Of course there were the night stocking crew, and the security men each night with us. Between us three women, we took turns who would be the night cashier and who would be "conditioning" the store. The two who conditioned simply straightened everything in the entire store all night. We had to wear plastic gloves as customers would put used personal products in glassware. When you'd reach your arms to the back of a shelf holding rumpled towels, and you'd spread your fingers out to smooth the towels back in place…often you'd get a gooey mess of toothpaste on your gloves that someone had squeezed out of a tube in obvious vandalism.…and we'd have to dispose of the towel.

One night when Audrey was the night checker, a young man stood in her line giggling. When it was his turn, she glanced at him and in not seeing anything he was about to purchase; said…"Well, what is it?"

He turned around, pulled his pants partially down, and mooned her. Laughing, he ran out of the store.

Security never found him, and she was too upset to work at the register anymore that night. She mentioned that this was a college town, and she didn't want to see another naked butt, and that another student might try it later…and once was enough for her. She rattled on and on. I took her place that night, and she finished working by helping Virginia condition the store.

A few hours later, they heard something in the broiler room as they walked by that side of the store. They knew the security officer, Mr. Helton, was with me by the cash register and they quietly approached us. Whatever they heard, they wanted him to check it out. They explained the sound came from behind two doors entering the broiler room. The three of them took off and they pointed to the correct two doors.

"Stand back." He advised.

They did.

He quickly kicked the doors open and there stood an employee who was supposed to be stocking groceries on shelves, and some girl in an embarrassing moment together.

He called the manager and told the couple to put their clothes back on.

The manager lived nearby and arrived within minutes.

43

After much discussion with the couple, Mr. Hollister fired the boy and hired the girl.

That's right. He hired the girl.

I reported this also.

Nothing could be done.

I later heard the girl was in the middle of a divorce, had two children and desperately needed a job.

She returned the following day, and I thought she looked to be about 20 years old. Mr. Hollister trained her in how to order from a handheld device on any products we were low on. She also was given the use of his upstairs office overlooking the checkout lanes for her two children. They would sleep on a pallet there at night while she worked ordering.

The main problem was the fact that she was still working at the store in the morning when customers were arriving.

The customers inquired how could this woman wearing short shorts and a halter top go all over the store obviously ordering something with a handheld machine? How could she get a job dressed like that?

And then it got worse.

This same woman would be seen by customers carrying her two children to and from that office late at night or early in the morning. And she dressed in skimpy clothing. Talk was spreading fast.

No employee dared talk about it.

The young woman kept her job.

I continued reporting what was wrong.

Most of the time it helped.

But what it did to us as a group of employees was to bring us closer together.

And then there was the can of chicken soup incident. An employee had married and moved to a town that didn't have a store to transfer to. After living there for years, she returned to our town. She wanted her job back with full seniority. Mr. Hollister told her they would work something out. She did get her job back ...with full seniority...but weeks later she approached me.

"I am sick of him coming to my apartment at night. I can't stand it any longer." She then told me about the situation. She was extremely nervous, and she wanted my help to stop it. As Union Steward, I considered many options.

We devised a plan.

She was recovering from a cold and informed him not to visit because she was still unwell. He was coming over that night anyway.... "just to check on her and bring a can of soup to help her feel better."

He would be arriving at her apartment at eight o'clock that night. I arrived there at 7:30 pm.

When he knocked at the door, she opened it, and I stood inside against the wall hidden from him behind the open door. He stepped inside and tried to embrace her.

She shut the door, and I looked him straight in the face.

I'll never forget his shocked expression upon seeing me.

He started stuttering and tried to smile. "I...I was bringing her a can of soup." He held the can of chicken noodle soup toward me from his other hand.

"I'll see that it gets heated. Thank you for bringing it over. I'll take care of it." I nodded at him as she motioned toward the door.

No one spoke.

He quickly left. And no, he didn't bother her again.

Your faith goes where you go.

45

We prayed and prayed and prayed. We grew great relationships. We listened to each other. We helped by being able to relate to what others were experiencing.

We knew how to keep our jobs and do the best we could. We learned how to do it without altering our values or morals. We learned that no one can be totally controlled. Mr. Hollister later passed away with a sudden illness. And when I left that job my divorce had been filed.

† † †

So often, we as believers, work with non-believers. When people are only for themselves…at any cost…we are to pray for them, but we do not join them. We work with them and usually must, but we can let them see the Christian that we are and see our Christian viewpoint by our actions. I wanted to share the following scripture as it also pertains to a marriage, and it is encouraging. Don't be unequally yoked!

II Corinthians 6:14-18 (NLT) 14: Don't team up with those who are unbelievers. How can righteousness be a partner with wickedness? How can light live with darkness? What harmony can there be between Christ and the devil? How can a believer be a partner with an unbeliever? And what union can there be between God's temple and idols? For we are the temple of the living God. As God said:

"I will live in them
And walk among them
I will be their God,
And they will be my people.
Therefore, come out from among unbelievers,
And separate yourselves from them," says the Lord.
Don't touch their filthy things,
And I will welcome you.
And I will be your Father,
And you will be my sons and daughters," says the Lord Almighty.

Moral of the story: Pray about everything! Stand for what you know is just and right. And don't lower your standards…you cannot please the enemy; they will lose respect for you and your values. Be true to yourself!

The End

Chapter Six

It Runs in The Family...

At 11 years old I was trusted to ride the city bus by myself. I would take my little sister with me. In those years it was perfectly safe to ride alone in the city without harm coming to anyone.

It was the summer of 1959 in Houston, Texas. My favorite place was all the way across town to the Heights Public Library. Inside, it had a winding staircase hugging the wall with only room for one person to walk up; if someone were coming down the stairs both had to turn sideways to pass each other on the stairs. We'd first look at the books in the children's section, check them out, and then begin climbing the stairs. We'd go to the third floor and sit on the carpet under a window curled up reading our books. It was quiet there and so cozy. A great place for two kids to feel comfortable and enjoy their time at the library.

We went often. Afterwards, we'd go to Rettig's Ice Cream Parlor and climb up on the row of stools in front of the counter. Eating our delicious ice cream would end the day and we'd take the city bus back home.

We continued our trips to the library and later added trips to the skating rink as well. Geraldine would stay home then, and I'd go to either an ice-skating rink or the roller-skating rink. And everyone in my neighborhood began skating on their concrete driveways daily. I raced up and down my own driveway and the neighbor girls and I would yell encouragement at each other. One family had 4 girls: Eloise, Esther, Elaine, and Evelyn. Sparks would fly off their metal wheels when they'd all skate at once and turn around at the end of the driveway.

But even with all the outdoor fun happening, I would read at night before going to sleep. Trips to the library were a big part of my life.

Years later, I began writing about what I'd experienced or what I'd seen firsthand happen to others. First in poetry, then in song lyrics. Wanting to write more in-depth, I then started writing short stories and finally writing entire novels.

I attended years of writing workshops and joined many writing groups. While learning the writing craft was vital, the opinions from my critique group were equally important.

The Lord blessed me with two remarkable sons, each unique and with their own talents.

One of my sons began writing. Jeff Brannon started writing in a school newspaper that he started himself in the fourth grade at South Marshall Elementary School in Marshall, Texas. He also began a ministry at seventeen years of age. Yes, I encouraged him, but he began writing all on his own. I told him that Yehovah had given him a gift of writing. He used my old Underwood Typewriter and later received one of the first portable word processors from me and his dad as a present.

My other son, Mike, was drawn more to engineering.

Fast forward to today, October 5, 2025.

 Mike is now an engineer and in big demand with several companies, traveling all over Texas and other states in his work, and internationally. His wife Kathryn is a licensed Texas realtor, and yes, they stay busy! And their son, Lake? His years of becoming an Eagle Scout and his years of flying remote control model airplanes have him now enjoying a career as a pilot! He also recently married Molly, who is so welcome in the family! I am so proud of all of them!

Jeff stayed with writing, and his ministry of 37 years has remained strong. He now has 5 published books available on Amazon in audio, e-book, and paperback versions.

(1.) The Priestly Garments: Who We Are in Messiah

(2.) The Priestly Service: How We Walk in the Spirit (just published)

(3.) Mark My Words: Yeshua Is Yehovah

The Watcher's Trilogy:

(4.) Book One: Before Adam: The Fall of Enlil

(5.) Book Two: The Nephilim, A Giant Walk Through History

I am so proud of him! He teaches the gospel and is a blessing to all. His writing just flows, and yes, it is anointed. Jeff is also my editor and publisher. He leads The Way Remnant- an online ministry reaching audiences on YouTube, Facebook, TikTok, X, and Rumble. He has also written songs and has made videos to accompany them for his weekly programs with his online ministry as well as the intros to each program aired. He and his wife, Miranda, also offer marriage counseling. They are genuine... the real deal... and dedicated to their ministry. They serve Yehovah and put Him first above everything while staying true to themselves and their beliefs. Connect with them on their website: http://TheWayRemnant.com or email them at: TheWayRemnant@Gmail.com. Their programs are a learning experience, and the work they are doing is heart-felt and scripturally researched. I highly recommend them!

And...along comes Jeff's daughter, Jessica .

She wrote short stories in elementary school. She loved it! This was done all on her own. I still have one of her earlier manuscripts that is unpublished. Two of her books were published in grade school. Her favorite name for a female character was Lucy. They were precious stories!

And let's not forget Jessica's half-brother, Austin! Watching him grow from a toddler seems like yesterday, but he is now a grown man! And yes, he wrote a book also! He continued into law enforcement as a career and is now a detective for the local police department. Happily married with a loving family and three children; I am so proud of the man he grew up to be!

As Jessica grew into her teenage years, she kept writing, chapter after chapter, and emailed them to me to read. Yes, I kept all of them! Each had such fascinating descriptions that I had to encourage her to continue her writing. She was excellent and without attending one writing workshop. I also told her that Yehovah had given her a gift for writing. She did enjoy going with me on two of my writing group meetings; one held in Pittsburg, Texas and another held in Longview, Texas. She was comfortable with meeting everyone, asking questions, and participated in a writing prompt at one of them. Fun times!

So that brings us to today. Jessica is married. Her name is now Jessica Todd.

I am happy to say that Jessica Todd has her first book now available on Amazon, "Orchard, Sown Among Thorns" and she created her own book Trailor, and book cover. It is a Christian Fiction book, and the best Christian Fiction I have read. It is a great book! All the artwork is created by her also on each chapter page. She immediately began on her next book. It just flows! And she is writing songs for Jeff's ministry as well. She has created videos to accompany them, and they air on the online ministry at The Way Remnant. She is so talented, and her writing is incredible!

She wrote her first book while being married and raising their three-year-old child and… while still working at her job. That is a major accomplishment in itself. Yes, I am so proud of her!

Where does she work?

She works at a library…it's full circle. In the genes…

To Yehovah be the glory!

Thank you, Yeshua!

† † †

Ephesians 4: 20 Giving thanks always for all things unto God and the Father in the Name of our Lord Jesus Christ.

Moral of the story: Raising your family is a Yehovah given blessing. Alway pray and seek His will and His guidance daily. Thank Yehovah earnestly for supplying your needs and providing protection for you and your family. We pray for His love, grace, mercy, and forgiveness to cover us and we give Him the glory!

The End

Chapter Seven

Laura Is Gone…

It's always encouraging to see someone who's struggled with anything to finally make progress. Especially when they try so hard to succeed.

And so it was with Johnny and Laura.

While other young couples would buy things on the spur of the moment, they were determined to stick with bare necessities and save their money.

And they prayed together. They studied the Bible. They were a team.

After many years with both working, they paid off the small house they had bought.

And Laura became pregnant.

The auto parts company where we worked was large enough to offer many positions in several departments. She didn't work in the office then. All that was available at that time was either pulling auto parts upstairs while walking on metal grates for eight hours and then taking your cart downstairs to the packers to pack each order for shipping; or being a packer downstairs on a concrete floor for eight hours. She decided to be a packer.

Unfortunately, the work proved to be too strenuous for Laura. By packing the heavy auto parts constantly all day, she developed blood clots in her legs that required surgery. And even worse, she had a tubal miscarriage.

Of course, the company's health insurance paid for everything. While she was off work, she submitted a written request for the first position that became available in the office. She was a key punch operator and often mentioned how she missed working at a computer.

Thankfully, she healed well from the surgery, and thankfully she got the new position of working in the office.

All she and Johnny talked about was having a baby. They prayed about it and even began saving their money for whatever expenses they encountered.

And she got pregnant. They were thrilled. We all were.

Most of the co-workers wanted to surprise her with a baby shower. They would try discreetly inquiring about what she might need. Laura was sort of evasive, as we muddled through our break times together.

Gail began talking about her seven-month-old daughter, Hope.

"Hope loves to go out to eat! She enjoys the attention. My husband and I were invited out to dinner last night by my husband's parents. We decided to let Hope eat some baked potato. She ended up eating the entire baked potato." Gail laid her sandwich down and started laughing.

"She wanted more and got upset. Then she put her foot on the table and kicked over my water glass! She got all wet!" Gail added.

"Oh no!" Suzi hollered.

"I was glad I brought another set of clothes for her." Gail solemnly announced and went back to her sandwich.

"What would we do without diaper bags?" Suzi laughed.

"I bought one the other day. This diaper bag has side pockets, and it is huge!" Laura told the group.

"Oh, you did? Well, Laura; what colors did you pick out for your nursery?" Gail asked.

"Oh, several colors." Laura smiled. "It won't be long now," Laura continued, "this is my last week before my maternity leave begins. I've been getting the nursery room ready."

"What do you still need to buy?" Felicia questioned.

54

"I've been going to rummage sales and getting just about everything." She explained.

"Didn't you say last week that you had to repair a baby swing that you bought at one of the sales?" I reminded her.

"Yes, I need to. I was going to the other day, but I haven't had enough time!" Laura admitted, as the buzzer went off.

Our fifteen-minute break was over.

Laura left.

"We must tell her about the shower! None of us can pinpoint what she has or doesn't have. I've reserved the recreation hall at my church. Her shower will be this weekend...this Saturday, at one o'clock. We have no choice!" Suzie groaned.

"I'll tell her." Sharon declared, as she and I walked down the hallway near the office she shared with Laura.

Gail went back to the switchboard room.

As Sharon entered that office, Laura was already deep into her work. She never took her eyes off her computer screen. She was excellent at her job.

I glanced through the window as I walked by the office.

Suzie was out in the hall.

"Sharon is going to tell her now." I assured Suzie.

"Good, I'll get back to my inventory, before I get behind." She grinned.

 Sharon must have told Laura about the shower, as Laura suddenly rolled her chair away from her desk. She had an exciting look on her face, and she was yelling happily! Then she wiped her eyes, and a smile spread across her face. I think everyone wanted Laura to be happy. She deserved it.

I left the hallway and continued to my work area.

Toward the end of the week, I told Laura I wouldn't be able to attend her baby shower. However, I would get her something after the baby was born. I wished her well and told her that we would all be waiting to hear from her husband.

"Tell him to be sure and call us here, the minute you have the baby!" I exclaimed.

Laura did have a nice baby shower. At one of our later office breaks, I did get to see the pictures that were taken at her shower. We missed her and were anxious for her baby to be born. I bought her some hand crocheted booties for her baby. I couldn't wait until the baby was born!

It wasn't long after that and THE DAY finally arrived! Laura's husband, Johnny, called and told our supervisor that they had a baby girl! The news raced through our wing of offices!

Imagine our surprise the very next day…settling back to our regular work routine…and seeing Laura walk into the warehouse! She nearly bounced! Her smile was from ear to ear.

"What are you doing here?" We all asked, astonished.

"I must talk to Mrs. Hyter. Oh, here she is." Laura approached our supervisor.

"Out of the hospital the next day? Laura, my goodness! How do you feel?" Mrs. Hyter blurted.

"I feel great. I had to bring some papers you forgot to fill out."

"How's your baby?" The supervisor asked as she took the insurance forms from Laura.

"She's perfect! I left her with my husband out in the car. I really do need you to fill out these forms, Mrs. Hyter. I know you are busy, but I hope you understand."

"No problem." She frowned and looked at the pages. "Let's get this over with, come on." Mrs. Hyter continued as she walked to her office.

Laura hugged us bye. We knew she was anxious to get home. We told her we would all get fired if we tried to sneak outside and see her baby.

"Plenty of time for that!" Laura laughed as she entered Mrs. Hyter's office.

"It really makes you feel so good inside to share someone's happiness." Suzie commented.

"It's the happiest time of her life." Sharon spoke reflectively.

With that remark, once again, we returned to our work.

Laura's six-week maternity leave went by fast. I happened to be near the manager's office, Mr. Spencer, when Laura returned to work. She had to give him the release form from her doctor. As I left that office, on my way back to the new office, I heard him tell her that she was no longer needed in the office.

I was shocked!

Laura was leaving the building when I hurried to stop her. It was obvious her feelings were crushed, but she wasn't crying.

"What is he doing? I heard him say you won't be working in the office anymore." I began slowly.

"No, he is sending me to the shipping and receiving department. He claims that several employees have quit that area and he needs me to work there. I asked him if this meant I could later return to my office job, and he said no. He said they hired a temporary girl in that office. Why is he trying to get rid of me?" Her voice was shaking.

"Laura, I know temporary employees do not get insurance. It seems like, if you left an office job you should be able to return to an office job after your maternity leave. He knows you can't handle the shipping and receiving department. Those parts they ship are too heavy. This is not a Union job, but you should have some rights." I told her.

"You mean call the Labor Board?" She bit her lip and straightened her posture.

"That's your decision. It's your job..."

"Oh, I will call them as soon as I get home." Laura interrupted me.

"Good. I can't believe you're being treated like this." I had to take a deep breath and hold it in a minute, or I'd lose my temper. My heart ached for her. This company should not treat her so cruelly. She'd always gone out of her way to work hard and be reliable.

"Well, I'm going to see what I can do about it before I start work in two days. I must go, see you later."

She turned instantly and left before I could say anything else.

I said a silent prayer for her.

I couldn't keep my mind on my work thinking how rotten the company was treating Laura. I wondered who else had experienced the same treatment that I knew nothing about. With any company like that, if they are cruel to one employee, they 'll be cruel to others.

I remembered what had happened to me. It was last year during one hot, summer at work, when I was working upstairs pulling parts off shelves into a shopping cart, when the weight pivoted the entire cart over pulling me with it onto the metal grated floor we walked on. The impact of the heavy cart falling over on my right arm broke it. I went to the Emergency Health Clinic where they took x-rays and put my arm in a cast. I returned to work with a doctor's excuse stating I could work, but light duty only.

I was sent outside to work wearing a cast on my right arm...with sweat rolling off me...while I counted two types of auto parts eight hours a day directly in the hot sun until my arm healed. I counted greasy, used alternators and used starters. I marked them individually and placed each in a separate pile picking them up with my left hand. Then adding to my total count on paper with my left hand and I was right-handed. I couldn't use my right hand or right arm. it looked like a childish scribble written with my left hand. But I stayed. They didn't run me off.

This is the same place that only had air conditioning inside the offices. In the summer, it felt as hot inside as outside the building with hot Texas temperatures in the 100's daily.

And the boss was a close friend of my ex-husband. The manager had gone to school with my ex-husband years ago. Between the two of them, someone put my mom's name, and my sister's name on several out of state companies' invoices showing parts ordered…to be packed and shipped. I took the invoices to the owner, and he called the businesses ordering, discovering no one by those names worked there. And I told him; it shouted of my ex-husband. My ex delighted in belittling and discrediting me. I asked the boss what did they expect me to think…that I was seeing things? He laughed, but it didn't happen again. Their being friends with my ex-husband explained a lot! I'd left the grocery store job and was recently divorced. At least I no longer had to support him and work all night long. He had enjoyed being at either of two restaurants every day in town; either Ward's or Gables…supposedly making contacts for his business while I worked all night and slept days. He once yelled at me, with his finger in my face, that I had to work. I might have to work but it sure wasn't for him. And his harassment followed me to this job, thanks to his friends. Naturally, I lost all respect for the boss and the manager. And yes, both men at my new job knew my mom and sister's name. It was a small town. My Mom had babysat for my boss and his first wife years earlier.

I continued remembering other incidents. Yes, it was a long day, and it didn't look good for the company. There had recently been an article about my auto parts boss in the local newspaper praising him for helping Habitat for Humanity. I laughed when I saw it. I instantly thought of my old boss at the grocery store, Mr. Hollister. This same small town thought he was also a great man with his military metals and how he helped the community as well. Yes, there are two sides to both of those men; one to show in public, and the other is their true selves. I'm not judging; merely pointing out they will have to answer for all of their actions one day.

Laura popped into our breakroom the next day. She sagged into a chair and in a voice quivering with emotion, she told us what was happening. I sat nearby and listened. Suzie left the room after hearing some of what happened. She told us it was making her upset, and she felt sick in her stomach.

The stress had to be overwhelming, and mentally exhausting for Laura. We were merely hearing about it, and Laura lived through it.

I felt my own stomach churn.

Laura told us she talked to the manager again, and her hours had changed. She'd still be working in the shipping and receiving department, but now she'd be working there late at night. She was breastfeeding her baby around her work schedule for the eight to five office job she thought she would have and still have the same hours in the shipping and receiving department. Now, she would have to get off work at ten o'clock at night from the shipping and receiving department. And she starts tomorrow. (It was not air conditioned and not as hot to work later hours. Often in the summer enduring the hot Texas heat, employees would experience a heat stroke and leave in an ambulance; and that was from working inside the building where the huge fans blew hot air along with dust.) She told Mr. Spencer that she had planned on going home for lunch and feeding her baby. Now, she would have to use a breast pump and let her husband give the baby a bottle.

"Your husband?" I blurted.

"Johnny got laid off from his job. I have to work." Laura swallowed hard.

"Did you call the Labor Board?" I inquired.

"Yes. They told me all the company had to do was give me a job when I returned from maternity leave." Laura yelled angrily, "I can't even sleep at night."

Her voice broke as she continued. "I need this job; they aren't going to run me off!" She whispered.

"Don't let them ruin your health, either. It's not good for you or the baby. Laura, this is not an endurance test." Gail's nostrils flared as her chest rose rapidly in anger, and she insisted even louder. "There are other jobs besides this company!"

"We are all concerned, Laura," Sharon rushed to her. "True, you must work, and it's not fair. Sooner or later, though, they'll have to pay for how they are treating you. Yehovah sees what's going on. And you're just as stubborn as anyone about the principal issue. If the situation continues, your baby will feel your tension. Then everything will get worse. Don't overdo yourself, okay?"

"I am going to try this job, for a while. Don't worry, I have my priorities, so does Johnny. He is my husband, we are a team, and we will not be defeated! Besides, we prayed and turned it over to the Lord." Laura assured us and suddenly had a slow smile. "Oh, I haven't had a chance to tell you about the chickens!" She gushed.

"Chickens?" We questioned her, as she had completely thrown us off our line of thought.

"Yes, chickens. A friend of Johnny's works at the Post Office. Every six weeks, crates of hybrid baby chickens arrive there. Some man that lives in the country raises them and later sells them when they are grown. Johnny happened to be inside the Post Office when he heard the baby chickens. He said you cannot imagine how much noise one hundred baby chickens can make, echoing inside those walls! Johnnies' friend introduced him to the chicken farmer, and Johnny is going to help him butcher the older chickens." She beamed and nodded at us as she left.

The following day, Laura returned to work. After a few hours, she went into the office and turned in her resignation. She was literally worn out.

A few days later, employees saw a sign posted by Mr. Spencer on the bulletin board. And yes, they told Laura. Mr. Spencer posted a sign listing various job positions that were available. One of those listed was that of data entry; Lauras old office job. As it turned out, though, Laura stopped looking for a job. She happily has one staying home and taking care of their baby…because the work Johnny obtained from the chicken farmer was just the beginning for him.

Johnny was in demand for other jobs in the entire area. He was kept busy and still is today.

Oh, and that company …I think they learned a lesson whether they will admit it or not. The big, bustling business is permanently closed now.

† † †

Galatians 6: 7 (King James Version) Be not deceived; God is not mocked: for whatsoever a man sows, that shall he also reap.

Moral of the story: Let the Lord fight your battles.

The End

Chapter Eight

Road Trip

I had traveled Highway 79 South to Round Rock, Texas, for several years. Trusting in the Lord, I always prayed for safety, and doubt never entered my mind. I enjoyed every road trip on that same stretch of highway…it never lost its charm! I knew each turn, each little town along the way, and could drive it by heart without even glancing at a map.

I knew where to stop for the best food, the best bargains, and be in absolutely no hurry! It was most relaxing and after I finally arrived near Austin,Texas; I could enjoy visiting my son and his family! That was the reason for the trip, and all else was extra. We'd do as much as possible in Austin, as we had time for. Restaurants, parks, and events were always so inviting.

I started out in a P. T. Cruiser in 2004.

At that time, I had two cats, and one dog.

When vacation time came around, two weeks off each year, the first thing I did was call to check for openings to board my animals in Marshall, Texas. The cats cried and howled all the way to the kennels but turned into "big babies" once they got there. Both were neutered males, and they played together like best buddies.

'Missy' is my AKC miniature Yorkie and considers herself to be my guard dog. (She is quick to learn anything!) However, she cannot tolerate cats. I had gone online looking for an AKC male Yorkie for her. She was only three months old, and I had plenty of time to get a male before I'd breed her at age two. (I became a registered AKC breeder for Yorkies for several years.)

I dropped the animals off the evening before the trip.

63

My mother would make the trip with me. We both lived in a rural town. We'd get up early, pack the car, and stop in Marshall, Tx. for breakfast. I always had the car serviced days before and started off with a full tank of gas. With our water bottles, and snacks within reach, we were off.

Let the shopping begin!

It's amazing how much you can get into a P.T. Cruser!

I had picked up a schedule for what weekends Jewett, Texas had their flea market open. That was just one of our stops, after which we'd have lemonade and corndogs.

The back seats were soon laid down flat, and our purchases were placed together. Next was an antique shop that always gave you 20% off at an already great price. Some furniture items were made of solid wood that you could hardly find anymore.

About an hour and a half before Austin, on the right-hand side of the road was another "must' stop. This was a flea market owned by an Egyptian woman who spoke broken English. I could talk to her for hours! She and I got along great. Most of her items were handmade in Guadalajara, Mexico. Through the years, I would buy a six-foot tall by four feet wide, metal coconut tree with coconuts and tree branches from her. All metal; later I'd buy metal armadillos, metal turtles, dog, etc. All would fit into the P.T. Cruiser.

Over the years, I also bought from her, two 6 feet tall ceramic vases, a huge ceramic frog, and a 5-foot-long metal fish to hang on the wall.

Anything medium to large was always forty-five dollars, I guess because of the quality and that it was homemade.

I can still picture her talking with her hands moving all around the air, and her voice becoming louder and louder. Then she'd smile and say, "I like you. You regular customer. I give that to you for good price. I give that to you for forty-five dollars."

And I'd smile knowing that was her standard price...to me, anyway. Sometimes she'd get upset and you'd experience her temper with her employees as she tried to get them to do exactly what she had in mind. None of them spoke the same language. They would look exasperated at her, and she'd go sit in her truck to "cool off."

She and I both wore a cross on a chain around our necks. I would walk over to her while her workers would load my car. Smiling at her, I'd touch my cross. She would immediately grin and touch hers.

"Everything alright! Sometimes you got to go and sit down!" She would exclaim. Then she'd laugh and get back to her helpers. They were very busy, and everyone finally understood how she wanted something done. It was lack of communication. They all made the best of it and went on with their day. No bitterness, no "I'm quitting!"

It was inspiring. With Spanish, Egyptian, and English languages coming from her helpers, all looked at her endearingly as she touched her cross.

After making that stop, we always plan to have lunch in Hearne, Texas. The Golden Chick restaurant had the best, crispiest, fried chicken I've ever had. The chicken is double dipped in milk, then in seasoned flour, creating great flavor!

On this trip, though, I traded off my P. T. Cruiser and had recently bought a brand new 2007 Toyota RAV 4, in Marshall, Tx. It had more room inside and got better gas milage. It was black with tinted windows and a great shine! (My P. T. Cruiser had been white and ended up with bug stains.)

Unfortunately, on this trip, we would go to Round Rock and have to return the next day. Something had come up after we arrived that cut our time short.

This time we left Round Rock, Tx. around two in the afternoon. Gas prices were high everywhere then. We stopped in Buffalo, Tx. to buy scrapbooking supplies. Buffalo was about halfway between Round Rock and Marshall, Tx. We ate at a deli there and got gas for the car. That's where I bought my Texas map. I had a sudden flash…this would be a great time to travel to Lufkin, Texas!

I could look at AKC male Yorkshire Terrier pups there! I had printed out a reputable list of them for sale in our area on the websites. With the price of gas being so terrible, it would be worthwhile to drive over to Lufkin and look at some. After all, I was halfway there now. That would justify not making a special trip there and back home.

I looked at the map again. That would have us arriving home around nine o'clock at night. If the owners happened to be home and happened to be available for a meeting. It could be worthwhile!

I called.

Yes, they were home, and yes, they could meet us after dinner in town. I agreed to call back after I got closer to them. I left Marquez, Tx. turning at the blinking, red light, and drove towards Lufkin, Tx.

The scenery was beautiful! Pastures and winding roads. Then, I noticed construction signs. It seemed like a one lane road that I ended up driving on. It was two lanes, but they were extremely narrow. I thought this wouldn't last long.

Wrong!

Gravel started hitting my new car and I could hear it bouncing off. I had just made my first car payment. I slowed down. Other cars that I met were apparently used to this as they were flying down the road.

I looked at Mom and told her there was no place to turn around.

Then I saw the freshly laid hot tar! I had to drive on it!

Usually, one lane will be blocked as traffic is shifted to the other lane without fresh tar, but, no, not here! I couldn't imagine what my new car would end up like, but I had no way to get off the road. No driveways to turn around in, nothing. This was one straight stretch of road. After fifteen minutes I drove out of it. The construction was over!

Thank the Lord my car was black!

An hour and a half later, I pulled off the highway and called again as I approached the loop in Lufkin. The owner (AKC registered breeder) agreed to meet me at a service station near an exit from the loop. I told her I was driving a black Toyota. She told me she was driving a black Hummer.

Okay! That wouldn't be hard to spot!

I parked and checked out my car during the short wait for her. Several bottles of spray tar and bug remover should get it back in shape in a day or two. Specks of tar were even on my tinted windows!

We went inside the station to get a cappuccino, discussing my car. I told Mom I was in a hurry to get this over with so I could start removing tar from my car. We walked back outside, and the Hummer drove up. She rolled down her window as I approached and we met each other. I agree to follow her to see the puppies.

After several minutes and many turns later, we arrived.

I couldn't get over how clean everything was!

She had the puppies in an air-conditioned building with a separate place for the mother to nurse them. I got to see all the parents of the pups as there were two litters available. I was astonished that they were just the size and color I had been looking for!

I was drawn to one puppy from the start.

He was fat with big eyes and a ring around his nose! It looked like he'd just gotten into something and got caught. She let me hold him and I simply melted! We let him run around and he was very active. He kept trying to get into things and I mentioned to her that he seemed mischievous.

"Oh yes, he is into everything!" She laughed.

I held him again, and walked around, checking out his parents. They were small, and blue in color. Alert, active, friendly, etc. I was so impressed with what I found.

There was no way I could leave without the puppy! This was the one for me! I was hooked. We talked about the price, and I went ahead and bought him. After the papers were completed and signed, I realized I didn't have anything to bring him home in.

I glanced around inside the car for anything that would temporarily work. Stores were closed at this time. We had duffel bags, large shopping bags, and one oblong, zip-up, overnight case.

Naturally, I dumped some belongings out of the overnight case and stuck him inside it. Mom held the case on her lap, with paper towels handy, if they were needed. We shook hands with the seller, left, and were on our way home!

The puppy turned out to be a good traveler with Mom petting and talking to him during the remainder of the trip.

Needless to say, we got home rather late that night!

The next morning, I took him to the vet. He checked out to be in excellent health. Then I bought supplies for him and went after the other animals I'd boarded out.

It didn't take long to discover 'Missy' ...my female Yorkie, was jealous of the new puppy. She chased him around the couch, then changed direction and he chased her around the couch!

He was short and fat, yet he'd run as fast as she did, with both sliding on the hardwood floors. They would lose traction and gallop to catch up, after sliding. It was very funny! She later bit him and I knew I'd have to keep them separated to protect him. He was eight weeks old, just a baby!

I asked Mom if she would like to take care of him while I went back to work.

Oh, she couldn't wait! We brought his kennel, toys, and food over. Mom turned out to be an exceptional trainer!

'Major Mischief' is what I named him, and we call him 'Major'. At first, he would try chewing on her heals or toes, when she would wear sandals. She'd turn around and say, "No!" to him.

He couldn't stand it! He would back up, stand on his hind legs, look her right in her eye, and bark at her! He was fussing at her!

She would have to turn her face away so he couldn't see her laughing at him. He is just too stinkin' cute! He only did this when she got onto him. He learned though and became better about it.

Major is now three months old and is completely house trained! He is so intelligent! He will not have an accident all night in his kennel. He also has his own ideas of how to do things. When he's out of his kennel and in the house, he wets on one puppy pad and always does his business on the other puppy pad!

Oh, how I love this rascal of a dog! I can't wait for him and Missy to have their own pups! There's no telling how smart they will be!

Who would have ever thought I'd return from a Round Rock trip with this little dog!

And yes, the tar came off my car! It was good as new!

And it never occurred to us how two women traveling across Texas could be in any danger on the road. After praying for safety, we knew without a doubt that we were safe.

† † †

Philippians 4:13 I can do all things through Christ Who strengthens me.

Matthew 19:26 With God all things are possible.

Moral of the story: Sometimes our best laid plans can develop an unwanted issue. Make the best of it and enjoy it anyway!

The End

Chapter Nine

Alesha

Alesha had lived in the Mid-West area of the U.S. most of her life. When her husband was transferred to Texas with his job, they were excited. Their small family of one son and one daughter soon arrived and moved into a medium-sized town.

The children were enrolled in school; the daughter was in the sixth grade at a local elementary school, and the son was in high school in the eleventh grade. Alesha found work at a large Methodist church as a bookkeeper.

As they prepared to settle into a new routine, her husband was needed at his old job for some technical issues only he could resolve.

He decided to leave for the weekend and return to Texas on Monday. Alesha couldn't join him as payroll was near, and she couldn't possibly leave her new job until it was done. The older son had a ball game and couldn't get out of it. But the little girl wanted to go. It was decided she could go with Daddy, and she was thrilled.

They left on a Friday morning, making the trip in his car.

Late Saturday night, Alesha heard a knock on her door. She opened the door and looked at two police officers with astonishment.

"Yes?" She cautiously asked.

They regretted informing her of a horrific wreck between her husband's car and a train. Unfortunately, her husband and daughter did not survive.

Alesha fainted. Her son ran towards her, lifted her and placed her on the couch.

She was groggy but came to fully conscious.

The officers wanted to request first aid for her, but she refused.

"No, I want to know what happened." Her voice broke as she stared at the two men.

She and her son both listened in shock as the officers continued.

"Your husband was stopped at a railroad crossing with your daughter, waiting for the train to go by...when a drunk driver drove up fast and rammed into the back of your husband's car...pushing them directly into the moving train. I'm so sorry...but they did die instantly."

She screamed and moaned in agony and her son was sobbing, holding onto his mother.

"And the drunk driver?" She yelled.

"He wasn't injured, but he is in jail."

They handed the son a card to call them if they could be of any further assistance, and the two officers left.

Her phone started ringing, family calling.

The wreck happened near their families' homes in the Midwest destination where he was going. He almost arrived.

It was beyond tragic. So very sad.

Alesha and her son drove up to stay with her family for the funerals. Her husband's family lived close by also.

Alesha later stated it was all a blur; it seemed surreal.

After the funerals, her son asked if he could stay there with relatives. He wanted to finish out the eleventh grade and remain there to graduate with his friends. He had known them all his life, and Alesha felt he needed their support instead of being with strangers in Texas.

She agreed but she could not live there anymore. Everywhere she looked she was reminded of the memories made by her, her husband, and

72

children. The park where the kids would play, and swing. Their old home. It was too painful. It was too much to handle.

Both sides of the family insisted she file charges against the drunk driver, and she agreed that it was necessary, so it wouldn't happen again to another family.

She obtained an attorney and had everything legalized.

She also contacted her son's school and signed papers that her family could take him for medical care if needed.

After many hugs, and among many tears, she left to return to Texas and her job.

It was a new beginning.

It took months, but she eventually packed up her daughter's belongings and saved them to remember her by.

Her husband's belongings were finally packed away also, but she took his clothes, shoes, etc. to the local Goodwill.

She led a quiet life, kept to herself, and kept a distance between herself and others… without becoming close to anyone.

Her co-workers respected her and were friendly.

One woman in particular reached out to Alesha in friendship. She mentioned how calm and peaceful it was at the lake. You could even rent a boat and go exploring.

Alesha perked up and was interested.

The following weekend, they arranged to meet at the local lake and bring picnic supplies.

Alesha was looking forwards to it and was not disappointed. The two women paddled about a mile offshore and anchored. Birds were chirping, a gentle breeze was blowing, and it was absolutely beautiful with the sun shimmering over the water. They visited for a while and began setting the food and drinks out in the boat.

Halfway through the meal, a boat approached.

A man waved and yelled, "Hello ladies."

Alesha had a mouthful of sandwich and merely nodded, blushing.

He grinned at her. "I'm Tom Kennedy. Don't think I've seen either of you out here before."

"No, this is our first trip out here, and it's beautiful. I'm Opal and this is Alesha. We're having a picnic." She returned the smile.

He tipped his hat at them and yelled, "Enjoy" as he maneuvered to the other side of the lake, obviously fishing.

They both dismissed him and had a relaxing day.

Weeks went by and Alesha was hurrying down a grocery aisle when someone called out her name. She turned and gazed right into the eyes of Tom Kennedy.

"I thought that was you." He grinned, "but I couldn't tell without that sandwich in your mouth."

They both laughed and Alesha blushed again.

They went their separate ways, and Alesha began feeling comfortable enough to get back into the public more.

She returned to the lake by herself on Saturday morning. Renting her own boat, she put on her life jacket and sunglasses and paddled away. The outboard motor would remain a challenge for another day. She ambled around and finally anchored.

Eating the sandwich and bag of potato chips she'd brought went perfectly with her container of iced tea. She retrieved the book from her bag she'd checked out of the library. The story was fascinating, and she quickly got caught up in it. Reading page after page, she lost track of time.

The sun began setting. Startled, she grabbed the paddle and headed back to the shore.

It was almost dark when she arrived. Another boat was heading in also and she chuckled when she heard Tom Kennedy's voice.

"You again. Lady, I think your name is Alesha, if I remember right?"

"Yes, that's me."

"Well, let me help you tie the boat up and get you out. You could stumble and fall on something. Hard to see out here, now."

"Thank you!"

The proprietor came to collect and lock the boat up as Tom helped her onto dry land.

Tom had his own boat. "Stand by the dock while I back my trailer in the water and haul my boat out."

"Okay."

He drove the trailer out of the water with the boat attached. He then drove his truck onto the pavement where Alesha stood.

He grinned at her. "I promise I am harmless. I do want to take you out to eat, if that is agreeable. You can follow me to the restaurant in your car. I'd really like to get to know you better."

She smiled at him. "Yes. I'd like that."

She did follow him in her car to the restaurant, and that was the beginning of them dating each other exclusively. They bonded together and grew closer. Eventually, she met all his friends and family. They were married before the year was out and remained happy.

She put in her two weeks' notice and quit her job. She wanted one closer to their home and was delighted to find one with a school district. For a year, she worked as Secretary to the High School Principal.

That is where I later met her. I also obtained a job there.

I got her old job. She preferred working where the younger students were. A vacancy came up for Secretary at the elementary school, and she took it. The Superintendent called me and wanted me to consider the job of Secretary at the High School. I thanked her but told her I couldn't type fast. She said I could learn and had me come to be interviewed by her and the high school principal. He turned out to also be a pastor. I got the job and gave Yehovah the glory! I loved the job!

For five years, Alesha and I would travel in the school vehicle once a week for state training. We both ended up completing over three hundred college credits to perform all our duties. She did the elementary programs, and I did the ones at the high school. We did everything from Business, Peims, Discipline, Attendance, Report Cards, Ard meetings for Special Ed., Mainstream Special Education, Bookkeeping, Nursing, and Ruby Payne Poverty Seminars, just to mention a few. There were many others.

And yes, we discussed everything we were learning and our daily lives. We became friends and shared a lot with each other. We prayed together over our meals when we stopped at the Mexican Restaurant after training sessions. It was not far from the Region Seven Training Center in Kilgore, Texas. And we prayed for each other.

Her son was now married and had children of his own. He never came to visit her, but she took a two-week vacation once and drove to visit him. She delighted in seeing her Grandchildren and she had visited her son and his family twice before. She hardly talked about her son to me.

But Alesha often mentioned how her husband wanted to change her. She was blond and he wanted her to have her hair dyed black.

I told her to discuss it with him. He probably didn't mean anything by it.

It got worse. She insisted he wanted her to do things she didn't feel comfortable with.

Again, I encouraged her to discuss it with him. Let him know how she felt, and more importantly…to pray about it.

She really loved him, and I felt they just had a lack of communication. After working for the school for five years, I retired early. Alesha kept her job at the elementary school.

76

A few years later, I was shocked to learn that Alesha and Tom had divorced. She quit her job and took some of her furniture with her and moved several states away to live near her sister.

After a while, Tom started dating, and eventually one girlfriend moved into his house.

I can only guess who might have told Alesha, maybe a neighbor, but someone called and told her about Tom's girlfriend living with him in his house.

Alesha still loved him and became very upset.

She called him and told him she wanted to come back home. She asked if he'd come and get her. He did.

They were both so happy to be back together, but they didn't remarry.

Then Alesha developed cancer. This was right in the middle of the COVID shutdown.

Tom made arrangements for Alesha to stay with a married couple that had been friends of his for years. They had a yacht anchored near Galveston Bay and were living on it. Alesha was welcome to stay with them, and they'd transport her back and worth to M.D. Anderson hospital for chemo treatments. Alesha agreed.

Her cancer became worse. She had surgery. Then she had surgery that wasn't even related to her cancer. She'd been staying on the yacht for nearly a year and a half.

And her condition continued to worsen. Tom would travel to see her often and was with her when the doctors gave her a few months to live.

It was heartbreaking for both of them.

Tom brought her back home.

She called one of her sisters to come and get her furniture before she passed away. They arrived from out of state and loaded up a small moving van. Her family went through the entire house grabbing anything Alesha

77

said was hers and carried it all out to the moving van. Tom finally got out of the house and stood outside. When they finished, Tom offered to go and get everyone bar-b-q and potato salad from a local restaurant. They thanked him, and Tom left. When he returned with the food, they were all gone.

Alesha had left him a note stating she wanted to be buried in the Mid-West by her husband and her daughter. Her family had come to take her there.

Tom was in shock.

She passed away a few days later and was buried by them. She even took back his last name, the one she had while they were married. Her obituary never mentioned Tom at all.

And in her will; she never gave Tom one penny.

Her investments paid off well though with the money she received from the settlement. She ended up with seven hundred thousand dollars and gave it all to the son who never came to see her.

† † †

Matthew 7: 1 (NLT): Do not judge others, and you will not be judged.

Moral of the story: Life isn't always fair. We never truly know what someone feels deep inside their heart. Did they become bitter? Have they prayed about their problem? Sometimes they leave Yehovah out completely. Sometimes they make up their mind about a major decision and refuse to listen to reason. Other times they follow bad advice that doesn't come from a true Christian viewpoint. Pray for them all, the ones who gave the advice, the ones who took it, and the one who was betrayed. And pray especially for the one left standing there, holding food for those who walked away. Pray that Yehovah blesses him with peace, comfort, and love surrounding his life.

The End

Chapter Ten

Grandpa

Wayne and Margie were such a loving couple. Always displayed thoughtfulness towards each other and made time for friends and family. It is an art of listening and knowing when to speak and when to be silent. You could say they mastered this, but those of us who had known them for years knew it was part of their genuine compassion. I often noticed a shared smile between the two of them, and a knowing glance exchanged when they preferred not to discuss something in public. Not only active in church, but they raised their children in a Christian environment.

Margie had cancer for many years, and Wayne was having issues with his health as well. They were on everyone's prayer list. Occasionally, I'd see the elderly couple at the grocery store. Both looking pale, he'd hold onto her arm and lead her down the grocery aisles while pushing the cart. You'd hear him quietly ask her if she'd like to try eating something he'd specifically point to. He tried hard to get her to eat but she continued losing weight. It was always good to see them and to stop and talk a moment, but difficult to see progress wasn't being made for her health. They were never seen apart in public and would quickly turn the conversation into how you were doing. Concern for others was part of who they were, along with praying.

Margie passed away over a month ago. One never gets over the shock of it, even though it is expected. I grieved for her. We raised our children together. We went to church together. We had fun times together. And now she's gone. I know her family is still grieving. She and Wayne had grown children, and many grandchildren whom they joyfully loved.

A few months later, Christmas arrived.

(Although I no longer practice Christmas or the other pagan holidays like Halloween or Easter; they are all around us. But they are not in the Bible.

I now practice God's Feasts He wants us to celebrate, and they are in the Bible.)

I can't imagine the pain the entire family experienced on their first Christmas without Margie. Oh, the grandchildren squealed and ran around the room excited to finally open their gifts from under the tree. Smiles were contagious.

No, I wasn't there, but I saw the pictures they shared on social media. Close up happy photos of the children rushing to show their parents a toy they'd just opened. Wrapping paper scattered across the floor as presents were opened by all. Lots of family togetherness. Joyful moments.

And then I saw the picture of Wayne. He sat near the back of the room in a recliner. All the activity and family were in front of him, yet he stared off to the side, obviously lost in thought. He no longer had his wife next to him. He looked tired and out of place. I could see what had happened. He suddenly became Grandpa for the grandchildren...where he loved that role in the past...it clearly wasn't enough of a role for him now.

No one seeking his advice, no priorities to help plan, no adult conversation, and feeling left out...I had seen this happen before in other families. Grandpa is put in his recliner to entertain the grandchildren. Oh, everyone asks if they can get him anything, and are courteous, but they get totally involved with their own little family group. He had that look on his face in the group picture they included in the Christmas photos.

Until you experience it yourself, you do not recognize it. If he gets up from the recliner, someone will rush over to grab his arm, "Here, let me help you. You don't need to fall."

He would quietly recall a few days ago he was helping his wife not fall, and my, how roles do change.

Yes, they change, but his mind is still alert, and his life isn't over.

It reminds me of past family get-togethers where adults ate at the table, and the children had a small children's table to eat with other children. You don't suddenly stop eating at the adults' table and be transferred to the children's table. Be careful how you treat the elderly. Thankfully, you will

81

be elderly someday and can enjoy a full life with many different parts to it. Being a Grandparent is a blessing but should not be all there is to your life.

†☐ †☐ †☐

This is a true story. It is also a gentle reminder that to everything there is a season. Ecclesiastes 3: 1-8.

Ecclesiastes 3:1 To everything there is a season, and a time to every purpose under the Heaven. 2. A time to be born, and a time to die; a time to plant, and a time to pluck up that which is planted; 3. A time to kill, and a time to heal; a time to break down, and a time to build up; 4. A time to weep, and a time to laugh; a time to mourn, and a time to dance; 5. A time to cast away stones, and a time to gather stones together; a time to embrace, and a time to refrain from embracing; 6. A time to get, and a time to lose; a time to keep, and a time to cast away; 7. A time to rend, and a time to sew; a time to keep silence. And a time to speak; 8. A time to love, and a time to hate; a time of war, and a time of peace.

Moral of the story: Treat others as you want to be treated.

The End

Chapter Eleven

What Day Is It?

This isn't just another true story. It's one showing a glimpse into the life of someone with Dementia and Alzheimer's; what all it does to them, and the love given by the caregiver. In this case, my 97-year-old mother and myself at age 76. There was no one available to help me with her or even stay at my house while I got a few hours of sleep. I took us to doctor's appointments, mowed the grass, washed laundry, cooked, cleaned, cut her hair and mine, did her fingernails, as well as cut my dog's hair, bought groceries, etc. all with no help...and I had to watch her constantly day and night. I'd have to sit her outside in a wheel chair with a book, on my front porch while I mowed the lawn. I completely give Yehovah the glory for my being able to care for her. I did not change anyone's names in this story.

And no, she was not always like this. I wrote a book about her inspiring life with pictures, titled: "Lillie, A Motherless Child." Her own mother passed away when she was seven years old, and she helped raise her two younger siblings. There was a total of sixteen siblings, and all were raised during The Great Depression in Texas. I remain humbled, and I give Yehovah the glory; it was His guidance to me and to my writing that led to "Lillie, A Motherless Child" being awarded first place in Biography in 2016 by the Texas Association of Authors. Her book is available on Amazon.

Too often those who haven't cared for someone with Alzheimer's and Dementia will picture the patient staring at a T.V. mindlessly for hours. That was not my mom.

I looked back at my daily journals, and from 2022 until this year, 2025; her behavior was that of keeping me up all night, hallucinating, arguing, could not be left alone for her own safety, sneaky, hiding food, lying, etc. The diseases worsened. It was no longer her anymore. Sometimes we'd talk and she seemed normal, and was even nice, but then I'd realize she thought she was a young girl still in school. So sad. It is frustrating to watch someone deteriorate. I could not have made it without prayer, and strong faith in Yehovah! Again, I give Him the glory for being able to care for her!

Through it all, I'd pick flowers from my outside Hibiscus and Gardenia plants and place a vase of them on my kitchen table. She loved them and enjoyed smelling them. Until I found a rotten, stinking cheeseburger she'd crammed down in the vase of flowers. And afterwards, she didn't know how that got into the vase. But I continued placing flowers on the table in a vase. I just sat there until she finished eating. She always loved them. At times, she'd say she loved me, and she would thank me for taking care of her. At other times, it was awful. It was not her then.

This was what I recorded in my journal from three years ago of what happened on October 18, 2022.

I was fine until I handwashed my car at 4:30 pm on Monday, the 18th, 2022...and I had not been around anyone to "catch" something. I looked up at the sky and saw a massive crisscross of chem-trails over my area. I later talked to Mom's wound-care nurse, and she saw it also. She said it was disturbing...not the few trails you normally notice. (I did have a very nice, wound care nurse for a very short time who taught me how to dress Mom's wounds when her thin skin burst open.)

 I finished washing my car as it was 73 degrees and I wanted to do it before the cold weather arrived the next day. So, next day it was 60 degrees and very windy. I went out and wrapped outside water faucets before the predicted freeze for Tuesday night. Brought my plants inside. And promptly got so sick in the middle of the night I could hardly breathe. It felt like two hands were twisting and pulling my guts about, and I started vomiting. Sudden waves of being hot and clammy kept draining me. I was never so weak! I called my doctor as soon as they opened. He wanted me to go to the hospital, but I told him I couldn't as Mom fell in the kitchen and couldn't walk. I had her back in the wheelchair. (She was 94 years old then.)

He called in two prescriptions for me, and I thank Yehovah for my 82-year-old neighbor, Jan, for driving into town to bring them to me. Also, I thank Yehovah for Mom's wound care nurse Mindi for surprising me with 3 bags of soup, crackers, sprite, and armor body drinks on my front porch! Unfortunately, Mom began hallucinating and kept me up all night. No sleep. She started spelling letters out loud like she was playing word search, her favorite pass time. She would chuckle and glance around at who she thought was in the room and spell out the letters again...t-a-v-i-s. The third time, I couldn't stand it and asked her what she was doing. She quickly turned her head and looked left and right exclaiming, "Where did everyone go? I had about 30 people in here!" "Playing the word game?" I asked. "Yes" I thought maybe she was playing with angels to pacify her while I tried to sleep! You never know. I had told her earlier that no, she could not read her word search book as it was in the middle of the night, and she needed to sleep. I felt bad after that, but it was 2 AM and we didn't need to continue going without sleep!

Wrong! So, I am lying in my bed with her wheelchair next to it, and she argues that she wants to get out of the chair. I remind her she cannot walk. She then talks to other people she sees in my room, doesn't like the 7 dogs that she thinks are hiding in there and wants me to turn on the light to see if they are gone...I do, and she promptly forgets and tries to get out of the chair again. Then she laughs and talks to a group of people that are in my bedroom. I told her she was dreaming and to go to sleep. She claimed they were shopping. Nothing would satisfy her, she argued all night. At 4am she demanded to lie on the floor. I finally did let her, thinking that she might fall asleep. No. It just got worse. Almost couldn't pick her up and put her back in the wheelchair, but I did. Ran to the bathroom sick often that night. Cramping so badly at times I could not move. The next morning, I got her doctor to send a prescription to make her sleep. No, it didn't work. More hallucinations again all night. She and I have not had any sleep now for 2 nights. Here it is 1:30 pm on Thursday and she is still hallucinating. Told me worms were on her tv tray and to get them off. Forgets constantly, and is still wide awake. I am concerned she may have a stroke.

85

 I thank Yehovah for the prayers! When my son Jeff and his wife Miranda began praying over the phone for me, my symptoms eased to the point where I could lay still and not hurt! Today, my nausea is gone, swollen belly is gone, and cramps are gone. My belly is just very sore from all the dry heaves that came after actual vomiting. I have not been sick in years, and certainly not that intense. I'm still sipping sprite and eating bland food. I firmly believe whatever was in the air from the massive chem-trails got into my system. Believe me, I will not be active outside when they are crisscrossed overhead! Now back to bed...and maybe some sleep for both me and Mom!

That's actual days and nights of what we experienced. Alzheimer's and Dementia are both horrible diseases, and she had both for years. There is so much more to both of them than simply being forgetful.

It began with her living next door to me. Mom used to knock on my window and bring me a plate of food while I was writing and editing my books. She encouraged me wholeheartedly and didn't want anything to interrupt my flow of writing. Before my seventh book was published, Mom developed Alzheimer's and Dementia. My writing came to a halt as I became her 24/7 caregiver. I had to move her into my home after I discovered a kitchen fire at her house she tried to hide. Her stove was against the wall, and something caught fire. She never said anything about it but tried to hide it from me. I went to her house to check on her and smelled smoke. Upon entering her kitchen, I saw a massive area on the wall next to the stove covered in grey duct tape. The rest of that wall was charred and burnt. It is a miracle that the entire house didn't catch fire. That is when and why I moved her in with me. And she really thought she hid it by applying duct tape over it. After that, she began putting items that should go into the freezer into the refrigerator. They would be ruined and sour, like frozen garlic bread, or frozen pizza; and I'd have to throw it away. I had to constantly watch what she might be putting in there daily.

She also developed what is commonly referred to as "Sundowner's." Each night she would dream out loud, talking in her sleep and trying to follow the people in her dreams wherever they were going. She would sleep-walk. Her behavior changed drastically to being mean. I had to stop her from trying to go out a window one night, another night she tried to go out the front door. I stopped her and she never knew she was asleep or dreaming. She announced she was going shopping with "those people." I seldom had a full night's sleep. Her doctor ordered a hospital bed with metal guard rails, and she'd try to climb out of that in her sleep. I ordered a bed alarm for three hundred dollars that was similar to an oversized heating pad. It went under her bed sheets and was plugged into a wall socket. A shrill, loud noise would alert me when she was trying to leave her bed and sleepwalk. This didn't work either as she had super strength at night and moved with a steady step and a fast-pace unknown to her during the day. She would be out of bed before I could leave my own bed and hurry across the hallway to stop her. She fell out of bed several nights. Her thin skin would burst open, and I'd have to call an ambulance. Once she broke her back, another time she broke her leg.

After it continued to worsen, her doctor instructed me to place her on a pallet at night to sleep. He said she is going to fall onto the floor anyway, so we will just put her on the floor. She would be safer there. I bought a 5-inch-thick memory form, twin -size mattress I placed on top of a folded king size foam resembling a large egg crate. Her place to sleep was well padded, and she was protected from herself, as I placed it against the corner of my room. My bed was opposite it. This worked for a while as she didn't know how to get up off the floor by herself. Then, she learned how to scoot across the floor. Her skin was so very thin and continued to burst open at the slightest impact against something hard. She rubbed the side of her leg on the floor one night trying to scoot into the hallway. It was horrible. It looked like a two-inch section of exposed raw meat. I called an ambulance and followed them into the nearest hospital. Unfortunately, the nurses used the wrong bandages on the open wound. I didn't realize it at the time, but they applied regular gauze to the open wound, and the doctor in charge did not supervise their work. We came home. I was told to change the bandage the next day.

I unwrapped it and was shocked to see the gauze patch the nurses had put over the wound had stuck into the leg. I took her back to the E.R. at the same hospital and told them what had happened. The doctor was very kind and gently unwrapped Mom's bandage. He quickly frowned when he saw the gauze stuck in the meat of her leg, and hollered out

87

loud, "This is torture! They knew this would torture her when it comes out!" Then he yelled in a foreign language, and several nurses came running to assist. He had one bring a tray of sterile instruments, and another nurse brought him a shot to deaden the area at the bandage site. He first sprayed a liquid wound cleaning solution over it that I would later learn was saline to loosen the gauze. Letting it sit for a minute; he liberally sprayed the gauze again. It was running off her leg and onto the floor.

Even with several injections to deaden the pain, Mom screamed bloody murder as he lifted the edges of the gauze up. It had turned as hard as concrete. He administered more injections to further deaden it.

I prayed this time it would work, and he could remove it. He sprayed liberally with liquid wound cleaner again and again. He pulled it out of her leg as she screamed in anguish. I had to turn my head so she couldn't see my tears, and I patted her as he removed it. A thin layer of flesh came out stuck onto the gauze. He was as upset as we were and took a deep breath. He then reported the nurses and assured me they would no longer be employed there. He was so apologetic to Mom and went into detail on how I was to dress her open wounds; even showing me how to do it correctly. He wrote what all I should buy when her thin skin ripped open again. And it did numerous times.

He said the elderly often get thin skin that can burst apart if scratched or bumped into rough objects. Mom was 95 at that time.

First, you apply saline wound wash, then pat the area dry with sterile gauze. Next, you apply a section of yellow pre-soaked gauze (looks like it is in Vaseline) that is sterile and will not stick to the wound; it has medicine that helps new skin develop and grow. Next step: you place a large non-adhesive pad over it, and finally wrap over that pad with regular gauze and secure it with tape onto the gauze without touching the skin. He instructed me to order this and keep it with my first aid items. I order "HEALQU Xeroform Gauze Dressings" 5 inch x 9 inch; then non-adhesive pads 3 x 12, and finally regular gauze and surgical tape. I order

88

these online from Amazon. Several different companies have these items available there in different sizes.

So, this became the new norm. It didn't shock me when it happened again. I calmly dressed her wounds. I also ordered Pro-Stat Concentrated Protein Drink from Amazon. She liked the grape flavor. It resembled honey, had 15 gs. of protein in a 30 oz. bottle and I mixed 2 tablespoons into 8 oz. of water daily for her. A nice Home Health nurse told me about it. I tried that company for a few months, and after she moved, I tried another company. They had a smart aleck attitude and began asking me probing questions about my personal life. I told them that my life had nothing to do with Mom's care and it was personal and none of their business. They became rude, and I must admit I did become rude also. I escorted them to my front door and told them not to ever come back again. So, I discussed it with Mom's doctor, and we cancelled Home Health care.

At the end of the year in November 2024, I went for my annual eye exam for new glasses and was told no new glasses at this time.(I had placed Mom in the wheel chair, put her in my car, and wheeled her inside the eye clinic, as was my routine unless I bought groceries; then I had to leave her in the car and shop super early so she wouldn't get hot in the car during the summer, or shop late in the day in the winter so she could sit in the car basking in the sun.) I needed cataract surgery on both eyes first, before I could get new eyeglasses.

I went to have both eyes examined again by another eye doctor, and yes, the surgery was badly needed. The doctor was the best in the entire area, and I told him to go ahead and schedule the surgeries. He did. The right eye was done Dec. 4, 2024, and the left eye was done Dec. 18, 2024.

All my family have moved to other locations. Some live a two hour drive away; and that's two hours coming here with two hours going back, some over eight hundred miles away, and others live thousands of miles away. It was hard to even find someone to take me to have the surgeries and follow up appointments immediately after the surgeries; as most of my friends have health issues, they can no longer drive or do not live close enough. I asked my neighbor, Aaron, and I was so relieved when she said of course she would. She has a restaurant and catering business and is very busy and still offered to drive me to have my eye surgeries, and watch Mom in her car while they waited for me to come out of anesthesia. She was a big blessing to me! I never could find anyone to help me daily with Mom, though, so I tried to continue taking care of her while my eyes healed. My doctor told me I could not bend down with my head below my waist or pick up anything over ten pounds.

So, I had to put Mom back into the hospital bed at night, as she could swing her legs over the side of the bed and get out instead of me picking her up off the floor.

It started out okay. At first, she didn't try getting out of bed in the dark in the middle of the night. She was too frail and weak to walk by herself, but at night she thought she was a superwoman. January 2025 started out with me continuing to put eye drops in both of my eyes daily. She started yelling at me at 2 AM that she was ready to get up. I'd go into her room, put her hearing aid in, and tell her to go back to sleep that it was two in the morning. She would nod at me, and then did the same thing at 3 AM, 4 AM, 5 AM, 6AM, and finally we'd get up for the day at 7 AM. I'd drink coffee, fix breakfast, yawn and leave her at the table slowly eating and working a Word Search book. I made a chart of when to put which eye drop into which eye and check them off as I completed each one. It was wonderful to lay on the couch those minutes doing eye-drops.

She had no memory of what happened during the night, and would sing gospel songs, or watch television until she began talking about the past as if we were still living in it. It was horrible to watch her slip back 50 or 60 years ago and ask me if I'd met my sister's boyfriend. My sister was married and over 70 years old.

So why didn't I put her in a nursing home?

1. Because I remember her screaming in anguish from how the E.R. nurses didn't bandage her correctly.
2. 2. Because she is so frail and weak. I knew it would be a matter of time when someone wouldn't watch her, and she'd try to walk

and fall breaking who knows what and then deteriorate until she passed away. I didn't want all of that pain and torture for her.

3. And when she lost control of her bowels and urinating, I knew no one would clean her up right away, and she'd get urinary tract infections or diaper rash. I had gloves, diapers, adult cleaning wipes, etc. and had developed a routine that was quick and sanitary.

At times, she'd tell me she loved me. Other times, she'd get mean, yell like a Comanche Indian, and curse me. I always rebuked the cursing and made her apologize and ask Yehovah to forgive her. She would. I knew I'd have to put her back on the floor on a pallet again (a simple bed made from a foam pad, folded blankets and quilts) as soon as my eyes healed. It just wasn't working out with her in the hospital bed and me running across the hallway all night to check on her.

So here we were in January 2025. At 88 pounds, she was so frail I could see the shoulder blades under her skin, and her thin skin draped over the bones of her arm. She has a history of hiding her food in a vase of flowers set on the table, or hidden under a couch cushion, or crammed into the toilet. I had to watch her every minute she was awake. (Later, in August 2025, she weighed 84 lbs.)

An arctic front was on its way sweeping down the United States with sub-freezing temps and bitter cold winds. She began talking out loud all night as she dreamed and hallucinated. The arctic weather approached. I had gone two nights with interrupted sleep. On January 6, 2025, her Dementia and Alzheimer's became too much for me.

At 3 AM, I heard a loud clanging sound coming from her room. I jumped out of my bed, ran across the hallway and saw her beating her hand into the metal guard rails and kicking her legs into them as well. I flipped on the light, put her hearing aid in and asked what she was doing. She promptly replied she wanted out.

(The night before she had wanted to go outside, I told her no it was too cold, and it was in the middle of the night. She argued for hours. No sleep for either of us. So, at 4 AM, I held her arm, walked her out to the back deck and let her see the pitch darkness of being outside. She was fine. I then brought her back inside telling her the warm bed was where she needed to be. She went back to bed then.)

So, here we were again in the middle of the night. She had wet her bed and somehow had managed to pull the large washable pad out from under her and throw it on the floor. I was so disappointed but knew this wasn't really her. This was what was left of her after this awful disease had her.

"I didn't want to do this now with the cold weather coming, but you can't stay in the hospital bed any longer. Your legs and your hand are purple from banging them in the guard rails...they are about to bleed. I must help you up and I want you to sit in this chair while I take your bed apart." She was fine with it. And so, that was the night I moved her out of the green bedroom that had the hospital bed, a television, and my desk computer.

I moved her into a small bedroom also across the hall from my bedroom. I called it the yellow room; it was bright and cheerful with a daybed against one wall that had teddy bears sitting on the yellow bedcover with metal trucks and stuffed dolls scattered about the room. This was the room I had originally fixed for when my young grandchildren spent the night. I moved the Tiffany style yellow floor lamp, and the yellow and white striped wing back chair with matching ottoman out of the room and into my room. I began to once again assemble a pallet for her. I folded the king- size, foam, egg crate in half longways, placed it in the now empty corner of the room and put her 5-inch thick, twin-size, memory foam mattress on top. I had to get a clean sheet as hers was wet. Got a clean pad for it also. Cleaned her up and helped her lay down on it. I put her sleep booties on her feet and three quilts over her. I explained she was not to try and get up, that she was 96 years old, and she needed to rest and get some sleep.

I tried to sleep on my bed and finally gave up the effort as she was still talking. I went into the yellow room where she was and tried to lay on the daybed. She talked out loud constantly from 3AM until 5 AM acting like she was talking to someone on a phone; but at least she couldn't fall out of bed to injure herself. At 5 AM, I left the daybed in that room and went to try and sleep on the couch in the living room.

I did sleep until my dog wanted to go out at 9 AM.

So here I am, writing and including this as one of my true, short stories. In two weeks, I will stop applying drops into my eyes. And my eyes? I give Yehovah the glory! I went from having to wear bifocals to not having to wear any glasses or contacts again!

Mom has awoken twice and both times I calmly explained she must rest her body and stay there on the pallet. She didn't. She'd try to scoot around in the dark. Once I caught her chewing something in her mouth at 2AM. I'd gone to check on her because she started talking out loud hallucinating. I couldn't believe what she was chewing. It was the bloody gauze bandage I'd placed over her arm where her skin had ripped open. Earlier, she'd hollered, "Ouch!" That must have been when she'd yanked the bandage off. Thankfully I found it and removed it from her mouth before the situation became worse.

At the beginning of August 2025, Mom lost all her strength in her legs. I tried to stand her up and help her walk by standing in front of her and holding her up under her arms. She was like a limp rag doll. But she tried. We'd take baby steps in the hallway for about three feet, and she'd say, "Lynn, I just don't think I can do this much longer." And she sounded so tired. I then began physically picking her up off the pallet on the floor at least twice a day, and sometimes at night. I was 76 years old …going to be 77 in December 2025…and could never have physically bent over and picked her body straight up like that if Yehovah hadn't given the strength to do it. Again, I give Him the glory. I then propped her up with pillows so she could sit up on the pallet, and she'd try to fall over to her side while I fed her soft food. She started sleeping more but continued hallucinating.

She kept talking about and to her imaginary little girl. It made me recall how over 40 years ago she took care of my sister's little girl. One of the cutest stories she told me much earlier that did happen was when her granddaughter, Donna, encountered an animal. Donna had been swinging in Mom's rural backyard by herself, when an armadillo came from the woods and meandered towards her. She ran from the swing to the back door of the house yelling, "AN AM-I-NAL, GRANNY, AN AM-I-NAL!" She was so terrified she couldn't say animal correctly. Mom ran to pick her up and comforted her. Donna was about five years old. Later, Mom enrolled her in school. Maybe Mom was remembering those years as if they were happening now. Sometimes she thinks she herself is a schoolgirl, other times that she is 55 years old instead of 97. I was once told another reason the disease is so horrible is to jumble all 97 years of her memories and mix them up out of order; with her remembering anything being similar to finding a needle in a haystack. I asked her during this time to repeat some German phrases to me that were taught to her by her family when she was younger. To my surprise, she told me four brand new phrases she'd never told me before! They must have been recessed way back in her mind.

Then a friend of mine from church who is also a caregiver to her 86-year-old mom with Dementia and Alzheimer's called me.

"How are you guys doing over there?" she asked.

"Well, Mom asks me so often all day, "What day is it?" that after about eighteen times I don't even know what day it is anymore." I laughed. Of course I was joking, but I knew she could relate to how they repeat the same thing over and over.

"I have just the thing for her and you both. I went through that with Mom, and it really helped. Are you still a notary?"

"Yes, I am. If you need something notarized bring it over."

"Great, I'll be there in a few minutes if that is convenient for you."

"Yes, that will work."

Tina's husband stayed with her mom, while she drove to my house. She had what looked like an electric tablet. She plugged it in and the date, the day, the time, and an icon showing the sun for AM and the moon for PM; all in large print appeared.

"It is perfect!"

We placed it near the table where Mom eats. She would still ask me what day it was, and I'd point to the clock. She'd smile and look at it. Each day she'd say how nice it was of that girl to bring the clock to us.

"Tina, her name is Tina." I'd remind her. Tina later told me her mother no longer knows me either. That is just part of it.

Mom is still sleeping on the pallet on the floor in the yellow room. She began telling me she loves me after I tuck her in at night with all the quilts. I assure her I love her also or I wouldn't be taking care of her. At this time, she also began thanking me for taking such good care of her, and she'd smile at me with a warm, loving smile. I'd give her a hug and try not to cry as all I could feel were her bones.

 Our routine each night was that after I wrapped her feet with a small, soft throw; keeping each foot warm and not touching the other foot so she wouldn't get pressure point sores, I'd tuck her sides in with 3 quilts. I'd blow her a kiss, and she'd do the same back to me. She always wanted to know what day is tomorrow and I tell her, then I'd say, "God bless you." She'd say, "God bless you" and we'd both smile. Then I'd tell her Yeshua loves her, Yehovah loves her, and I love her, and we want her to rest now. Then I'd take out her hearing aid, turn out the light, close the door, and begin my nightly prayers.

Toward the end, she forgot how to swallow water, or pills. I had to show her how to tilt her head back and how to swallow. It worked. She'd gulp air and then finally swallow. She had also begun to hallucinate about having a little girl for the past two months, and she was becoming weaker. She constantly wanted to know if I'd seen her little girl, and I told her no. At times, the little girl was in the room with her…or so she thought, and other times she decided the lady down the road was taking care of her little girl. She covered the little girl up at night acting like the child was sleeping next to her. She still hallucinated about other thing, but mainly "her little girl."

 I called my sister Geraldine, her daughter Donna, and her son Ross, and her grandson Dustin, my two sons Mike and Jeff and my granddaughter Jessica; and had them talk to Mom one at a time over the speaker phone. I told them she wasn't doing well, and I thought they'd like to talk to her and tell her hi. They all appreciated me doing that so they could hear her little voice and talk to her. My sister and most of her family lived two hours away in Louisiana. Her husband had health problems so they could only visit Mom at Christmas or her birthday/Mother's Day. Mom's birthday was close to Mother's Day. And one of my sons lived in West Virginia as did his daughter, so they couldn't visit often. My other son lived near the Texas border about 8 hours away, so he couldn't visit often either. She smiled through all the phone calls, and then my sister and her daughter came the following day to visit Mom.

Before they arrived, Mom was talking about her little girl again. I asked her what the little girl's name was, and she replied happily, "Donna!"

So here comes Geraldine, age 72, and her daughter Donna, about 53 years old, into the yellow room at my house. Mom is lying on her pallet. Donna sat next to the pallet on the floor Indian style with legs folded under her and kissed her granny's hands.

"This is Donna! She's all grown up now." I motioned to Donna who was holding Mom's hands, kissing them, and telling Granny that she loved her.

Mom glowed with love and admiration for her. Mom looked at her with so much happiness and love! And kept it up! Geraldine bent over and hugged and kissed her mother and then sat beside me on the yellow daybed.

I put my arm around Geraldine's back and looked at Mother. "Do you know who this is?" I asked. "This is Geraldine." I smiled.

"Yes, I know who she is." She returned the smile and quickly focused on Donna again.

"My little girl! Look at you! You are beautiful!" Mom glowed with happiness and love as Donna continued to kiss her Granny's hands.

"You used to keep her for Geraldine when she was a little girl. When Geraldine went to Florida. You even started her in school. Remember?" (Mom had said for years Geraldine was in Florida.)

96

"Oh yes! You have grown up, Donna! My little girl!"

Geraldine corrected me, and said "Dallas, I was in Dallas."

I nodded yes to my sister, but I wasn't going to correct Mom. If she wanted to keep thinking it was Florida, it wouldn't hurt anything. I knew Geraldine felt the same way. Years earlier, Geraldine had called Mom long distance and collect. That same day, Mom wanted to play with my oldest son, Mike, who was about three or four years old at the time. I lived next door and had just put my youngest son, Jeff, down for his nap. Mom ran over to my house to get something and told Mike to sit in a chair and not get up, that she'd be right back.

As soon as she left, the phone rang. It was Geraldine calling collect on a long-distance call. Mike answered the phone, and Geraldine told the operator that it was her young nephew and to please tell him to go get Granny. The operator relayed the message, and Mike solemnly replied, "Ain't nobody he-ah but me and duh dogs."

We all laughed about that later. So, whether it was her trip to Dallas or Florida, it didn't really matter. The memory was still a sweet one.

Needless to say, Mom loved the visit we had that day in the yellow room. Donna and Geraldine left, went to the store, and brought back snacks and groceries she and I could both eat. Mom even fed herself chocolate pudding with her right hand as her left hand shook. (She was left-handed.) We were all impressed and told her so. It made her feel so good about herself. They promised to return soon for another visit, and hugs and kisses were exchanged. It was a treasured moment shared together. She passed away three days later.

Yes, it took a lot of patience, and a lot of love. One of the worse things I experienced was when I heard her saying something over and over. I ran into the yellow room to check on her, and I cried when I saw her. It was so pitiful! She lay sideways with her back on the hardwood floor, legs across the pallet, and she had taken her shirt off. She kept staring in space; the only part of her moving was her head going up and down, and saying "What day is it? What day is it? What day is it?" I lost it! She reminded me of a broken wind-up children's toy that fell over and still had

97

one part moving. I cried so hard as I picked her up, dressed her, and put her back on the pallet. She never knew what happened.

Of course, the only thing worse than that was finding she had passed away. She had called for me by name three times that night. I was up and down with her a lot. Once, she told me to help her up…that she needed to cook supper. I told her she didn't have to cook anymore that I did all of that. Her face lit up, and she grinned. "Oh, I don't have to!" She was excited. The other two times she thought she needed help with something else, and I told her it was okay, everything would be fine, and to rest and get some sleep. Then she hallucinated the rest of the night. At 5 am she sounded excited and gasped out loud 4 times in a row. (It did not sound like anything painful.) I knew she'd swallowed air with that and went to check on her. She belched out the air, and no, it was not like a death rattle. She was sound asleep, and I didn't dare wake her up to ask what or who she had seen when she had gasped excitedly. She had finally gone to sleep after being up for so many hours. At 8 am she had been quiet for about an hour when I went to check on her again. Her forehead and neck were cool, it looked like she wasn't breathing, but her arm was still very warm. I called my son Jeff, and he said to put a mirror below her nose. I did, and there was no fog on the mirror by her nose. She had just then passed away peacefully in her sleep as her arm was still so warm. That was so final. It was painful for us, exactly like it was later for me to see the funeral home's hearse back up to my front door. They covered her up, placed her on a stretcher and rolled the stretcher into the hearse. I cried as the hearse left my house and drove off down my country road. That was her last time travelling on this road that she and I had been on together for decades. It was a sight I will never forget. It was such a sad moment to see the hearse going away with her in it.

Earlier, after I had called 911, the Sheriff's Department sent the EMS, and a deputy arrived. EMS took an EKG. I saw the straight line. The Justice of The Peace arrived. The people from the funeral home arrived in a hearse. And one special detective from the local Police Department heard the call on the radio and also came.

The Justice of The Peace officer looked at the detective and asked, "Why are you here?" (As this was a county jurisdiction.) The officer and detective were friends. The detective smiled and nodded towards me and said, "That's my grandma."

I was so glad to see my Grandson, Austin! I got the biggest hug from him, and I was so relieved I had family with me. He told me when he heard my address on the radio, he had to come and be with me. He was such a blessing.

Mom passed away on the morning of September 9, 2025. She was 97 years old. She also passed away on my oldest son's birthday. We will celebrate both of them then. It is odd to get into my car and not have her sitting in the passenger seat. She was my passenger in my car for over ten years, and yes, my house seems so quiet now. She and I were together 24/7 for well over ten years also. I keep waking up hourly all night as both of my dogs do; we were so used to her calling out to me or hallucinating and talking out loud to others in her dreams each night. She is greatly missed but is finally at peace and resting in a much better place. I give Yehovah the glory I was able to care for her while she was still here! One of the German phrases she taught me from her German family was "Sas ist alles" that means "That is all." That is not all for her though, her journey with our Lord Jesus Christ has just begun!

†☐ †☐ †☐

Exodus 20: 12 "Honor your father and your mother that your days may be long upon the land which the LORD your God gives you."

Ephesians 6: 2-3 "Honor your father and mother (which is the first Commandment with Promise,) That it may be well with you, and you may live long on the earth.

Moral of the story: Give flowers to the living for them to enjoy, don't wait to give flowers at their funeral. Spend quality time with your parents and be thankful to Yah for your time together.

The End

Chapter Twelve

She Likes to Talk Like That...

A few days ago, at a local restaurant, I couldn't help but overhear two men talking loudly at the next table. I didn't know them and had never seen them before. Their conversation was rough, filled with foul language, complaints, and stories that made it clear they weren't thinking about the Lord.

Those at my table and I were waiting for our food to arrive. We tried to visit among ourselves, but the men's voices carried through the room. We smiled politely at each other, trying to ignore them, but it was hard not to hear every word.

Then something changed in their tone. One of the men laughed and said, "We moved my mother-in-law in with us, and I even invited the pastor to come have dinner at our house after church Sunday."

The other man looked shocked. "At your house?" he asked.

The first man chuckled again, lifted his hand toward the ceiling, and said mockingly, "Hallelujah!" Then, shaking his head, he told his friend with a grin, "Yes, she talks like that!"

His friend laughed, and they went right back to their coarse conversation as if nothing had happened.

But that phrase stayed with me.
"She talks like that."

It echoed in my heart for the rest of the day.

Wow. Brings to mind different scenarios, and so many ways to look at them.

None of us are perfect, but I question why this dramatic display.

This phrase keeps staying fresh on my mind. I have a strong belief in my faith and have strong convictions. I try to treat others as I would like to be treated also.

Would a stranger think that I "liked to talk like that?" Or would my actions speak for themselves? Would they know me for my Christian faith, and my Christian values? I would pray to be a friend and a Christian example to others.

Was the first man telling his friend about his mother-in-law as a way to "break the ice" and discuss spiritual beliefs? Or was he embarrassed by her faith?

Was the other man having lunch to keep a "valuable contact"? A guess would be a waste of time. Never assume anything.

I hope that if someone ever says about me, "She talks like that," it's because they see an unwavering devotion to my God. I pray that even in mockery, they recognize the truth behind my words and the sincerity in my actions. May my life speak as loudly as my faith, and may everything I say and do reflect the One I serve.

†☐ †☐ †☐

Psalms 32: 10 (New Living Translation) Many sorrows come to the wicked, but unfailing love surrounds those who trust the LORD.

Psalms 118: 8 It is better to take refuge in the LORD than to trust in people.

Psalms 56: 3-4 But when I am afraid, I will put my trust in You. I praise God for what He has promised. I trust in God, so why should I be afraid? What can mere mortals do to me?

Psalms 18: 2 The LORD is my rock, my fortress, and my Savior; my God is my rock, in whom I find protection. He is my shield, the power that saves me, and my place of safety.

Moral of the story: We have no idea how many non-Christians are around us daily. Wherever you are, and whoever you encounter, pray earnestly for all to want to receive Yeshua as their Lord and Savior. If possible, ask them what their spiritual beliefs are, and share yours.

The End

Chapter Thirteen

Emma

In many small towns across the USA, generations of black and white families grow up side by side. Neighbors know each other's parents and grandparents and often see one another almost every day. There's a sense of familiarity and comfort that comes with small-town life where everyone knows everyone.

If the town is large enough to have a Family Dollar store, it quickly becomes the local gathering spot, something like a small shopping mall or community center. Teens with cars lean against them in the parking lot, laughing and talking, while others stroll around visiting with friends. Friday night football games, school events, and baseball games bring the community together, filling the stands with cheering families and the smell of popcorn.

It all seems simple and wholesome, and in many ways it is. But not every story that starts in a small town has an innocent ending. When young people don't understand the difference between lust and love, the choices they make can ripple through their lives and disrupt entire families for years to come.

Emma had gone to a party in a nearby town with her friends. One young man, who was a few years older than Emma, was instantly attracted to her. She wasn't used to the rush of attention he gave her. After the party, he drove her home assuring her he'd be seeing her often.

And he did.

In time, she discovered he was a drug dealer. She soon became addicted and pregnant. After several years and raising three children together, she continued to live with him in the same nearby town. On this particular day though, she happened to be riding in the car with him and the children when a police officer pulled them over.

The father of her children quickly shoved his bag of drugs into her purse.

The officer had a warrant for him and discovered Emma had drugs in her possession. Both went to jail, and child protection services came for the children.

The two older children, aged five and seven, gave the authorities their mother's parents' names and phone numbers. The baby was one and a half years old.

Arrangements were made before the Judge for the grandparents to keep the children until their parents obtained an attorney.

Emma finally agreed to treatment at a local drug rehab center. She later moved in with her parents.

The children's father remained in custody for several months. Upon receiving probation, he immediately drove to Emma's parents' house and got Emma. They left in a hurry.

Emma's parents were furious. Her father drove around trying to find them. He finally found them in a local motel, and he escorted Emma out of the motel room and into his car. Emma was already so drugged she could hardly stand up to walk.

He took her home and put her to bed before the children could see her.

"I can't have this. She can't take off like that and leave the kids to be with him." He told his wife and his anger raged. "We're getting custody of the kids. She's no good for them, and neither is he."

"I wouldn't have it any other way. They are our Grandkids." She assured him.

They got an attorney.

And yes, they got legal custody of all three children.

Emma went back to a drug rehab facility.

The children's father could still visit them once a month. And no, he and Emma were never married.

The first time he came to see them, he took all three kids to eat ice cream, and then over to the public park to swing. He brought them back at the correct time. No problem.

The following month he picked the children up again. This time he drove out of town and into the country. The two older children testified they had stopped on a dirt road near the river where a car was parked. They watched in horror as their father shot and killed the two people in the parked car. Screaming, they held onto each other as their father raced back to their Grandparents house and let them out in the front yard, baby and all.

His motive for the killings was never discovered. Authorities did consider his lifestyle as well as that of the victims and speculated it could have easily been a drug deal gone bad.

And that trauma for the kids began years of counseling. And yes, their father was arrested and sent to prison for forty years.

Understandably, the Grandparents became overly protective of the kids. They took them everywhere. Those kids felt their Grandparents love and felt safe with them. Years before, the baby had been locked in a closet for hours by his father when he was under a year old. The father even named the child a name from a foreign country as he believed that was not his child. He began hitting Emma and accusing her of having boyfriends from foreign countries. Both older children later related this to their Grandparents.

They had all been through so much turmoil and chaos.

Emma was still in rehab. Her father decided it was time for them to start going to church and bring the children up with Christian values.

The first time they went, everyone in the church turned around to look at them as they walked in. They smiled, and people smiled back.

The next time they went, people stared at them. Some would nudge the one sitting next to them and nod towards the Grandparents and their Grandchildren.

The congregation saw two very white Grandparents walking in with three very black Grandchildren.

Emma's parents were uncomfortable as people kept staring at them. Even the children asked why people were staring at them.

After three times of the same type of reception, they quit going to church. They bought children picture story Bibles and began reading with them. School resumed after the summer, and life became a busy routine.

Emma was released and returned to her parents' home.

Mr. Woods was helpful in obtaining a job for his daughter. Emma took the job in an office, and loved it. She would come home from work, spend time with her children, and help her mother cook dinner. It was enjoyable for all.

Until she happened to see an old school chum she hadn't seen in years at the Post Office one evening. He wasn't working, didn't even have a car, had kids of his own though…by three different women…and was living at his mother's house. His kids lived with their own respective mother's.

Of course he was happy Emma had a great job, and wanted to see her again, soon.

And so begins the story of Emma Woods and LaMar Morris.

It was at this point in time that Mr. Woods heard from a friend of his who desperately needed someone with Emma's training to supervise the part-time help at his business. He was out of town often and needed someone he could trust.

Emma was excited and turned in her two weeks' notice at her present job. It was a fantastic opportunity. She enjoyed having more responsibility at this job and spoke highly of it.

Mr. and Mrs. Woods were so proud of the change in her, they purchased a house for her and her children to live in and be their own family for the first time.

Emma and her children were thrilled. With her parents' help, Emma began obtaining furniture for the house and decorating it. Each child had their own bedroom for the first time in their life. The school bus picked the kids up in the morning and Emma then left for work. She arrived home shortly after they returned home from school. They did homework from school until she came home from work.

And then the unthinkable happened.

The owner of the business at her new job called Emma's parents. Emma had left in her car after only working a few hours that morning and had not returned. It was two o'clock in the afternoon and he was worried about her.

Mr. Woods told him he hadn't heard from her, but she had may have become ill and was at a doctor's clinic. He assured them that Emma was independent and enjoyed taking care of her own problems. He thought she would return before the five o'clock rush on the store.

He put the issue out of his mind and returned to his own work at his job.

That evening his oldest Grandchild phoned.

It was nine o'clock at night.

His voice quivered as he spoke to his grandfather. "Mom hasn't come home...and we're hungry."

"We'll be right there, hang on."

Mr. Woods cringed as he ended the call.

Where was she?

He told his wife what happened, and they hurried to get hamburgers for the kids and took the meal to them. Mrs. Woods stayed with them while Mr. Woods went in search of his daughter.

Surely, she wouldn't just leave her kids, her job, her own home...for time alone with some man!

He recalled her mentioning something about LaMar Morris living with his mother.

He spun his car around and drove to LaMar's mother's house.

Thank God this is a small town, and everyone knows everyone here.

He caught his breath as he approached the Morris house.

There it was.

Emma's car was parked in the driveway.

His chest instantly hurt, and tears filled his eyes.

Dear Lord, not again, he prayed, as he parked his own car, and walked to the front door.

Suddenly the front door of the house was flung open. The couple stood together half dressed.

Didn't his daughter have respect enough for herself but to wait for marriage? Or consider her children?

No, she wanted the drugs that he provided.

LaMar had his arm behind Emma, obviously holding her up. He looked boldly at Mr. Woods with defiance. And Emma? She could hardly focus her eyes. She smiled sheepishly.

Their odor hit him with full force then. He grimaced.

They stunk!

"I'm done, Emma. This is your choice for your new life, and your new home."

He turned and walked away.

No, he didn't look back at them.

And LaMar's mother?

She was elderly and senile. She probably didn't know Emma was even there.

And so it continued.

The children moved back in with their Grandparents. Their home with their mother was now history. Someone else took Emma's place at her job.

At school events, Emma's kids would see their mother sitting in the bleachers with LaMar and his children.

No, Emma never went to them. Never even waved at them.

Friends told Mr. & Mrs. Woods she still couldn't focus her eyes, and she laughed a lot.

It continued for years.

The two older children graduated from high school and then graduated college. The younger one just graduated from high school.

And Emma?

She and LaMar are no longer living together.

Emma has some gray hair now.

She works at a truck stop in another town.

Mr. Woods once asked the children if they wanted to see their mother for Christmas. He told them if they did, he would invite her over. They took a vote, writing their answer on a slip of paper and dropping the paper into Mr. Woods' hat.

He opened each folded slip of paper.

All three children voted no.

And they are all quite happy today.

And the Grandparents? They give God the glory for the Christian values and morals the children now have…in spite of everything that was against them.

They remain a close-knit family.

†□ †□ †□

John 10: 1-15 (New Living Translation)

The Good Shepherd and His Sheep

"I tell you the truth, anyone one sneaks over the wall of a sheepfold, rather than going through the gate, must surely be a thief and a robber! But the one who enters through the gate is the shepherd of the sheep. The gatekeeper opens the gate for him, and the sheep recognize his voice and come to him. He calls his own sheep by name and leads them out. After he has gathered his own flock, he walks ahead of them, and they follow him because they know his voice. They won't follow a stranger, they will run from him because they don't know his voice. Those who heard Jesus use this illustration didn't understand what he meant, so he explained it to them: "I tell you the truth, I am the gate for the sheep. All who came before me were thieves and robbers. But the true sheep did not listen to them. Yes, I am the gate. Those who come in through me will be saved. They will come and go freely and will find good pastures. The thief's purpose is to steal, and kill, and destroy. My purpose is to give them a rich and satisfying life. I am the good shepherd. The good shepherd sacrifices his life for his sheep. A hired hand will run when he sees a wolf coming. He will abandon the sheep because they don't belong to him and he isn't their shepherd. And so the wolf attacks them and scatters the flock. The hired hand runs away because he's working only for money and doesn't really care about the sheep. I am the good shepherd. I know my own sheep, and they know me, just as my Father knows me and I know the Father. So I sacrifice my life for the sheep.

Moral of the story: An old saying is true here; believe half of what you see, and none of what you hear. The couple did their best to raise their grandchildren and help their rebellious daughter in the midst of small town gossip and racial prejudice. My son Jeff once said, "Don't be quick to point a finger at anyone; when you do, four more of your own fingers are pointing back at you." I like that saying also!

The End

Chapter Fourteen

Kicking Tires

Heat shimmered from the pavement as the scorching sun blazed. It was bad. The glare on the cars blinded me as we stepped from the grocery store. Scanning the sweltering parking lot for my car, I gave a half-hearted shrug. Squinting, I cupped my hand against my forehead and continued searching.

"There it is, Ne-Ne. I see the P.T. Cruiser." Lake, my seven-year-old Grandson, calmly announced and pointed at the vehicle. It was parked in the next row and looked magnificent. Hand-washed with Turtle Wax Car Wash, the dead bugs came off, and the white paint shined beautifully. It was well worth my effort. And the sunroof was a bonus. Both my Grandson Lake, and my Granddaughter Jessica, enjoyed gazing at the clouds as I drove.

Today it was the three of us; Lake, my mother, and myself. We had left my home full of energy. After a few hours, though, we were drained from completing errands-entirely too many stops at various businesses; the pharmacy, cleaners, and now the grocery store. It was pleasant, but we were done...totally zapped.

I clicked the remote unlocking the car and we made a slow advance towards it. Lake walked straight to the front passenger door, and opened it for my 80-year-old mother. She slipped in and sank into the padded seat. "Thank you so much, Lake. You are such a gentleman."

"You are welcome, and thank you, Ging-Ging," He solemnly stated, and climbed into the back seat. Busy, he quietly adjusted the head rest and buckled his seat belt.

I waited as the carry-out employee unloaded bags of groceries into the rear of the car. Sweat rolled down his face, and he tried to smile. I felt like hugging him for working in such conditions but refrained. Instead, I helped him unload the bags from the cart into my car. Ripping open a package of paper towels I'd just bought, I handed him several paper towel sheets. He wiped sweat off his entire face.

"Thank you, Ma'am." He nodded.

"I know how that can sting your eyes. Here, put some in your pocket for later." I unrolled several more sheets and shoved them at him. He snatched onto them, smiled, and left.

Hastening to the front of the car, I plopped down in the driver's seat and turned on the ignition. It seemed to take forever before slightly cool air blasted out of the air conditioner vents.

"It's getting cooler." Mom declared. She stretched her legs out and sighed deeply.

Lake folded his hands behind his head, a half-smile growing-obviously savoring the improved degree of coolness filtering through the car.

Sensitive feelings tugged at my heart as I observed each of them relax-with no complaints, no rudeness. That was something that wasn't in their nature. Both caring and both helpful. I smiled with love at them.

"Is anyone getting hungry?" I inquired.

"I am." Mom blurted.

"Me too, Ne-Ne."

"Fried chicken, okay?" I backed the car, veered to the exit and blended into the traffic on the main road.

"Golden Chick's?" Mom raised her eyebrows.

"Sure. I like their crunchy chicken. What about you two?"

"I'd like the dark meat, mostly legs." Mom replied.

"Chicken strips for me." Lake chimed in.

"Sounds good, we'll be there in less than ten minutes." I changed lanes while I had a chance. Traffic moved smoothly. Two blocks away from

114

Golden Chick's Fried Chicken restaurant, my car suddenly made a horrible squealing noise.

I gasped. Shocked, Mom and Lake looked at me wide eyed. The instant I drove into the parking lot, the sound stopped.

Quickly, I glanced in the restaurant windows and noticed standing room only. All of the tables were taken with other customers.

"That noise must have been a fan belt. I remember that's what it was years ago when Pop's old truck conked out…sounded about the same…" I frowned at my own conclusion.

Making my way to the drive-in window, I dismissed the thought and quickly ordered our meal.

"It's too crowded inside; we'll have to eat in the car. Try not to make a mess but don't worry about it. I can clean the car, later. At least the A.C. is blowing ice-cold air. I'll leave the car on while we eat."

Two weary faces responded with a quiet nod.

After waiting several minutes our order was ready, and I finally found a parking space. Food and drinks were distributed. We all ate hungrily, crumbs falling about as our appetites kicked into high gear.

As we ate, I recalled 'the sound' first began a week ago. It was frightening to say the least. I called the dealership, and they suggested I bring it to the service department. My neighbor thought it was the main fan belt. Our small-town, local, shade tree mechanic mentioned it could be the axel weakening. No one could understand why it happened, but all agreed I should wait for another occurrence before returning to the dealership. Not being knowledgeable about cars, I took their advice but felt uneasy about it.

However, I investigated other brands of vehicles for gas milage, safety, etc. My car was recently paid for, and in the back of my mind, I knew I'd have to use it for a trade in, eventually.

Silently debating the issue, I finished eating and passed the bag around for trash and empty food containers.

115

"I'm done, Ne-Ne." Lake through his induvial box into the bag with the others. Mom opened small, disposable, wet towels, and we cleaned our hands. Full and refreshed, we perked up, almost as energetic as when we first left home earlier.

"Let's go." I announced, and everyone quickly buckled their seat belt. I backed out of the slot and left the parking lot. Minutes later, a few blocks away, the sound' returned worse than ever.

"Lord, protect us," I said half-aloud, and paused. "This is a safety issue. I don't care what anyone else thinks. I'm going by my first instincts." I glanced at my passengers and spoke in a steady low-pitch voice. "We are going straight to the Toyota dealership to look at cars."

"Woo-hoo!" Lake sat up straight in his seat.

"Good idea." Mom, with strong eye contact, nodded at me.

Driving a few more miles on Highway 80, I was amazed when 'the sound' grew quieter. Eventually it disappeared altogether.

Searching for the Toyota business, I drove further and decided it was not on this highway. Slowing my car, I signaled to turn. Lake leaned forward.

"What are you turning for, Ne-Ne? It's on down the highway,"

"I don't remember it being this far."

"It is, Ne-Ne. Keep going we're almost there."

My Grandson is seven, going on twenty. Smart, alert, he takes in information like water soaks into a sponge. I knew he had to be right. He knew what he was talking about.

"Okay, I'll keep going straight."

Three miles later the tall Toyota sign jutted above all the rest.

"There it is," Lake yelled.

"Thank you, Lake…woo-hoo!" I veered my car into their driveway and passed the many rows of parked vehicles. All three of us looked in a different direction as I came to a complete stop at the main office. Cars, trucks, and SUV's surrounded us in every color currently available. It was an awesome assortment.

Mom was the first one out of the car. Lake was a close second, and the salesman approached as I exited the P. T. Cruiser.

"Good afternoon, ma'am. May I help you?"

"Oh, no, thank you. We're just looking."

"Well, if you find anything you like let me know."

"I sure will." I pivoted to address Mom and Lake only to find Mom intently examining a nearby car. Lake had spotted a small compact car and motioned towards it. I shook my head in a negative response and pointed to the far corner of the lot.

"We have to find something that's not so low to the ground. When you get older you will understand. It's hard climbing in and out of anything whether it's a couch, a chair, or a vehicle."

"Okay, Ne-Ne." He sprinted to the lot I'd shown him.

"Mom, come over here." I waved to her, and she eased by several cars to get to me.

We strolled to the area that had RAV 4 vehicles. Lake opened the driver's door on one and sat inside. He examined the instrument panel and the seat adjustments.

"What do you think, Ne-Ne?"

"I like the size. It's not a low ride close to the ground." I peeped and took a long, hard look at the interior. "No, I can't drive a stick shift. I did years ago, but I don't like it now. Let's look at some others."

"It's not a stick shift, Ne-Ne. That's the way they make them now."

I studied his young, serious face and realized he was up to date on the latest models of cars.

I sighed. "What are you talking about?"

"See? It does not have the H pattern of the old stick shift. This just shifts to drive, park, neutral, and reverse. There is no clutch."

"Well, you are so right. I didn't notice."

He grinned.

"Okay, I know I want a Rav 4. I googled it online and like what I saw. It gets great gas mileage, the price is reasonable, and you don't feel like you are sitting on the ground."

I glanced at Mom. "Try getting into this car and tell me if you need help." I stood nearby ready to assist her.

Mom opened the passenger door and ran her hand above the side window for the pull-down hand grip. She grabbed a hold of it and lowered herself into the car with no problem.
"Okay, that confirms it. Let's go in the dealer showroom."

We walked in and there on display was a brand new, sparkling RAV 4. Being super shiny, and jet black, it stood out above the rest. We three were all over it.

"Ma'am, I see you found something. Do you mind if I test drive your car? In case we use it as a trade-in today?"

"Oh, you don't want to drive my car. It's not clean right now and..."

He interrupted. "It will help to know what the boss will offer for your car."

"Well, it's not acting right but here you go." I handed him my car keys.

Lake narrowed his eyes and studied the RAV 4. Stepping close, he drew his leg back and started kicking the tires. Satisfied all was well, he nodded at Mom and me.

The salesman mumbled as he walked off." That kid is checking out the tires...those really are new Toyota tires..."

I considered how much this car could haul in the back. "Let's put the back seats down." We did, and I was hooked. All three of us were. This was the perfect vehicle for me.

I meandered to the front of the showroom, waiting for the salesman to return with my P. T. Cruiser. Picking up a magazine, I thumbed through it and glanced up at the wall clock.

He's been gone for fifteen minutes...surely the car didn't break down somewhere...

Mom and Lake joined me, and we wandered to the waiting room, complete with coffee and a television broadcasting a popular food channel. I went towards the service area and asked for the remote. The employee gladly handed it to me. I scrambled back to the waiting room. At this time, others sat waiting for their cars to be serviced. Some read newspapers while others gazed at their smart phones, and no one was watching the television.

"Do you mind if I watch the national news?"

"No, go ahead." Everyone was in agreement, so I settled into a chair and changed the channel.

Got to stay informed...

I listened to a reverse mortgage commercial and forgot we weren't alone in the waiting room when I commented to Mom.

"Can you believe that propaganda? I wonder how much that actor was paid to look and act so sincerely."

"Mrs. Helen's daughter talked her into having a reverse mortgage on her home, then got power of attorney, and put Mrs. Helen in a nursing home. The daughter got the money and moved back up north. Mrs. Helen can't play her piano anymore, her daughter sold it, and her home went to the state." Mom's face grew flushed discussing her friend and the problems she had with a reverse mortgage and her daughter.

"Excuse me, but I believe a reverse mortgage on your home is very helpful to our senior citizens." I glanced at the stranger sitting proud and straight in his chair. He had obviously overheard our conversation.

"Do you have children?" I asked.

"No ma'am, I don't, and with prices sky high our seniors are anxiously struggling with their low, fixed income from social security. If they can get the money for their house now, when they need it, who cares if the state does get the house later?"

"I'm trying to be broadminded," I told him. "But I do have children. I don't know what your spiritual beliefs are, but I am a Christian. It is biblical to leave an inheritance to your children, and that is my plan. Even if it wasn't biblical, I want my children to always have a home they can go to if the need arises, and I am no longer here."

"I think we both understand each other's views." He sighed. "This economy has us all walking on eggs."

Another man spoke up. "Sometimes it's hard not to throw those eggs." He laughed and everyone seemed to identify with that statement.

"I sure don't want to be around if that happens." Lake shook his head, and the adults quickly changed the subject. I was glad the experience wasn't lost on my Grandson.

I obtained another cup of coffee and provided Lake with money to purchase bottled water for both him and Mom from the nearby vending machine.

Where is the salesman who left with my car?

The manager approached and invited me into his office. There sat the salesman. I guess he entered through another door. I was presented with a terrific contract, and I signed it. Thankful for such a great deal, I could now drive a safe car in warranty.

Lake and Mom met me in the hallway. Excited, we swiftly made our way outside to my RAV 4 to transfer belongings from the old car to the new one. The salesman followed us and pulled me to the side.

"Would you believe that kid checked out the tires on your new car?" He grinned.

"Yes, he's pretty thorough." I beamed.

Taking Lake at face value-the salesman had been impressed with his actions- a young boy kicking tires. That's fine, but I realized the depth of what he missed by not *knowing* Lake. He didn't know the reasoning, beliefs, kindness, character, or values that made my Grandson the exceptional young man he is. Of course, the salesman didn't have time, but with anyone it's a missed opportunity unless you make the effort.

And the car? With regular maintenance and new tires and batteries, I drove that as my only transportation for 17 years! And yes, I stayed with the model and car company; I now have a 2022 Toyota Hybrid RAV4! Good to go!

†☐ †☐ †☐

NKJV: Proverbs 3:5 "Trust in the Lord with all your heart and lean not on your own understanding."

Moral of the story: I didn't come unglued when my car began making noises. When you get lemons, make lemonade. Trust in the Lord. You are part of His plan!

The End

Chapter Fifteen

Restricted From a Social Media Platform

I enjoyed the social media platform for many years as a Christian writer connecting with friends, family, writers, readers, and I loved the gardening and canning tips. I am also the caregiver to my 96-year-old mother who lives with me. She will be 97 on May 21, 2025.

Before she moved in with me, she lived next door. While writing my books, she'd knock on my window and bring me a plate of food. She didn't want me to be interrupted from writing by having to stop and fix a meal. Always encouraging me to write and she loved reading them. I give God the glory that I have authored seven published Christian books, and that four of them received first place awards in Christian Fiction and Biography by The Texas Association of Authors.

After she moved in with me, we both looked forward to the online posts, comments, and videos on my desk computer daily. It was instant entertainment to share with her. I'd position two chairs in front of my desk computer, and I'd have snacks on a tray for her to eat.

Then one day it all stopped. I went to the social media site, and they informed me I could no longer post or comment.

How unfair! I could not speak to anyone about it, could not argue…I could only select one of their reasons as to why I was done unjustly…and none of their reasons applied to me. I did as they requested and waited for days. They had stated I could not comment or post for 30 days. Several days later, I tried to comment again on someone's post, and it suddenly let me post!

So, I'm back...before the end of the restriction of no post and no comments from Dec. 29, 2024, until Jan. 29, 2025.

And what happened? To begin with, I first posted the post of the Bible stating marriage was only between a man and a woman. That is what started this. I had two gay women comment on my Christian page that there was nothing wrong with two women being intimate with each other (my way of describing the awful words they used). They graphically described what they did to each other, and that I was being horrible to them. I blocked them immediately and deleted their comment off my page. Instantly, a man comments that he does not like what I write (I am a published author of Christian Fiction and Christian Biography.) He then used the F--- word and the S---word in describing how awful my writing and I are. I immediately reported him for hate speech and blocked him as well. The social media platform fact checkers had no problem with what they posted on my page. That did not upset their community standards. With that in mind, I have decided that group is how I got restricted. Those three must have a lot of pull with this social media platform!

The day before, in my social media memories, a Shabbat Shalom post came up that I shared to my media page. It had been in my memories in the previous years also. THIS IS WHAT THE FACT CHECKERS SAID WAS AGAINST THEIR COMMUNITY STANDARDS AND WAS WAY TOO SEXUAL TO BE POSTED!!! It was the face of a young girl blowing a kiss with her hand and the STAR of DAVID was at the top of the post with the only words, SHABBAT SHALOM. That is why I was restricted! Nothing sexual about it, and it made it the last two years as a memory that was posted with no problem! So, while I was denied access to wish friends Happy New Year, or comment on anything; I began writing...and yes, this whole episode is documented for future reference, if it happens again. I have another Bible scripture that pertains to this perfectly, and I will share that with you. Isaiah 5: 20 "Woe unto them who call evil good and good evil; who put darkness for light, and light for darkness, who put bitter for sweet, and sweet for bitter!" Do I forgive them? Yes, I do. And I will warn others, and I will not be silent. Psalms 32: 18 is another reference, "Let the lying lips be put to silence which speak grievous things proudly and contemptuously against the righteous." Also, Isaiah 54: 17 "No weapon that is formed against you shall prosper; and every tongue that shall rise against you in judgement you shall condemn. This is the heritage of the servants of the Lord, and their righteousness is of

Me, saith the Lord." I do pray for my enemies to accept Jesus Christ as their Lord, Master, and Savior. The Bible also states that in the latter days Christians will be persecuted. They may still persecute me on this social media platform, but they cannot rob me of my joy!

In January 2025, the owner of the social media platform decided to no longer have fact checkers. He stated that they were often biased against other religions, against other political parties, and against health information…who… were in fact for the corrupt misinformation given in propaganda announcements they…along with the countries and companies …. would profit from.

†☐ †☐ †☐

Romans 12: 2 And be not conformed to this world but be ye transformed by the renewing of your mind, that you may prove what is that good and acceptable, and perfect, Will of God.

Moral of the story: Don't give up! Keep your faith and continue praying. We are living in the evil world that the Bible warned about. It is indeed in the later days …now…where some call evil good and good evil. And it is becoming worse. But we win in the end! Yeshua will return! Halleluyah!

The End

Chapter Sixteen

Getting Groceries

Upon entering, I immediately spotted him. He drove a handicap scooter through the grocery store, and I didn't notice anyone with him. Other customers would dart in front of him, snatching an item off a shelf and hurry on their way. He went in one direction, and I went in another. Later, after selecting everything on my list, I went to the front of the store and stood in line with my cart. Two people were ahead of me. The cashier called for a manager, and we all waited patiently for her to arrive. She made her way through the crowded store and placed her key into the side of the cash register to unlock it. The two employees exchanged a brief smile, and the manager made a hasty retreat inside the glass walled office by the entrance. That customer paid, gathered her grocery bags into her cart and left the store.

The cashier was new. I watched her emit a friendliness that was refreshing to witness. It was Senior Citizen Day. She'd tell the customer in front of me that she gave them their discount, and how much they saved. I began placing my items on the conveyer belt with cold items together, and canned goods in a separate group. I put all my produce last on the belt and grabbed a divider rod setting it across the end of my purchases.

It's a habit held over from my own grocery cashier days. I worked as a cashier many years ago. I knew firsthand how a mess could develop when customers got their groceries mixed into someone else's order.

That'd when I spotted him again. I had placed the divider rod after my groceries when he drove up behind me in the scooter. I noticed he had a few items in his cart. I also noticed he wasn't grey headed, but he was elderly. He had plump, round cheeks on his face and a pleasant smile. He seemed so naïve and innocent and reminded me of paintings of a happy cherub.

Still bent over, I reached into his cart and grabbed his carton of eggs.

"You don't have to get up. I'll put your things here for you." I said as I quickly put them on the conveyer belt.

The sides of his eyes crinkled into tiny lines with the smile he gave me.

"Thank you, that would be nice." He nodded.

My groceries were soon bagged, and I paid for them. I moved forward as I dug through my purse for my car keys. By the time I retrieved them, he had paid for his order without leaving the scooter. I glanced at him again.

"No need to get up. Here," I said, "I'll put your bags back into the carrier for you."

I put his bags into the scooter's front carrier area, nodded at him and left. He was smiling as he drove the scooter out of the store in the opposite direction of where my car was parked.

He seems like such a nice older man, I thought.

I located my car and opened the trunk. Standing next to it, I knew the two cases of 24 bottles of water were going to be heavy. I lifted one end of a case and struggled to get the entire case out of the grocery cart. The other case fell on top of it causing it to drop back into the cart. Pushing my silver white hair out of my face, I tried again. Determined, I shoved the other case a few inches away and attempted to lift the other one again.

"Can I help you, ma'am?"

I turned and faced a young man about eighteen years old.

Surprised at the offer of help, I breathed a sigh of relief, "yes, thank you."

He had three bags hanging from his hands that I reached over and held as he effortlessly put both cases of water in the back of my car.

"Thank you so very much!" I looked at him and handed him his bags back. "God bless you."

126

"Well, thank you, ma'am." He grinned and took off to his vehicle.

I was still so thrilled at the unexpected help I had received; I kept saying, "Thank You, Lord Jesus" as I slipped into my own car. The overpowering peace and happiness I felt then was as big a blessing as the young man's help.

That's the joy no one can rob you of, it comes from within.

†☐ †☐ †☐

Galatians 6: 7-10   7. Be not deceived; God is not mocked: for whatsoever a man sows, that shall he also reap. 8. For he who sows to his flesh shall of the flesh reap corruption; but he who sows to the Spirit shall of the Spirit reap life everlasting. 9. And let us not be weary in well doing for in due season we shall reap, if we faint not. 10. As we have therefore opportunity; let us do good unto all men, especially unto them who are of the household of Faith.

Psalm 34: 1, 8-9, 14. 1. I will bless the LORD at all times: His praise shall continually be in my mouth. 8. O taste and see that the Lord is good: blessed is the man who trusts in Him. 9. O fear the Lord, ye His saints: for there is no want to them who fear Him. 14. Depart from evil; and do good; seek peace, and pursue it.

Moral of the story: Treat others as want to be treated!

The End

Chapter Seventeen

The Hot Water Heater

It was almost freezing outside. I had washed dishes earlier and wanted to wash my hair in the kitchen sink. There should be enough hot water in the 40-gallon hot water heater near the kitchen for me to wash my hair. I knew the hot water wouldn't last long after it traveled all the way to the back of the house to the shower.

Letting the warm water run, I leaned over, wet my hair and applied shampoo. Suds grew in between my fingers as I moved them through my hair and onto my scalp. It felt wonderful! Even the sink I was leaning against was ice cold with air filtering in from the kitchen window. I lingered for a moment enjoying the warm water on my scalp as I rinsed the shampoo out.

Then I heard it.

A deep rumble, and another, quicker this time…then a loud groan that sounded like metal ripping against metal from the hot water heater. Instantly, I heard water gurgling in the pipes. I watched in horror as water began leaking out of the bottom of the hot water heater.

I gasped! Except for the utility room, my entire house had hard wood floors!

I had to stop the water!

I quickly called my next-door neighbor to cut the water off as I began mopping and throwing towels over the floor.

He answered with a calm, "Hello."

I blurted, "my hot water heater has burst open."

"Ms. Lynn, I'd cut your water off but I'm in town now. Let me call a buddy of mine, he's fishing near your house right now. I'll get him to come and cut it off. He's the one who has the kayak rental down the road from us."

"Ok. Thank you so much!" I ran to the back of the house and scanned across the river until I saw a boat headed straight to my place.

"Are you Lynn?" He yelled over the purring boat motor.

"Yes."

"Your neighbor called me. I'll have your water off in just a second."

He tied his boat up and ran up the hill to my house. I let him inside the house, and we ran to the utility room. Water was climbing higher from the floor. He reached behind the hot water heater and turned some valves.

"There, that should stop water from flowing into the tank. And you still have water; cold water but that's fine. You can heat water on your stove until you get this replaced." He smiled and nodded at me as he was leaving. I thanked him for helping and walked him to the back door. Relieved, I waved to him as he climbed back into his boat and left.

Now for the mess. I had soggy bath towels lying across the floor of the utility room. And I was still putting drops in my eye from recent cataract surgery and wasn't supposed to lift more than ten pounds or lower my head below my hips. Okay, I'll try. Wringing the towels out into a bucket was a chore but I was so thankful none of my hardwood floors got wet.

"Thank You, Lord Jesus!" I yelled. "And Praise God if it had to happen, at least I was here to protect my floors! And help was nearby! Thank God for all the help!" I started mopping the floor when I heard water trickling into the water heater. I froze and listened. Yes, it was a small steady stream of water still going into the heater. Something must have happened.

I called my neighbor again and gave him an update on the situation. He was still in town. He and his wife were picking their child up from school. He assured me they were coming straight home, and he'd stop and cut off my water at the main water meter. He reminded me to draw water into pots and bowls to flush the toilet with. I got busy. He soon arrived and shut all my water off. I would have to call a licensed plumber now. Thankfully, there was one I had used before, and I called leaving a message on his answering machine. I figured he'd probably return my call at the end of the day. Wrong.

To my surprise, he called about an hour later telling me he was on his way from a nearby town and would be at my house within twenty minutes. Again, I was so relieved. He arrived and went to the hot water heater, frowning as he inspected it.

"How old is it, and where did you buy it?"

"Twelve years old." I answered, "and it was bought at Lowes."

"Hot water heaters at Lowes are no good. And whoever installed it made a mess. These valves are stripped out, and there are by-passes behind the tank that should not be here at all." He shined his light behind the hot water heater and shook his head.

"How much for a new one?" I asked.

"Well, I only recommend one that is about a thousand and a half. You will never have a problem with it, and it has a great warranty. Your problem will be the labor. All these valves and bypasses must be removed and reworked. I would say you are looking at least a thousand for labor. It won't pass inspection without all of that being removed and reworked."

"It'll have to wait. I don't have that kind of money. I'm retired and on a fixed income. I'll have to save for it and call you much later. Meanwhile, I'll heat water on the stove when I need it."

"Well, I hate to leave you without any water. I can stop all water from entering your tank and drain it for you, right now, and turn your water back on. At least you'd have water then.

"How much for that?"

"Two hundred."

130

"Okay, it'll be worth it. Go ahead."

He got his helper from the truck and hooked a machine onto the hot water heater. They put pressure on it to push the remaining water out. It was too loud to talk over. He worked behind the heater, and I sat in the kitchen watching them. When they finished, he handed me an invoice, and I gave him a check for doing the job.

"Sorry, this happened ma'am. Let me know when you are ready, and I'll give you a written bid for a new hot water heater including labor." He walked outside to his truck.

"I'll let you know, and thanks for coming so soon."

He nodded and waved as he drove off.

"So much for that." I thought, "I'll be heating water on the stove for quite a while."

And I did. I got organized with it. Worked it into my schedule as if it were a new way to clean. I had both kitchen sinks half full of cold water and kept two large pots of water on the stove ready to boil. I placed tubs at the bottom of the bathroom shower ready for hot water to bathe with. The shower had a seat to sit on. As for washing clothes in my machine, I used cold water only and added Lysol to my detergent.

It took a lot longer to wash anything or bathe, but it worked. I could do it and save money for a new hot water heater at the same time. I prayed for it to work out smoothly. I turned it over to God and stopped worrying about it.

I found a great homemade recipe by googling on my computer for making your own laundry detergent. You use borax, baking soda, washing soda, oxy-clean, three 5.5oz bars of Fels-Naptha grated, and one 28 oz. container of Unstoppables for scent. I bought the ingredients, mixed them together, and loved it. Everything was cleaner and smelled great. I felt better about washing clothes without hot water now.

Two weeks later my 92-year-old Baptist preacher phoned. (We had to stop going to church four years earlier as my then 93-year-old Mom lost control of going to the bathroom. She could no longer tell if or when it might happen, and it was daily. His late wife also had Dementia and Alzheimer's, so he could relate to what was happening with my mom. Prior to that, Mom and I attended that church for over 15 years.)

"How are you doing over there?" Bro. Bob inquired.

"Mom is still waking up at night wanting to get up, but she is eating. How are you doing?"

"I'm good. Still on my walker, but they installed a ramp at church for me. They push me up the ramp and help me to sit in front of the podium. I am thankful to God to still be of use to preach." He announced with emphasis on being thankful to God. I could hear in his voice he was still able to get his point across.

"I thank God for you, Bro. Bob. They keep getting you back from retirement when the younger pastors move on. You are a blessing to our church." I told him.

"Well, you are a blessing to your mother. We pray for both of you. I am trying to record my sermons so those like you who can't come to church can still hear the sermons. I will start sending them to you on Facebook."

"We will look forward to them. That is such a good idea, we can listen to them when we can, day or night."

"That's what I thought. I know you stay busy there."

"Yes, I do. Especially with boiling water now. It takes a while, but it works."

"I don't know what you are referring to. Why are you boiling water?"

"Oh, I thought you'd heard about it. My hot water heater burst open and I'm saving for a new one."

"No, I didn't know. When did this happen?"

"About two weeks ago."

"Well, we can't have you boiling water with everything else you're doing taking care of your momma. Let me see what I can do. What kind of hot water heater do you need? Gas or electric?"

"Gas."

"We have two of them in the parsonage and we are fixing to tear it down. I don't know if the heaters are gas or electric. I'll find out. Either way, we'll try and get you going again."

"This is the answer to prayer." My voice broke and the thought was overwhelming that help was about to happen.

"That's what we do, we try to help each other. I'll call you back." His deep voice, firm and positive, spoke assuring me.

"Okay, and thank you so much." I ended the call, and immediately yelled "Thank You, Lord Jesus! Thank You Heavenly Father!"

I was energized and happy and felt so blessed.

Bro. Bob called back within an hour.

"I'm sending someone from the church to look at your hot water heater to see if this will work. His name is Jesse Cooper. He can do plumbing and electrical work and has contracted to tear down the parsonage for us. We do have an electric and a gas hot water heater, but I want to make sure if you need parts, Jesse can get them too. He'll be there in about thirty minutes. Jesse will also install it, and there will no charge for anything."

"Thanks again, Bro. Bob. This is so incredible. I am so thankful!"

"Well, you deserve it. Give God the glory."

"Oh, I have, and I will continue doing so." I told him cheerfully.

We ended the call, and for a moment, I stood by the cordless phone shaking my head. I was in awe of this huge blessing! It was not only a tremendous help but showed me to never limit God. Turn a situation over to Him and forgetting it is the best way to solve a problem.

Jesse Cooper arrived, noticed I needed a new valve, and left to purchase it and remove the hot water heater from the parsonage.

This happened in the coldest winter. The heater had to be unhooked from servicing the empty parsonage, then drained, before removing it and brought to my house to install. It was 35 degrees and cold in the parsonage. He called hours later and stated he'd be back early in the morning to remove my old heater and install the new one.

He did, and it turned out the heater from the parsonage was only used for a short time. It was almost brand new. He made certain everything worked well before he left. He did say the plumber that estimated a price of about three thousand dollars was wrong. He said even two thousand dollars was too much for the job.

Even my son told me that the price was entirely too high. He and my daughter-in-law came to visit a week after my hot water heater burst open. They lived over four hundred miles away, and he had told me not to let that plumber ever do the job. He said I could get a new hot water heater for four or five hundred dollars and get a warranty from the store and have them install it for about two hundred. He even said it was meant to be for them to make this trip and stop me from spending too much money on a new heater. God's plans do work smoothly and do come together perfectly on time.

Once again, I give God the glory! And yes, I sent a thank you card to the church for the tremendous blessing they gave me. I prayed for God to bless Bro. Bob, and all the members with whatever their needs may be, and to bless the church with growth. I could never make it without Yehovah!

†☐ †☐ †☐

Deuteronomy 28: 1-2

And it shall come to pass, if you shall hearken diligently unto the voice of the LORD your God, to observe and to do all His Commandments which I command you this day, that the LORD your God will set you on high above all the nations of the Earth. 2. And all these Blessings shall come on you, and overtake you, if you shall harken unto the voice of the LORD your God.

Moral to the story: Don't ever limit Yehovah! He is in control of everything! Praise His name and give Him thanks!

The End

Chapter Eighteen

Three Years

The red light flashing from my telephone answering machine appeared to be urgent. Arms full of groceries, I continued to the kitchen unloading them onto the table. Stopping into the living room, I grabbed the handlebars of Mom's wheelchair and maneuvered it to the foyer and outside. She sat alone in my car gazing at the blooming flowers in various size pots on my front porch. Short, round pots and tall slender ones displayed a bright profusion of color from red hibiscuses, yellow ruffled ones, and pink ones with large round petals to a white one with a red center.

Hibiscus is my favorite flower with Geraniums in second place.

Opening the car door, I helped her into the wheelchair.

"You'll have to put some flowers in a vase. That would be so beautiful on the kitchen table." Her voice trailed as I escorted her into the house.

"Yes, I agree." I answered, remembering the last time I tried that. I had cut several fragrant and delicate purple and white flowers from my Magnolia Tulip tree. After a few days of enjoying their beauty on the table, I smelled something rotten. The closer I came to the vase the worse the smell became. Upon examining it, I discovered she'd crammed most of her hamburger down into the vase. She could be sneaky throwing her food away. I'd found food hidden under a couch cushion, as well as in her clothes. Alzheimer's and Dementia were also slipping into her life. I had to watch her every move 24/7, for both our safety. And her short-term memory was horrible, but she could remember details with amazing accuracy from fifty years ago.

Wheeling her past the blinking answering machine on the piano, Mom glanced at it.

136

"Aren't you going to answer it?"

"Yes, I am when I put these groceries away."

I wheeled her to the table and began my task. Her eyes followed me as she watched in silence.

"Is that…is that my ice-cream?" She asked timidly.

I had to smile at her innocent question.

"Yes, just for you! Vanilla Bean; your favorite!"

I put the last of the groceries where they belonged and fixed her a bowl of vanilla ice cream with chocolate syrup drizzled over it. Placing the bowl and a spoon in front of her on the table, I turned to the answering machine. Holding the cordless in my hand, I punched the play option. I smiled at Mom as she dove into her bowl of ice cream.

"Hello?" A deep baritone voice echoed through my large house. "Lynn?"

I gripped the phone, gasping, and sat in a nearby chair as my heart suddenly pounded in my ears. I realized my entire body was trembling.

"Could it be him?" The thought raced through my mind. I felt my face flush. I stared at the answering machine as I listened in unbelief.

"I hope this is you. I've been looking for you for a mighty long time. If this is you, you used to be Lynn Miller, now you are Lynn Hobbs. My daughter found you on Facebook after I told her I wanted to buy some land from you. She has no idea I've been trying to locate you for years. I sure want to talk to you. Call me at this number." He gave me the phone number and repeated how much he wanted to talk to me.

Memories of the past flooded my mind as I recalled the last time I saw him.

Of course, I'll call him. I quickly did the math, and it had been over 45 years since I'd seen or heard from him. I played the answering machine again, and my eyes welled up with tears at the sound of his voice.

Dear Lord, why was his voice affecting me like this? And after 45 years? Yes, I had to return his call.

I waited until I had Mom in bed for the night. Hopefully, no interruptions will be made during the phone call.

I tried to remain calm and dialed the number.

"Hello" he answered.

"Keith, it's me, Lynn." I blurted.

His deep voice boomed. "Lynn? I'd know your voice anytime. I was hoping you'd call me back." His voice broke and he stopped momentarily. "I-I have so much to tell you, so much to talk to you about." I could hear the emotion in his words. He was struggling with this as much as I was.

"I just want to know one thing first." He continued. "My daughter told me you are married. I want to know if you are happily married?"

"No, I'm not. He left years ago."

"That's all I need to know. When can I see you?"

"Anytime is fine with me."

"Tomorrow?"

"Yes, I'd like that."

"Let's meet in Jonesville at the Dairy Queen, say at 10:00?"

"Okay, that's fine, but I must bring my mom. She has Alzheimer's and Dementia and lives with me. For her safety, I can't leave her by herself."

"No problem. We'll fill her up with ice cream." He laughed.

"Oh, she'll love that. What are you driving?"

"I'm in a white Jeep. What about you?"

"I drive a black Rav4 Toyota."

"And I'll be sitting in my car watching for you to drive into the parking lot." He sounded so sincere, and unless he'd changed, I knew he was sincere.

I couldn't keep my mind off him for the rest of the evening. Later, sleep became a series of vivid memories thrust back at me from so many years ago. Turbulent years. Growing years, and yes, heartbreaking years. I learned a lot from all the unexpected twists and turns I would experience. And yes, I am now a better, more cautious person than that naïve young woman, but more importantly, I trust my Lord and Savior Jesus Christ and not mortal man.

I drove into the parking lot and spotted his white jeep immediately. It had a few minor dents in it; what we here in Texas refer to as a whiskey bruise. Hmm. Instant red flag. My nostalgic emotions froze as my suspicions grew to high alert. I had to be careful until I could see the whole picture of who he is today, not the man he was 45 years ago.

He was talking to someone on his cellphone when he saw me drive in. He quickly ended the call and left his car. I exited my car as he hurried towards me.

I looked into those eyes and saw the same kindness, the same gentleness, and the same steady strength I had always known. He was still that person. No nonsense. No lies. No hidden motives. No using or belittling anyone. No silver-tongued devil.

A silver-tongued devil is someone who is charming and persuasive but often deceptive or manipulative, using smooth words to get their way. I should add, usually good-looking too. That description fits my ex-husband, not Keith, even though Keith was, and still is, a handsome man.

We stood in front of each other and smiled.

"May I hug you?"

I nodded "yes."

His arms surrounded me gently pulling me closer into the embrace as I felt the hug tighten and I hugged him back. He patted my back as he held me in his arms. His cheek brushed against mine, and I caught the scent of his aftershave. I hadn't been hugged in years. It was an overwhelming moment for me. Not only the hug, but to be hugged by him.

We pulled apart, tears visible in our eyes.

"Did you feel that?" He grinned.

I answered in a shaky voice, "Yes, I did."

"Come on, let's go inside."

"Let me get Mother out of my car."

"I forgot about her." He gave a sheepish smile.

He followed me to my car, and I introduced them while we walked to the entrance of the Dairy Queen. Mom did not remember him, of course.

He opened the door, and Mom and I went in first. He was right behind us. We found an empty booth, and I placed Mom by the window. I sat down beside her. Keith sat across from me. The waitress came and after much discussion on how we weren't very hungry, we ordered Mom a dish of ice-cream and French fries with drinks for us.

"I can't get over finding you. Lynn, do you know how long I've been looking for you?"

"I didn't know you were looking. When I didn't hear from you, I thought you didn't care."

"Didn't care?" he exclaimed. "Your sister and your stepbrother came into my house and held a shotgun on me while I was still in the shower. Told me to stay away from you!"

"What? My sister? And stepbrother? No one told me about that. There was nothing for them to even know about you and me period. Nothing happened. I did tell my mother you asked if I needed anything ...after my

140

husband was gone overnight…and I said I was out of milk for my little boys. You brought me a gallon of milk and left. I said you were my neighbor and how nice you were. That was it. And that got turned around into them holding a gun on you and telling you to leave me alone?"   My voice rose in anger.

Mom looked up from her ice cream. "Gun? What gun?"

Keith glanced at Mom. "We better continue this conversation in private."

"Oh yes, we will." I fumed. "Trust me, Keith, no one in my family has ever held a gun on anyone. We are not a rough family. It is mind boggling that those two did this to you!"

"Lynn, I know your family isn't like that, but those two were." Keith paused and frowned. "I asked everyone we knew where you were. No one would tell me. Especially your husband's family, and they knew he was seen with other women, and often. All you ever did was work. I could believe you left him, but I couldn't believe you just disappeared. Weeks after you left, I overheard someone say you moved to Jonesville."

"I did. And what happened to your ex-wife?"

"She slept with over 5 men in that town. She would leave our two kids with strangers for days and go off with some man. I didn't know about this until my oldest was afraid to be left with a babysitter."

"Those poor kids."

"Yep. They have been through all kinds of cruelty. Their mother has probably got the record for marriages in Texas, eleven at last count. She married some in Oklahoma and others in Arkansas. She got mad and shot at some, most divorced her. At one point, she took a pickax to the back of our house immediately after our own divorce. She was bi-polar, and I didn't know it."

"Wow! I shouldn't be surprised though. As your neighbor while you two were married, I often saw men coming and going. One even had a tractor and pushed dirt around for a few days. No project happening, just pushing dirt around. No rhyme or reason."

"Lynn, that was his excuse for being there, I'm sure."

"Yes, in all appearances to the community; he seemed to be working."

"And what about you? Are you retired or still working?"

"Officially retired from working at a public high school. And I give God the glory, I am a published Christian Fiction and Non-Fiction author. I was awarded first place in Texas for several years for my books. I'm still writing."

"Good for you! It seems we both took a Christian path with our lives. I sang in a quartet that traveled to Baptist churches to give concerts."

"You did? That is a big change. I'm happy for you!"

"And you too, lady. A Christian writer, how rewarding. Telling stories, planting gospel seeds."

"I love it."

He leaned back and looked at me smiling. "Well, I'm retired. I was co-owner with your ex-husbands brother, Clayton, in a business that fell apart when Clayton died. I ended up broke. The employees maxed out the company credit cards. I had to pay all of them off. But my deceased business partner, Clayton, did not. Clayton's second wife and your ex-husband insisted that Clayton receive his fair share to the point where I had enough of it. They would not listen to any facts I gave them proving large debt. So, I paid off massive amounts owed by the business and was completely broke, but Clayton got what they insisted was his fair share. I still have the documentation for all of it. After that, I took care of my wife."

"I heard you married Sandra." I emphasized.

"Only after I couldn't have you in my life. She and I were breaking up the night your sister and stepbrother barged into my house. They pushed past her and found me in the shower."

I shook my head. "We have so much to talk about. I can't get over them doing that to you, and my sister interfering in my life like that. I never interfered in her divorce with her ex-husband. So, what happened to Sandra?"

"I told her I would marry her. That's what she wanted, but I told her I would always love you. She said I would learn to love her. And that's how we married."

"She was a lot older than you, wasn't she?"

"Yes. I didn't know it until she died, and I saw her driver's license. She was twelve years older than me. And her ex-husband was the first man my ex-wife married. It didn't last long. I threw myself into my work, and Sandra did her crafts. She was out of control on spending money. We ended up with about nine storage buildings full of her craft supplies. She'd buy everything for a sewing project, grow tired of it, and jump into another project. Making dolls, painting, making jewelry, sewing quilts, making flower arrangements; always buying something. She had tons of clothing material. At the end, I went with her to estate sales, and we'd look for antiques to start an antique store for her. I figured that would be cheaper than all the craft projects. Anyway, that's where my money went. She just wasn't content with anything very long. She passed away with cancer. We taught Sunday School in a nondenominational church for years, even picked kids up in a church bus and brought them there."

"That had to be rewarding."

"It was." He kept smiling at me. "So, what did you do after your divorce?"

"I worked a full-time job and worked on my property. And I got burned too badly from my divorce to trust again. I didn't even date anyone for twelve years. Stayed single all that time."

He instantly raised his head in shock, squinting at me and his mouth fell open. He groaned.

Mom abruptly pushed her empty ice cream bowl to the middle of the table and yawned. "I'm ready to go."

He frowned and reached for my hand. "I let you get away once before and I'm not letting that happen again."

143

I reflected on the experiences we each had since our last encounter. "It's hard to believe we're here together after forty-five years."

He nodded. "I have looked for you for years. I know how I feel."

He was so solemn. I knew I could believe him.

"I would like to follow you to your home. Is it okay for me to visit you?"

"Yes, of course."

He squeezed my hand, and we stood up to leave.

We walked to my car, and he opened the passenger door for Mom. I buckled her in, and he shut the door.

"I'm right behind you." His voice rang out as he went to his car. We each drove off in our own vehicle and my mind was racing about my being a married woman. Legally, I was a married woman…whose husband had abandoned her years ago. Unknown to me at the time, but my husband had a woman living with him in a distant town since 2007. She had been in prison three times for substance abuse, and they were rough characters; both heavily into the drug world. He was living a double life.

I live in a small neighboring town from the Dairy Queen where Keith and I met. The journey to my house in the countryside took approximately twenty minutes.

Keith parked his car behind mine.

We came inside and I poured both of us a glass of iced tea and sat them on the coffee table in the living room. Mom was happy to watch television in the den. We sat down on the couch.

"I need to tell you" … he began.

"I have so much" … I interrupted him.

Laughter erupted.

"Okay, you go first." I chuckled.

"Thanks. I would say ladies first, but I do have serious issues to inform you of."

I nodded and gave him my full attention.

He sighed. "I have a lot of health problems." He stared ahead and glanced across the room. Turning to focus on me, he smiled and looked into my eyes. "You may not want to get involved. It may be too much for you. I would completely understand."

I tried to smile.

"Ever hear of Myasthenia Gravis?"

"No, I haven't." I answered.

"Your muscles give out, and you could end up in a wheelchair. And I've been a diabetic for years. I go to the V. A. hospital, and my doctors recently told me I am now in stage four kidney failure. So, I will start weekly dialysis soon. I take over 23 prescription pills daily for everything that is wrong with me."

I listened to him as sadness overcame me and my instinct to comfort him had to wait.

"I was in the Navy and was placed in Agent Orange in the war in Vietnam. Not sure how much of that caused what's happening to me today. I still drive a car, but I am now legally blind. Sometimes when I try to merge onto a highway, all I see is a large shadow and I know that is a car or truck, so I wait to merge."

"Keith, that is way too dangerous! You should not be driving at all, anywhere! "

"Well, I can still do it." He tried to assure me.

"What about your family? Can't someone drive you?"

"I lost my son in a horrific accident, and my daughter is married taking care of all the grandkids from herself having five kids. Her five are all grown, some married, some left their kids with her, and they all need her

145

help babysitting daily while they work. She cannot help me at all. And that's all the family I have. Everyone means well, but they all work."

"I'm so sorry to hear about your son. And so sorry of all you are going through." I shook my head as silence filled the room.

He hesitated and spoke firmly. "I don't want your pity. I just wanted you to know."

"Okay. Fair enough. What's your daughter's name? I don't remember."

"Irene."

"Irene sure has her hands full."

"That's what she wanted. A big family. After my son passed away, and her mother left; she and I were all that's left of the family. My Mom had passed away as well as my aunt. I was raised in an orphanage. Irene told me she was going to have five kids and have her own big family, and her husband loved kids. When they were raising their five little ones, my second wife, Sandra, babysat for them at our house while Irene worked. Then I would help on weekends when I was off work those two days. Irene and her husband needed help."

"So, she is paying it forward. Helping them now by taking care of their own children."

"Yes."

"How many does she take care of?"

"Seven with three on the way."

"That is a lot at one time for one person to take care of!"

"She loves it. It's her whole life."

"Sounds like Irene is happy with her big family. Good for her!"

"She is. She and her husband are both happy. But getting back to me. I did not contact you because of my health issues. I started looking for you

146

years ago. At one time I was told you worked at Walmart. I didn't know what shift you worked, or which days, so I drove to Walmart two and three times a week. I walked through the aisles in search of you and examined all the checkout counter employees. Ha! You don't know how many bags of dogfood I bought!"

"Aww. And I never worked there."

"Then I heard you moved to the lake. I immediately drove all over that area searching for you and asking strangers if they knew of you, or where I could find you. Nothing."

"You were so close.'

"I can't believe it. Finding out you were single for 12 years feels like a cruel twist of fate. We could have been married, shared our lives, and built so many memories together. The thought of those lost years, the time we could have spent with each other is almost too much to bear. But now that we've found each other, I don't want to waste another moment. What do you say? Could you please clarify with a yes, or no?"

"Of course it's a yes. I can't believe we have this chance to be together. It's been 45 years! And once again, I'm married but all alone. Abuse, abandonment and adultery are the only Biblical reasons to divorce and remarry. My first ex-husband committed adultery, he was also controlling and mentally abusive. He had many girlfriends while I worked. I even had a woman at church tell me a few years ago, how she had an affair with my husband over twenty years earlier, until she found out he was married to me. He didn't want her to break up with him and tried to choke her. They were in a motel. I believed her because that is what he would do…try to choke you when he was horribly angry. He even tried to choke our kids in a fit of anger. My second husband is the one who abused and abandoned me for a drug lifestyle he chose. The scripture about that one is 1Corinthians 7:15. Keith, I feel like God has his hand in this for both of us. To show me what it could have been for two likeminded people to marry…no longer unequally yoked with an unbeliever."

I paused and frowned at Keith. "I must admit I am afraid of my husband. Especially living in an isolated area like this is."

147

Keith leaned towards me and raised his eyebrows. "What…" He began.

"Let me explain." I blurted.

"When I married him, he resembled a clean-cut man straight from the Marines. Short crew cut, no beard, no tattoos, no drugs, and he went to church with me. After working away at other towns, he changed completely. His friends were now bikers who shared their "Biker Babes" and were heavy drug users. He joined a biker group with members from Mexico. He became a man with a long, unkept beard, a longer, gray ponytail hanging down his back; and his body was covered in tattoos. The last time I saw him he physically abused me. I could not walk for three days. I told him to leave and never come back. He did. I was afraid to press charges for retaliation by him and his biker friends. I just wanted to be left alone, and I sure didn't care about ever marrying again."

"How long since you have seen him?"

"Over five years."

"And he hasn't contacted you in any way?"

"No, Keith. He chose an entirely different way of life and is so hooked on drugs now I don't think he could ever stop. When he left, he was taking two hydrocodone pills before breakfast and chasing them down with whiskey. He'd try to hide it at first, then didn't seem to care. He wasn't the man I knew anymore and certainly not the man I married. When he left, he filled two long-bed trailers full of high dollar items. He took both of his Harley Davidson motorcycles, two trucks, a Buick, a zero-turn lawn mower, a tractor and some implements, oh and lots of guns. He wasn't coming back. And he didn't."

"Do you have any protection for yourself?"

"Oh yes. I took a concealed handgun course two years ago. I possess a license and have legally purchased firearms at a store with an authorized shooting range."

"Good safety measure. Hopefully you won't ever need to use one."

148

"So do I." I chuckled. "I did have a rabid dog run out of the woods at me when I first had my gun and was about to target practice. I couldn't flip the safety lever to the off position and the dog started running in circles and returned to the woods. I never saw it again. After that, I would practice on an armadillo digging holes under my rent house. Someone told me not to shoot at the shell on their body; that the bullet would ricochet, so I focused on hitting the nose. I didn't know they were teasing me at the time. It's difficult to hit a moving target in that spot. The first time I tried, I overshot. Then I took aim, followed the animals' movements, and tried again. Perfect shot. Right in the nose. I was thrilled to get rid of the destructive animal. They had destroyed my neighbor's barn by digging holes six feet deep around the concrete blocks that held up the building. It fell to the ground. And my neighbor had no insurance. Some animals in the country can be destructive."

"That was a great shot." Keith nodded. "But that rabid dog could have got you."

"I know. That never happened again. I learned it took force to flip it from safety. Since we're discussing guns, tell me about my sister and stepbrother pointing a gun at you."

His shoulders hardened and he ran his hand through his hair.

"That was a wild night."

"I had no idea they did that. My stepbrother lives in Houston, and I hardly ever see him. He is older and married. My sister is younger than me by five years. She was divorced at that time with a daughter of her own."

"Well, they knocked at the door and Sandra answered it. They shoved her aside and barged in the house. She and I were breaking up. We had a long talk just minutes earlier and ended our relationship. I was in the shower and didn't hear anything. Suddenly, the shower curtain was pulled back, and I was looking at a man and a young woman yelling at me.

"Stay away from Lynn. She is married. Leave her alone." They both yelled and the guy raised a shotgun into my face. I couldn't believe what

149

was happening. I did not do anything to provoke this. They were in a rage and kept yelling. They left as fast as they came. Water was still running from the shower on me, and I was sopping wet. Sandra was yelling, "They're gone."

"I dried off and dressed. My mind was reeling. Here I was, a divorced man, breaking up with a girlfriend, in love with a woman I wanted to spend the rest of my life with, and this happens. Did she want to keep trying with her husband? Did she send them over here? I had no idea. Did she have any idea how I felt about her? I didn't know. I walked into the kitchen where Sandra sat at the table. She was shaking. I told her I don't know why that happened, but it looks like I don't have a chance with Lynn. She jumped at that remark." Forget about Lynn, let's try again," she spoke firmly. That's when I told her I would always love you, Lynn. She just wanted me to marry her so badly that she told me I would learn to love her. I tried finding you the next day and you were gone. So, Sandra and I got back together. That was 45 years ago."

"They should never have interfered with my life! It wasn't Sandra that came between us, it was them!" My eyes welled up in tears and Keith hugged me.

"I moved and filed for divorce that next day after you brought me a gallon of milk. Someone had mailed me a copy of the local newspaper. The image depicted my husband seated and leaning over the table at the grand opening of a new catfish restaurant in town. He looked asleep. I think my sister-in-law sent it to me, as he was drinking a lot and she and her husband saw him with different woman often. He acted single partying with his friends. The kids and I were an obstacle to him."

"I know." Keith quietly assured me.

"Keith, all I did was tell Mom you brought me a gallon of milk while my husband was gone. You were a neighbor asking if I needed anything. That was all. And that got twisted into a home invasion with a shotgun held on you…and my sister and stepbrother yelling for you to leave me alone…the one man that cared about me. I am so very sorry that happened to you!"

Keith spoke softly, "and ultimately happened to us." He reached for me and held me close.

I could only think of the years we lost because of their unneeded interference in our lives.

"That's over now. We can't change it." Keith bit his bottom lip. "I had to tell my daughter I was trying to find you to buy some property. She found you on Facebook. I lied to her, but she found you. I asked God to forgive me, and I want us to make the best of this."

"Oh, we will." I grinned. "It really is amazing after all we have been through. I've been caregiver to Mom for years now. I never thought anyone would be in my life but her. Guess I was wrong."

"You were bad wrong." He smiled.

"I do have to get her dinner and then prepare her for bed. Can I see you tomorrow?"

"How early can I return?" He asked.

I laughed. "Ten o'clock would work. That will give me time to help her in the morning."

We stood and walked around the coffee table. He hugged me bye and left.

I sat down and this time my mind was reeling.

I woke up the next morning and poured myself a cup of coffee. I was relaxing with it and recalling the conversations that Keith and I had shared when Mom woke up. I helped her out of bed and fixed her breakfast. Glancing out the kitchen window I almost tripped on my own feet. Keith's car was parked outside. I had to smile. How nice to have him here.

I took him a cup of coffee and we sat on the front porch enjoying the early morning. Birds were chirping, squirrels were running up trees and chattering and barking at each other. A slight breeze eased by us.

151

How nice to enjoy this time together. After I showed Keith my fruit trees, grapes, thornless berries, and the river in my backyard, he was eager to start. He drove Mom and I to his house, struggling to stay in his lane. We arrived and he fed his dogs and cats.

"Since you like antiques, there are some here I want to give you. I saw you glancing at the Toledo Scales. They still work. Do you want it?"

"I would be thrilled to have it, but don't you think your daughter would like that?"

"Irene couldn't keep the kids from jumping on it and ruining it. It has a delicate balance of weights. I have another one also, if you want it. The other one has the "pees" you lift and add to distribute to measure your weight."

"In that case, yes! I want them both. They will look great on my covered porch by the climbing roses and bench."

He retrieved a trailer, and we loaded them onto it by ourselves. Before we left, he added an old trunk that was still in mint condition. He strapped everything securely onto the trailer.

"Wait a minute, there's something else I want you to have. I'll be right back."

Before I could say anything, he went into his house. He soon emerged carrying a large brown object and he was grinning from ear to ear.

He opened the car door and handed it to me. "Here, you'll have to hold this in your lap. It's very delicate." He had held it on its side and turned it around for me to see it.

"An antique clock with a long, swinging pendulum!" I gasped. "I have never had one. Thank you, Keith. This is all so special. I will always treasure your gifts to me today."

"I knew you would, that's why I wanted you to have them." He climbed into the driver's seat, and we took off. Keith managed to keep the vehicle in the lane, but he struggled with curves, often going off the road. I knew this was the first and last time I'd let him drive us anywhere. Thankfully we were on a back, less traveled road; we soon made it to my house.

We positioned the scales onto the porch, and he hung the three-foot long, brown clock on a wall in the living room. He showed me how to wind it and where the key was kept.

I fixed a quick lunch and we all three ate. After the meal, Mom took her afternoon nap.

"Keith, I need to talk to you. You are not driving safely. From now on, if we go anywhere, I will be the driver."

"It was that bad?"

"Yes, it was. When do you go back to the doctor?"

"I have three appointments tomorrow at the Overton Brooks V.A. Medical Center in Shreveport, La."

"Then I'm driving you."

He let out a deep sigh. "Only if you'll let me treat you and your mom to lunch afterward."

"That's a deal." I grinned.

"We'll go to my favorite Chinese Buffet. You'll love it."

"Sounds great, but you'll have to give me directions. I don't travel to Shreveport often and don't know my way around that town."

He began telling me how to drive to Greenwood, La. Then he referred to roads that were unfamiliar to me; Burt Kountz, 70th Street, Youree Drive, Kings Hwy., Shreveport Barksdale Blvd., and Stoner Blvd.

I smiled. "Well, you'll be in the car if I make a wrong turn."

He laughed. "It will be easy." He assured me.

And it was.

We entered the massive V. A. hospital packed with people coming in and going to various doctor appointments. He checked himself in at the Kiosk machine and it shot out a ticket. He noted the number, and we waited in the sitting area, watching the screens on the wall for his number to be called. Making three appointments was time consuming, but informative. In between, we stopped in the lobby and bought bags of popcorn. Then at his last appointment of the day, he took Mom and I to a gift shop on the second floor where we could shop. We shopped and walked around. Upon concluding his consultation with the last physician, we proceeded to the pharmacy to obtain his medication and then departed.

The Chinese buffet at Imperial Cathay on Youree Drive was amazing! In fact, it was the best I'd ever experienced. We returned to my home tired but happy. It was a good day.

"Thanks for everything. It has been enjoyable, but it is late, and I need to drive home. I have animals to feed." He grinned.

"We enjoyed the day too. Are you sure you can drive home?"

"If I leave now, I will be able to drive home."

"Well, please be careful."

"I will. I'll see you tomorrow." He waved and drove off. I said a prayer for his safety.

And that soon became our routine.

Weeks later, I invited Irene and her husband over for dinner. Keith met them at the front door, and they appeared to be cordial and relaxed. We sat at the table, everything ready.

I had prepared an extra-large pot of Cajun Chicken Spaghetti with garlic bread and a salad. Everyone was jovial as I dished it out. I genuinely liked his daughter and her husband. Conversation flowed freely and I looked forward to becoming more acquainted with them. Then Irene and her dad seemed to square off.

"So, you were considering purchasing property from Lynn, correct dad?"

"Sorry, but I did lie. I knew you could find her, and I'd had no success for over 45 years."

"Forty-five years? Really dad?" She raised her eyebrows and appeared amused.

Keith gave her an incredible look of surprise. "Irene, I loved Lynn then, and I love her now."

She laughed. "And I thought Mom was the player in the family. So, you are both players."

I had heard enough. I interrupted their conversation. "Irene, you have no idea what we have been through. It happens to be a blessing we can even see each other after all this time. We are both sorry he lied to you to find me. Come on, let's eat."

Her husband began small talk, light and cheerful. We all chimed in then and it turned out to be a pleasant evening while we ate.

After the meal, they rose to leave. Everyone was smiling. That's when Keith told Irene he wanted to marry me. She jerked her head up to him and exclaimed, "Oh no. There won't be any more marriages."

Keith and I stared at her, stunned. Her husband escorted her to the door, expressed their gratitude for the evening, and departed.

"Why doesn't she like you?" Keith asked incredibly.

"I don't know. She doesn't even know me. Maybe she doesn't want to share you with anyone."

"She always tells everyone she is the Monarch of the family. Looks like it went to her head."

"I'm sorry, Keith., and I certainly don't want to be a Monarch."

He chuckled. "She'll have to get used to you. And I will be with you."

Keith bumped into the table as we returned to the kitchen. Initially, I did not perceive it as significant. I began washing dishes and jumped when he put his arms around my waist.

"I'm not used to hugs." I laughed.

"Well, I love you and I'm sorry my daughter treated you that way."

"Oh, Keith. That was so sweet. But you have no control over her, or her actions. Don't worry about it."

"Thank you. I just don't want her interfering with us."

I hugged him back and returned to washing dishes. He turned to leave the room and bumped into a chair.

"Keith. I've noticed your eyesight is getting worse. I don't want you driving to your home tonight."

"And if I stay? I don't want the neighbors talking about you."

"They know me. They have known me for many years. They know if you are here nothing immoral will happen."

"You are sure?"

"Yes, I am. And I have a spare bedroom."

"No, I don't want a bedroom. A recliner will work fine for me. I can be comfortable there. And I thank you. I haven't mentioned it to you, but yes, you are right. My sight is much worse."

I placed sheets, blankets, and a pillow on the couch.

"Thank you." He was so sincere.

"Goodnight then. I'll lock up. Mom and I are going to bed. See you in the morning."

"Thanks again. Goodnight."

I left him alone in the living room and went to the other part of the house. I added nightlights in the long hallway to the bathroom and put another one in the kitchen that opened into the living room. Keith was settled in a recliner, and I turned the TV on and handed him the remote. I smiled and checked on Mom in her bedroom, and I went to mine. It was a quiet night until I later heard a man snoring. I had to smile again. It had been a long day for all of us. I prayed for God to forgive me if I was doing wrong by having Keith here and taking care of him. The last thing I wanted to do was to disappoint my Heavenly Father.

The next day, Keith suggested digging up my grape vines around the deck behind my house. They had almost taken over the entire area. He built a grape arbor on the property I had down the road. It was perfect. We replanted them and took pictures of the completed project. Once again, we were worn out, but happy.

We both enjoyed canning, and a friend provided us with three buckets of cucumbers. They were the "Straight Eight" variety. We canned garlic pickles, bread and butter pickles, and spicy Cajun pickles. Yum! They were good!

Between taking him to his doctors, and Mom to hers; we were extremely busy. It was at this time we received bad news from the V.A. doctors.

He had to have a port installed for dialysis to begin. It would be in his chest. A dialysis port, also called a central venous catheter (CVC) or hemodialysis catheter, is a flexible tube inserted into a large vein in the chest or neck for dialysis treatments. The catheter is tunneled under the skin, and the tip is positioned in a large vein near the heart. This allows for easy and frequent access to the bloodstream for removing waste and excess fluid during dialysis. The appointment was scheduled.

We arrived for the procedure in Shreveport at the V.A. hospital, and went back to Texas with a lot of instructions. This port didn't work as we were told. It continued to get infected. Next, we went to Longview, Tx. for a new portal installed in his wrist. The first port was still in his chest.

Also, this began dialysis three times a week in Marshall, Texas. I would take him to Marshall at 8 A.M. and return at 2pm to bring him back to my house. Four doctor appointments were now scheduled each month in Shreveport, La. as well. We stayed on the road.

At one of Mom's doctor appointments, her doctor discussed with Mom and I the importance of having me as her legal power of attorney and legal medical power of attorney. We agreed. I made an appointment with an attorney and had both done.

Within two weeks, Mom had gone to her home for something and nearly burnt it down. I didn't know about it until the following day. Her home was next to mine, but for her safety she had been living with me. I entered her house and smelled charred wood. I found the results of the almost fatal fire in the kitchen. Her stove was against a wall. She must have tried to cook something and forgot about it. When she found it, she tried to cover the burnt wall with duct tape. Of course, the duct tape stood out even worse.

It was time for the house to go. Thankfully it was a mobile home. I discussed it with her and told her it had to be sold. Between removing her belongings from the home, and going to doctor appointments, I was looking forward to our Shreveport meals at the Chinese buffets. We enjoyed taking turns at Imperial Cathay on Youree Drive and Sumo Buffet on the same street. There were others but these were our favorite.

Mom's home sold before the month was over. She now had more of her belongings in my 1,900 sq ft, three-bedroom house. We had stuff everywhere for a while. Keith tried to help me place some of her belongings in my shop across the street. I used it strictly for storage. His strength was nothing compared to when he first arrived. His muscles were deteriorating. He was a trooper though and wanted to help. He did.

Christmas was approaching and I still practiced the holiday then. (I now know Jesus wasn't born then and the decorated tree is an abomination to our Heavenly Father. It is pagan.)

I bought presents for all of Keith's grandchildren, great grandchildren and Irene and her husband. I loved picking out what I thought each would really like, and had grown fond of all of them, especially the great grandchildren. It later took two trips to Irene's house to drop all the presents off for the get together later at her house. It was fun, and yes, everyone enjoyed it.

At the next trip to the V.A. Hospital, they gave Keith a walker, a light wheelchair called a transport, and a machine for blind patients to enlarge print with to read. He knew he needed help and was excited about the reading machine. He was also signed up for the government program Audible Books for The Blind.

He would sit on my back porch and listen to the stories where he'd eventually fall asleep. Boats were going by often on the river and some people would wave at him. Even when he was awake, he could not see them.

Motorcycles began driving by my home. Probably because this was a country road, but I cringed every time I heard one. Even today, I still do. I couldn't stop picturing my husband with his biker buddies and him coming back. Keith didn't like them either.

Keith suggested insurance for us.

"Insurance? For us?"

"Yes, think about it. If he does come back and shoots me, you need the money to move away from him. Criminals aren't in prison long anymore. Parole and all."

I looked at Keith and shared my thoughts on the subject. "And if he shoots me, you'll need the money for a down payment on a new home. Your home needs so much repair, it would be cheaper to buy a new one. Or rent an apartment. And you would be taken care of. You could hire a housekeeper."

"Bless you, Lynn. No one else thinks of me. Let's do this. Call a life insurance company. Have a representative make an appointment with us here."

"Okay. I agree. That's a great idea."

Within a week, we signed the contracts for our new life insurance policies. Each was $20,000. He was my beneficiary, and I was his. I had other policies with my children as beneficiaries. He told me he also had other policies where his daughter was the beneficiary. We both felt better about the motorcycles driving by, but even today, I still cringe when I hear one.

The employees at the Marshall Dialysis Center began telling him they could train me to do his dialysis at my home. I had a zero-water filter on my kitchen counter for the water we drank, but filtered water for his blood to be removed, cleaned, and returned to his body in my living room would not work. My electricity goes out often, and I live in a rural area. If something went wrong while I did his dialysis, I lived too far from town to receive help very fast.

I had to refuse. Keith wanted me to try. I couldn't do it. A few days later, the water was turned off at the Dialysis Center he attended in Marshall, Texas while patients were hooked up to the machines. It was a full-blown emergency for each patient. They had to be placed in ambulances and driven to a Longview, Tx. hospital.

That ended the idea of me being trained and doing his dialysis from my house.

Keith was able to read his Bible with the new machine from the V.A. We enjoyed great in-depth discussions on what chapters he'd read recently. It was such a blessing to have discussions about scripture with a Christian man. I never had that with either of my husbands.

One day driving into Marshall for dialysis, Keith told me to turn into the cemetery on the main highway. I did. We were early and had enough time. He had me stop at the grave site of his son. We got out of the car. Then he nodded at the stone next to it. It said "Mam-Maw and Pap-Paw" with Sandra's name and the stone also had Keith's name. I looked at him and realized that was what he was to Irene; a Pap-Paw. Not a man with a life of his own. Someone for the kids. Yes, it is a blessing to be a grandfather, but an older man still has a mind, goals, and a private life besides their grandchildren. I remained quiet and kept my thoughts to myself.

Keith turned to face me. "I wanted you to see this. I do not want to be buried here by Sandra. Where are you going to be buried?"

"I bought four plots in the cemetery of the town where I live. "

"Well, I don't want you to be buried by yourself. I want to be buried next to you."

"Keith, that's not going to happen. Everything is ready here, the stone, the engraving. Yes, I'd be honored to have you next to me, but Irene would never agree."

"You could bury me."

"Irene won't let that happen. She will be in charge."

"Well, we'd better go. Let's talk about this later."

I nodded, and we returned to the car.

Keith wasn't happy with his relationship with Irene. It was not close like he wanted it to be. He would phone Irene during dialysis. Sometimes she couldn't talk; she was getting her hair done, or buying groceries, or at a grandkids ball game, etc. But she would call him at times. It bothered him that she didn't drive over to visit us. We stopped off at her house often on our way to the Shreveport doctor appointments. I gave her autographed copies of all my books. Her husband seemed more excited to get them than she did.

 He told her about the life insurance policies, and she didn't like it.

"Dad, that is an awful lot of money."

Keith looked at her and frowned. "You don't understand what it's for. If Lynn's husband goes crazy …as drug addicts are known to do…and shoots one of us, the other will be taken care of financially.

She shook her head and changed the subject.

On the way home, Keith had me promise that when he did die, for me not to give Irene his dog.

"Lynn, she won't take care of it, and it will run out into the highway by her house and get run over."

I promised. When the time did come, I took the dog to a no-kill shelter, and they found it a good home with a fenced yard and a barn. I couldn't keep the dog as he was not house broke and would urinate out of the metal kennel in my living room onto my hardwood floors.

 Irene also invited us to all the dinners they gave for the family. They were enjoyable and relaxing, but Irenes' husband seemed to be Keith's relative instead of Irene; and was a lot friendlier. Of course, we continued driving to Keith's home to feed the cats and dogs and then we'd drop by Irenes' house. Busy times.

(Because this is a short story I cannot continue with three years' worth of dialog. I had no choice but to summarize many instances.)

It was hard to believe Keith had been here with me for almost three years. We had met in 2018 at that Dairy Queen a day after Valentines Day. The following year, he was in the V.A. hospital during Valentines Day. I spent the day with him and the V.A. treated all couples to a steak dinner that day. That was our second Valentines Day. He had swollen legs, and they wanted to run some tests. He was released the next day.

We managed to keep up the fast pace of our lives. The VA decided Keith needed a sleep aphthae overnight test. I drove him to a different town for this test. It was across the stateline into Louisiana in a small town not far from Smithland, Tx. I was taking the wheelchair with us at this time. I'd help him in and out of it and the car. He stayed overnight at that hospital, and I returned the following day and brought him back.

That night he fell onto the bathroom floor. He couldn't get up, and blood was all around him on the floor. He yelled for me to call Irenes' husband for help. I did. He came right over. I gave him towels to put on top of Keith as he was covered in a mess. His son-in-law lifted him up and tried to clean him as best as he could. I informed him that I would dispose of the towels, and that he should not be concerned about it.

Keith had hit his forehead on the sharp corner of the sink and that's where most of the blood came from. I helped then with first aid. Soon, Keith was up and about. Walking slowly though. We thanked his son-in-law, and he left.

162

We continued dialysis 3 times a week in Marshall, Tx. and going to Keith's house in a different town to feed his animals. Then he wanted to bring his gun collection to my house. We did. We even stopped at the pharmacy in his town and Mom, Keith and I took the Shingles shot. Then returned to take the second one. It was a fast-paced schedule with several Shreveport doctor appointments added each month when Mom's behavior changed. Even Keith was surprised about the difference. "I've never seen a mother be so hateful to her daughter as your mother is to you," Keith often said.

I discussed the sudden hatefulness with her doctor and was told to expect that to become much worse as both the disease of Alzheimer's and Dementia were progressing. She began sleepwalking and hallucinating. Talking out loud all night. Falling out of bed. Broke a leg. Had to have a hospital bed with metal rails. It did not help. She would climb over the rails and fall. I bought a 300-dollar bed alarm similar to an extra-large heating pad. It would activate when she moved off of it, but she was fast as lightning. I once caught her trying to climb out the window. I had to cover the window with a blanket. Finally, her doctor said make a pallet on the floor for her to sleep there. No more bed so I rearranged my bedroom and bought her a 5-inch thick memory foam twin size mattress. I put it in the corner of my room with a king-size eggshell foam folded in half under it. Since she always ended up on the floor she would now sleep there. Then she began hiding her food more often. Where she had hidden her food under couch cushions, and in her clothes or in a flower vase full of flowers; she now became destructive with it. She crammed a sandwich into the commode and ruined my septic system. I had to get a new system. I was so thankful for Keith's help with her. He watched her as best he could when I was busy with chores in a different part of the house. We continued our pace of at least 5 doctor appointments that included coming and going from 3 dialysis sessions a week. Besides me cleaning the house, cooking, washing clothes, mowing the grass, paying bills, going to feed Keith's animals; we would nearly fall asleep at the end of the day as soon as we sat down. On a day not so hectic, Keith and I looked forward to sitting on the patio in the afternoon …when we were here and not on the road, to simply rest and talk. Keith was a fantastic conversationalist. He was inspiring to me. This was happening in 2020. It got worse with Mom the following year. Her skin became thin and would bust open when she 'd twist it against the wooden floor in my bedroom. She would scoot on her rear end in the dark and not talk. I'd hear a bump into the wall and turned on the light. She'd be on the other side of the room with a bloody arm. I'd get out of bed, get my first aid supplies, and clean and dress her arm.

I tried Home Health Care twice a week to dress her wounds, and the first employees were wonderful people; so friendly. They were transferred to other areas though. The new employees were not friendly, and I decided I didn't want them in my house. So, my doctor cancelled them. I bought the wound care supplies from Amazon and did it all myself. Keith grew weaker but would still come up behind me and give me a hug. He was a light in the middle of darkness for me. We grew closer if that could be possible. When Mom would get upset, she would scream like a Commanche Indian and Keith would look at me and say "That's not her. That's the sickness trying to get a rection out of you. Don't holler at her."

So, I would smile at her, and she'd glare at me. After a few months of that, she changed again. She began singing gospel hymns and we never knew what year she would wake up in. She developed a nicer attitude. She'd look at everyone when we went to the VA hospital, and I was glad she was a people watcher. When we'd go eat at the Chinese restaurants she'd eat and enjoy it. 2021 arrived and we bought Christmas presents for everyone again. As for progress, at this time, Keith would put Tinkerbell, (nicknamed Doggie Girl, my little Yorkie dog) on his walker and push her down my long hallway to the bathroom. The dog would wait patiently for him to return from the bathroom.

My son came to visit and enjoyed talking to Keith about stories of fishing and hunting with family. My granddaughter also came over and cooked us a meal. It was delicious and we enjoyed the company.

I needed car repair then and Irene's husband took my car to Shreveport to have it done. Keith insisted on paying the $800 costs for the repair. I was driving a rental while the work was done. My son came from another town to get me when it was completed. He picked me up from the rental company (in a second different town) and took me to Irene's house (in a third different town) to get my car back. Everyone was so helpful. It was a blessing.

I had no idea that Keith would soon pass away by the upcoming Valentines Day.

His downfall began by the VA scheduling him a COVID vaccination. He felt strange afterward, but they insisted he take the follow up shot the next week. They cancelled his dialysis appointment in Marshall, Tx. to take this second COVID shot in Shreveport, La. That one finished him off. He told me he felt like ants were crawling all over him after we returned to my home on that Saturday.

"Keith, I'm filling your overnight bag. We're going right back there." Countless other times when he'd felt bad, I'd want to drive him to the V.A. Hospital, and he always refused. "No, if they ever keep me all night I'll never come home." But this time was different. He was quickly becoming worse.

"Okay. I'll go back."

I threw shaving equipment, toothpaste and brush, after shave, hair comb and brush, and deodorant, into the bag along with underwear, shirts, a pair of blue jeans, and house slippers.

I returned to the living room. "Do you want your billfold?"

"No," he gasped. "You" …he paused, "You keep all the money." He spoke firmly then.

"I have enough for the bills." I didn't think he had much in his billfold. It later turned out he didn't.

He raised his head and stared at me.

"Okay," I looked back at him. "I'll leave your billfold here." I dismissed it.

"I'll prepare Mom and load the car."

He nodded. "I have to go to the bathroom."

I backed the car to the entrance of my home. Hurriedly, I put his overnight bag and Mom in the car and returned to the house.

He then called out to me.

"Lynn, Lynn! Help!"

I was in the foyer grabbing his jacket.

I barged into the bathroom, and he sat on the commode, shaking. Blood and huge, round blood clots, the size of a silver dollar, flowed out of him and down the side of the toilet bowl onto the floor. The clots were thick and not bright red, but dark, nearly black resembling old blood.

I cleaned him up, got him out of there and phoned the V.A. Hospital in Shreveport.

He was sitting in the recliner then.

I was still on the phone with the V.A., giving his last four of his social security number when it happened again. I told them we were on our way. I hung up and ran to get towels for him.

"Get a trash can, I'm getting sick." He yelled.

I had to get him there fast. I snatched a trash can from the bathroom along with an armful of towels and put them in the front seat of the car. I carefully sat him on his walker and pushed him to the car. He sat on top of several towels. By this time, diarrhea began along with the blood and blood clots. He started vomiting. He laid his head on my shoulder and threw up away from me into the trash can all the way to Shreveport.

He was alert and talked. He kept saying he'd never felt anything like this before. He grew weak and his feet and legs began swelling.

I knew toxins were building up in his body from the missed dialysis session.

When we arrived at the VA 's emergency entrance, a stretcher was brought out for him. Two men helped him out of my car and onto the stretcher. I told them the COVID shot caused blood and blood clots and he needed his dialysis done as it had to be missed to get the shot. They thanked me and told me I could not go into the hospital with him. No visitors were allowed.

I told him I loved him, and I was praying for him. He told me he loved me too. He sounded so weak. That was the last time I saw him.

It was late and we drove home. I put Mom to bed and cleaned the car and the bathroom.

I called Irenes' husband early the next morning and told him what had happened. He said he would go immediately to the VA hospital and try to see him.

 I then called Keith at the hospital (this was the next day) and they wouldn't let me talk to him. I called the second day and couldn't get him. I called a nurse's station then and demanded to talk to him. They said a phone was not in his room, and I told them to locate one and plug it in to his room. They did. I finally got to talk to him. He sounded better. Talked like normal.

"You don't know how happy I am you called." He told me in a rush.

"I've been trying! It was hard to get through to you since you arrived there." I answered.

"I'm not surprised. It is so crowded here and complete chaos. They've been running all kind of tests on me …trying to find out where the blood is coming from."

"It's still happening?"

"Yes."

"Have you had dialysis yet?"

"No, not yet, it was scheduled for tomorrow morning."

"Keith, you will swell up worse with toxins if they didn't hurry and do it."

"I know. I'll make sure they do it in the morning as they claimed they would."

"Good." I suddenly heard several muffled voices.

Keith instantly spoke quietly," A group of foreigner doctors are here. They are discussing me now. I got to go. I love you."

"I love you too." I told him.

That was the last time I talked to him.

The following day I called again, and the call went to the nurse's station.

A male nurse answered.

"I'd like to talk to Keith in room 2007, please." I stated.

"I'm sorry, but he's too weak to talk."

"Really? He was fine yesterday. Strong firm voice, not weak at all. "

"Well, you ought to get him out of here, this team of doctors can't get it together. Some want to schedule surgery, and some want to put him in a coma. He needs to go to LSU. "

I was caught off guard and instantly became upset. "Give me his doctor's phone number. I want to talk to him right now."

He took a moment and gave me the phone number.

 I got a recording to leave a number and message. I did.

I left a detailed message on who I was calling for and what all I wanted to know and to please return my call right away.

He called alright. And right away. But he didn't call me, the one who took care of him for 3 years. The doctor called Irene. She was listed as his next of kin on the who to call list. Irene was at a ballgame.

Apparently, the doctor told her that Keith wasn't going to make it much longer, and she should come to the hospital now.

She never called me. Her husband never called me.

She went to the hospital with her husband, but they only let her in. They told her he was in a coma, that they did tests and unfortunately, there was no brain activity. She told them if they were sure then go ahead and pull the plug. They did.

He died the next morning. No one called and told me. Late that night about 9 pm, Irene's husband called me and told me he had passed. I could not believe it. I told him he was fine when I last talked to him. We got off the phone.

Keith had only been in the hospital for less than a week.

Irene put a pitiful post on Facebook. She asked everyone to pray for her, that her dad had died, and she had gone to the VA hospital alone to see him. She mentioned her husband was not allowed in the hospital. She said it was so disturbing for her to go in there alone. Comments flooded in with prayer for her.

Keith would have been so upset. It was all about her.

"Snowmageddon 2021" occurred then. It was during mid-February and began on Valentines Day. Two winter storms emerged in our Ark-La-Tex area. Shreveport usually receives 1 inch of snow a year. This time our area received 2 feet of snow, Shreveport having 8 inches. It was from 1 degree below freezing to -5 below freezing for way over a week. It cripped the area with impassable roads, power outages, heavy snow and ice caving in roofs and carports, frozen water pipes…this was record cold!

Keiths body remained at the V A Hospital during the entire time. No one could travel anywhere. After it finally began to thaw out, Irene began planning her father's funeral. It was stated on her Facebook page that only family members were allowed at the graveside. Irene planned the funeral at the church he and Sandra used to attend that had been permanently closed for some time. Irene made arrangements for the church to be opened for Keith's funeral, and again, no one told me anything.

I later found out about it. Everyone gave condolences to Irene on Facebook and told her what a good daughter she was.

In the brochure to give out at the funeral, the obit stated his military years, his surviving family, his ministry work, and then at the very last, it stated; Keith is now at rest and has joined the love of his life; Sandra.

That was done deliberately to hurt me.

A few days later, Irene's husband phoned. They wanted his belonging.

I agree to gather as much as I could. They were coming that night.

It was raining. Irenes' husband and his grown son, and son-in-law arrived. They began taking over 30 rifles and over 25 pistols that were Keith's collection. Then several large boxes of medicine; ointment, bandages, and pills. I told them how he placed the pills in order around the inside of the boxes because he was blind and couldn't see or read what was what. They looked at me as if that was news. They took boxes of personal papers, clothes, etc.

Then Irenes' husband stopped and glanced at me. "I'll be back tomorrow for the rest of it."

His son glanced around the inside of my house and looked at the high cathedral ceiling. "You have a really nice home, no wonder Papaw liked staying here."

With that remark, they left.

The next day, Irenes' husband returned with two pre-teen grandsons to help him. They went through the shop where many of my family had belongings stored. He would pick up different items and tell the boys; "Here take this, I know Papaw had one like it, it must be his. Go put it in the truck."

Both boys took a lot to the truck. I didn't stop him. I didn't care about material things. I did give him Keith's Bible for Irene. I told him Keith was reading 2nd Timothy when he left here.

"Thank you. I don't know if anyone in the family has contacted you or told you this, but I want to thank you for all that you have done for Keith, and I do mean everything."

No one had done either of that, so I just looked at him and nodded.

After he had finished going through everything, he seriously announced, "We won't be seeing you anymore."

They walked to his truck and then as a parting remark, he said, ""Oh, Irene said to tell you they don't make pine boxes to bury people with anymore and you should not have kept the insurance money." Before I could say anything, they climbed into the truck and left.

That was the last time I saw or had any contact with them.

That hurt, but I should have been prepared for it with Irene's attitude.

A few weeks later I had to remove Keith's recliner from the living room. I kept turning my head away from it. I couldn't stand to look at it without him in it. I gave it away. It was too painful to see it.

I tried writing about Keith and kept crying each time I started. It has now been 4 years since he died (I should say killed by the VA) Even now I cry but I wanted this told.

Do I forgive everyone involved? Yes, of course. God won't forgive me of my sins if I don't forgive others of their sins. Am I perfect? No. No one is.

I even forgive my sister and my stepbrother from keeping Keith and I apart all those years ago. She came to visit last year, and I had a talk with her. "Remember the man I told you I was taking care of? He was blind and had to have 3 dialysis treatments each week?"

"Yes, I do." She answered.

"Well, that's the same man you and Wendell held a shotgun on and told him to stay away from me."

"What? "She exclaimed.

"That's right. You kept us apart. But 45 years later, he found me."

"Lynn, I am so sorry." She cried. "I was only a kid then."

"Sister, you were in your early 20's and had a child. But I forgive you. I forgive everyone. I thank God Keith, and I at least had three years together. And if it was wrong for me to take him in and take care of him, I pray for forgiveness. I don't know what you were told, or by whom, but whatever it was, it was wrong. You reacted to wrong information and never asked me about anything…you and Wendell should never have taken it upon yourselves to do that. I can't control how others treat me, but I can control how I treat you. Always treat others as you want them to treat you. And if you think holding a gun on someone and taking control of two people's lives is right; you need to stop and think about your actions before you jump to conclusions. I never interfered in your divorce with your ex-husband. I never told you to go back to him. But I do forgive you, I forgive everyone for everything. We can't change the past, and we have all made mistakes. I love you sister, and I always will."

She didn't offer any information on what she and my stepbrother were told, or by whom…my mother or my estranged husband, or both. I didn't ask, it didn't matter. It was a mighty big lesson learned that others could also learn from.

So, it's all behind us now. And I am divorced from my current husband. His girlfriend since 2007 has now been in prison three times for substance abuse. His drug habits have destroyed his mind. That was the lifestyle he chose.

And for me… had I not taken Keith in… I would have deeply regretted it. I am glad I didn't pass up the opportunity to be with Keith and help him. Married or not, I followed my Christian values.

†☐ †☐ †☐

Philippians 4:13: I can do all things through Christ who strengthens me.

 Matthew 19: 26: But Jesus beheld them, and said unto them, with men this is impossible; but with God all things are possible.

John 7:24 (NLT): Look beneath the surface so you can judge correctly.

James 1:19 (NLT): Understand this, my dear brothers and sisters: You must all be quick to listen, slow to speak, and slow to get angry.

Moral to the story: Walk in someone's shoes before jumping to conclusions.

The End

Chapter Nineteen

A Cat Named Brother

I did not change his name; it really is Brother.

I noticed the cat for over a year. It would come from my neighbor's house who lived farther down the road. The first time I noticed the cat was when he crouched on the ground for seemingly hours. As he lay still, birds would land on the concrete birdbath near my Tulip Tree. I'd see him from my kitchen window. I'd later return to the same window, and he was still there. Determined.

Some days I'd see a few blue feathers on the ground where the cat had been, and I was intrigued by the cat's skill. I knew the cat couldn't be hungry, because my neighbors were animal lovers, and took excellent care of them. They had dogs as well.

A month later, I hired a contractor to replace my deck. It was ten feet off the ground and attached to the back of my house. After removing the old wooden planks, one of the crew stopped working and knocked on my door.

"Do you have a cat?" He asked.

"Well, no, but I do have a neighbor's cat who comes and goes around the area. "

"You need to get him before he gets hurt. He's batting his paws constantly with a water moccasin. Each time the snake leaps toward the cat to bite it, the cat paws at the snake."

I ran outside and looked down at the ground and there the cat was, casually laying and pawing at the curled, long, thick snake. I instantly yelled, "Get out of here!" and the cat ran off.

I hated to scare it, but that was the only way I knew for it to leave and be safe.

One of the men took a shovel and killed the venomous snake, pitched it into the river, and returned to working on the deck.

I waved at my neighbor the following day as he was driving by my house. I told him what the cat was doing with the snake.
"That crazy cat! He's already been bitten twice by a snake. He won't leave them alone. Oh, and his name is Brother. He likes to ride with my wife and I in the go-cart. He will roll over for a belly rub, and meow at you wanting attention. He is something else." The man grinned.

"Well, he visits me often and has rolled over for a belly rub on my porch. He sure is friendly."

"That is amazing. He is usually skittish around other people. I guess he feels comfortable at your place." He laughed.

"I think he does." I smiled as he drove off.

I would put good leftovers in a paper plate on my bench on the front porch for Brother when I had them. He always stopped by to check out the bench as he strolled by. He seemed to enjoy exploring. I could see him across the street at times. On other days he'd be roaming at the neighbor's yard on the other side of me. Busy cat.

Then I bought the boneless chicken breast at the grocery store that changed everything.

It was on sale. I was surprised at the price and bought three family packs of it. My intentions were to freeze most of it and cook some that day. I unwrapped the cellophane off the first package and took the skin off one of the pieces of meat.

Yikes! It was shredded meat under the first layer of skin! It looked like spaghetti!

I smelled it, and it smelt okay.

I was not about to eat it though. I had heard on television how some consumers had recently had the same kind of chicken, and it was reported on the national news to have had hormones inserted into the chickens and they grew too fast. It was also reported that it was safe to eat.

"Brother is going to get some Southern Fried Chicken." I thought.

I fried it in flour with seasonings and set it out on the bench. Brother would eat and leave only to return later and eat again.

"Well, he sure is enjoying it." I decided to fry the other two packages the next day and let him have that also.

I did.

I put two paper plates out on the bench then. You could smell that fried chicken all over my front lawn. It was as strong as if you walked into a grocery store that had fried chicken wafting through the air in their deli area.

I smiled as Brother returned. He jumped onto the bench and started eating.

I was baking cookies then and left Brother alone. Something caught my eye as I walked past the kitchen window, it was Brother running into my front yard again.

"Hmm, he must be incredibly hungry, or he loves fried chicken." I thought.

Curious, I opened my front door and to my amazement there were five cats all identical to Brother eating fried chicken! Each one was dark gray with black stripes!

I later found out that Brother was the only one who loved belly rubs, the others were merely his brothers and sisters from the same litter.

So, I had been seeing five cats instead of the one who seemed so extremely busy!

Note: How often do you assume something because that is how it appeared? We all need to be careful with assuming anything!

And what became of the other cats?

Brother was joined by the same neighbor's (Aaron and Justin) other cat; Hector, a male black cat. And another one of Brother's twins. These three have claimed lounging rights on my long, concrete, covered porch with a kitten that is a bit shy. The others come over briefly to check for leftovers and return home. On this particular day, Thursday, October 23, 2025; I had to cover my only outside water faucet. A cold front was predicted along with rain. It was time to wrap it up for the upcoming winter. I took heavy material, a large roll of duct tape, plastic trash bags, and scissors outside. I didn't notice any cats around. I set everything by the 2-foot-tall pipe extending out of the ground the water faucet was on. I started at the bottom of the pipe, wrapping the heavy material round and round until I made it to the top and then secured it tightly with lots of duct tape. I grabbed the roll of black trash bags and ripped them apart at their pre-marked sections as I held them in the air. That's when I noticed the cats. They appeared out of nowhere. Hector was stretched out in a crouching position about to smell the roll of duck tape. Brother was laying on top of the unused material, and the twin had climbed into the box of trash bags. I had to laugh! They were all three quietly inspecting what I had going on! I talked to them as I finished my project, gathered the remaining supplies for the job, and went back inside. Once again, they slowly meandered down the middle of our country road and headed back home.

Update on Brother: Once a year I rake and burn leaves from the many trees on my property. I always spend several days with this task as you cannot burn leaves when it is windy. On this day, I had five huge piles of leaves to burn. Knowing I'd be tired at the end of the day, I put a glass of iced tea and a bowl of popcorn on the front porch bench for my break. I placed a paper towel over the popcorn to keep flies, etc. out. Halfway through burning leaves, I saw Brother walking down the road, then he headed straight to the bench on my front porch. Before I could stop him, he ate a piece of popcorn, spit it out on top of the paper towel and stuck his mouth on the top of the glass of iced tea. His body quivered at it, and he went back home walking down the middle of the road like he owned it. I could not be upset with him. That was his place to eat!

†☐ †☐ †☐

Exodus 23:4–5 (NLT): "If you come upon your enemy's ox or donkey that has strayed away, take it back to its owner. If you see that the donkey of someone who hates you has collapsed under its load, do not walk by. Instead, stop and help."

Moral of that story: Be careful of even the least significant thing you teach to someone or some animal. Brother was taught that the food on that bench was for him. He learned that quickly, and I learned a lesson as well!

The End

Chapter Twenty

Why I Have a Gun

Home invasion. One hears this phrase often on the news almost daily.

What is your first thought?

Do you simply picture the family giving their money and valuables to the thieves and no one is harmed? Sorry, but during the chaos thugs do not have manners, and they do not want any witnesses to their crime.

Police cannot appear instantly in emergencies.

Could you protect yourself or protect your family?

Are you someone who prefers to give consoling to the criminal and not call 911 for help? Ensure your will is filed at the courthouse, and your business affairs are in order. Your life means nothing to a criminal. You are an interruption to their plan.

Again, as in each of my stories, the names have been changed.

Two home invasions happened in my area, each in a different small town, and only a few miles apart.

In one, I personally knew the three survivors.

In the other one, I personally knew all three who invaded the home.

Both had significant impacts. Both involved guns, and none of the innocent victims had guns.

Life changing? Yes.

Horrific abuse? Yes.

This is another true story. It begins in 2004 and ends in 2009.

I was secretary to the Jr./Sr. High School Principal in a small Texas town.

I first heard of Ladarius when he was in the sixth grade. He forcibly pushed a little girl down on a moving school bus and raped her. It was at the end of that school term.

No cameras were on school buses in those years.

No rape kit was used.

But the little girl was hurt, and many children saw what happened.

No charges were filed.

(I later discovered most small school districts refrained from reporting bad discipline problems with students as their government funding would be seriously reduced. If a student needed to be criminally charged with anything; it had to be made by a parent of the victimized child…not by the school.)

Nothing happened to him. He thought he got away with it.

He did, but summer was over. Everyone was watching him.

And now, he was coming to the Jr./Sr. High School to start the 7th grade.

I had taken over 340 credited hours in at Region 7 Educational Training Center for my school district. I did Peims, Attendance, Discipline, Bookkeeping, Report Cards, Poverty seminars, etc, and I was the school nurse.

This is how I met Ladarius. He had medication to take daily while at school, and I gave it to him from my office.

One day, he came into my office and quietly moved away from the front of my desk so I could see his exposed, protruding penis.

One cannot predict their reaction to such circumstances; in my situation, I responded with anger.

I grabbed him by the back of his neck and shoved him into the principal's office that adjoined mine.

"I don't have to work like this." I shouted, as I pushed the boy in front of the principal. His penis was still exposed.

"No, ma'am, you don't! I'm calling Mrs. Maxwell in the detention room to come and get him. Then, I'm calling the sheriff's office."

I pivoted and returned to my office.

Mrs. Maxwell soon arrived and escorted the boy to her detention room. His pants were now zipped up. Within five minutes, her shrill voice filled my room from the intercom. He just exposed himself to her. The principal heard it and took off in her direction. He remained there until a deputy came to remove the boy.

We were shocked it had happened, and I wasn't the only one angry about it.

The principal pressed charges.

Nothing like that had happened at our school and he didn't want it to happen again.

So, within two weeks, a hearing was held at the county Juvenile Detention Center. Mrs. Maxwell and I both had to testify in front of him and his family about what happened. His family claimed we were lying because we were white, and they were black.

I spoke up fast and addressed his mother. "Excuse me, but I happen to be one of very few white people on this campus, much less who work here. I love my job. I love people. I have made great lasting friendships here. You don't even know me. First, I am a Christian. Second, I am a sponsor of the FBLA. If you don't know what that organization is, it's the Future Business Leaders of America. We are encouraging and concerned for the students' future welfare. Third, I mentor numerous students here and I do not consider their race, as I view each student individually. Do not throw race at me. I don't care if your son is black or white; he needs to be held accountable for his actions."

A county attorney spoke up then. "The poor boy is misunderstood. I recommend treatment at the Behavior Center in Shreveport, La."

And that is how it ended.

Ladarius snickered at Mrs. Maxwell and me and left with his family.

For the following two weeks, each morning, Monday through Friday, Ladarius sat in the school transportation car waiting for a bus driver to finish his route and drive him to Shreveport to the Behavior Center. I had to walk in front of that car each morning on my way to my office. Ladarious would glare at me each time. The school's parking lot was located across a public street from the school building.

After two weeks of attending behavior classes, Ladarious fought a woman guard and was expelled. He returned to our school.

His mother found my phone number and called me. She apologized for saying I lied about her son. She said when he fought and hurt the female guard, she saw a side of him she had never seen before. I accepted her apology and our conversation ended friendly despite the circumstances.

At this time, my mother had an appointment with the hospital in a nearby town for an x-ray on her back. Upon entering the hospital that day, I was shocked to see Ladarious and two of his friends leaving the hospital. I immediately thought of where I parked my car, as I knew his hatred for me could result in my tires being slashed, or worse. I had parked out in the open in plain sight. I decided it was safe.

Why they weren't in school, I don't know. I had taken a vacation day off work to help Mom.

I was glad Ladarious was no longer needing medicine daily. He stayed away from my office. His two friends were well known in our small community. The first one, Coby, was a student at our school. His mother left him often and he was raised by a relative…off and on. He seemed well behaved and was liked by most of the students. The second one, Julius, was a student in the town where the hospital is. He was distant, not friendly at all. Julius would often appear at our school the instant the last bell would ring, I often wondered what his school attendance record was like. He was the leader of the three.

Since Julius was with Ladarious and Coby so often, I noticed a change in both boys. Coby started wearing silk walking shorts with a matching tank top. He had a different attitude; and suddenly acted older. His way of dress was so out of character for him. And Ladarius appeared sneaky. Julius was quiet but was clearly the leader of the three.

Two weeks later, on a Saturday morning, I noticed an older model truck drive slowly past my house. I got cold chills immediately.

It was Ladarius, Cody, and Julius.

My house is on a dead-end road in the country. Thankfully, there were houses on both sides of my house and a house across the street. I was relieved when they turned around at the end of the road and left the area.

I prayed for protection.

A few days later… those three choose a home in the country in a nearby town …without many houses around…and performed a home invasion on an unsuspecting elderly white couple.

It was horrific.

The woman, who was eighty-two years old at the time the crime occurred, testified that she and her husband had been married sixty-two years and had lived in the same house for forty years. On September 20, 2009, the elderly couple awoke in bed to see 16-year-old Ladarius, with his face covered by a bandanna, pointing a gun at them. Cody, 20 years old and Julius, 18 years old, were also in the bedroom, and all three intruders had guns. Ladarius demanded "to know where [her] money was." She was ordered out of the bed, tied to a nearby lawn chair, and had her pajama top ripped open. As Ladarius grabbed the woman's ankles and started to drag her out of the bedroom, her husband, who was resisting, was shot by Julius. Ladarius dragged the woman into the bathroom where he raped her while she was still tied to the collapsed lawn chair.

The woman testified that Ladarius left the bathroom to talk with the other intruders. When Ladarius returned, he had the woman dress and then taped her hands. She was escorted into the garage and ordered into the trunk of her car. The intruders drove her to a deserted tract of land, backed the car into some bushes, locked the car, and abandoned the car with the motor running. She testified that her husband had shown her, a long time ago, where a lever in the trunk of the car would release the trunk. Although she could not find the lever in the dark, she was able to observe a wire by light from the brake lights reflecting into the trunk. When pulled, the wire released the trunk. Then the woman, seeing the intruders had left, used the car's keyless entry to unlock the car and drove away hitting a tree in the process.

She testified that she passed the three intruders walking on the side of the road as she drove to the police station. A Police Officer observed three African American males, matching the description given by the elderly woman walking along some railroad tracks. All three complied with the Officers' command to get on the ground but Cody fled while the Officer was cuffing him. Another Officer pursued and detained Cody after a brief chase. The elderly man's wallet and driver's license were found in Cody's pocket. One weapon, a handgun, was discovered near Julius' feet. Ladarius had gloves and the elderly man's prescription medicine bottle in his pocket.

During a police interrogation, Cody admitted to participating in the burglary. The revolver found at Julius' feet had one fired cartridge and five unfired. A forensic analysis on the gun determined it fired the bullet recovered from the couple's mattress. DNA reports were admitted.

Cody was convicted of murder and sentenced to life imprisonment.

Ladarius took a plea bargain agreement, pled guilty to murder, receiving a 60-year sentence in prison. If he ever gets paroled, he will have to register as a sex offender for the rest of his life.

Julius was sentenced to death.

I first heard about this violent crime on television. The local newspaper kept giving the latest updates. Word of mouth in this community was constant about it.

Such a waste of so many lives.

It is mind-boggling that those three young men were capable of doing this to that poor, innocent elderly couple.

I then read about another local home invasion that took place at night. Several grown men broke into the home of an elderly couple and their two adult children. The 90-year-old man was beaten brutally, pistol-whipped again and again on the head with a .45-caliber handgun. It took more than ninety-five staples to close the wounds on his head.

His wife ran to another building on the property and grabbed an old rifle. She pointed it out the window toward the men, hoping to scare them off. The gun was unloaded, but they didn't know that. One man chased after her while another began shooting. Somehow, every shot missed. Her skin was thin and tore easily, and blood began to flow from where it had ripped open.

One of their adult children entered the room, saw what was happening, and ran for help. The other child fought back, pushing one of the men out the front door. As he stumbled outside, he fired his gun, and the bullet grazed the side of her head. In the chaos, the mother managed to call for help. Within minutes, the sound of sirens filled the night as law enforcement rushed to the scene.

They now have the outside of their home, at night, lit up like a football field on a Friday night. They also have several large dogs they constantly keep inside, day and night.

And the invaders?

They were never caught.

After this happened, I and another female school employee enrolled in a certified concealed handgun course. We passed and obtained our license. At that time, you were trained to take your weapon apart and put it back together. You could also purchase weapons there. I decided a 9mm Glock was easier for me to take apart (the purpose was to know how to clean it properly). I bought it and a shotgun. Later I bought what I call a cowboy gun; a long barreled 22 single shot pistol. It is great for target practice. We took written tests on laws of owning a gun, when and

185

when not to shoot, and where and where not to carry a weapon. Extensive training is a must.

You only shoot if your life is in danger.

Hopefully you won't ever have to protect yourself, but if you do…have a gun with stopping power. We were taught the larger caliber will stop somebody from coming after you, where a smaller caliber will only make them angry and they will keep coming after you. So, I bought a long barrel 357 Magnum pistol. It is under my bed, and it is loaded.

No, there are no children here.

And yes, you now know why I have a gun.

And it all started when Ladarius was in the sixth grade and raped a little girl on a school bus…

†☐ †☐ †☐

Isaiah 54:17 No weapon that is formed against you shall prosper; and every tongue that shall rise against you in judgement you shall condemn. This is the heritage of the servants of the LORD, and their righteousness is of Me, saith the LORD.

Nehemiah 4:14 And I looked, and rose up, and said unto the nobles, and to the rulers, and to the rest of the people, Be not ye afraid of them: remember the LORD, which is great and terrible, and fight for your brethren, your sons, and your daughters, your wives, and your houses.

Luke11:21 When a strong man armed keeps his palace, his goods are in peace.

Moral to the story: We need guns to protect ourselves. If gun were banned, no one would have guns except the criminals. The black market would be flooded with them. Every drug dealer, human trafficator, burglar, pimp, pedophile, felon, gang member, illegal; any criminal…could get weapons from their buddies. Law abiding citizens must have weapons for protection. We must protect ourselves. If anyone has ever been brutally raped, I assure you if that victim had a gun, no one would ever rape them again.

The End

Chapter Twenty-One

When Remodeling Becomes a Necessity

It looked like no one had ever lived there. Termites were swarming around the rotten boards at the front door. When I walked inside, I noticed a bird's nest sitting on one of the exposed rafters in the kitchen. The electrical wiring hung loosely, looped through the two by fours, and there was no ceiling, only a roof.

The back bedroom had no gas line. There were no closets, no shelves in the bathroom, no bathtub, and no hot water heater.

Trying to stay positive about my new home, I had to smile. I had never remodeled before, and there were only three rooms in this cabin, three rooms of pure mess to make livable. On my limited budget, I couldn't afford much, so I silently prayed for strength.

I went across the road to my late stepfather's tool shed beside the house where he and Mom had lived. Sorting through his old tools, I used whatever I could find and began replacing the rotten boards on the cabin. I was determined to make it into a decent home. Pulling out damaged boards with a crowbar and hammer wasn't hard. After spraying for termites, I started replacing the entire damaged area. I didn't even have a roll-up tape measure, just a three-foot wooden yardstick.

Once again, I made do with what I had. By salvaging scraps of leftover lumber my ex-husband had discarded, I managed to gather enough material without buying new supplies.

Finally, the exterior was ready for my vinyl siding crew. Not knowing how skilled we might be, I turned around proudly to face both members of my team.

They grinned at me, eager to get started.

Mother was sixty at the time and newly widowed. Aunt Bernice was fifty-eight and wore nitroglycerin patches for her heart. She was visiting from another town and couldn't overexert herself. I was recently divorced, and no, there was not a boyfriend in sight.

I smiled back at them, picked up my tools, and together we began the vinyl siding.

The vinyl siding had also been discarded. Most of it was usable; but a few of the panels were damaged in a fire. My ex-husband had the siding left over in his building business and had forgotten about it.

This cabin was part of my divorce settlement, along with the only car on his lot that was rusted underneath from years of saltwater at the beach. Across the road sat the home my parents lived in, and that house was paid for. A customer had given it to my then-husband as payment for a construction job he had done.

Years earlier, I had told my parents they could live in that home for free if they could help me. I had four thousand dollars saved for the down payment on the land but needed one more thousand. They agreed to help, and I made the loan through my job, paying it off through the employee purchase plan taken from my paycheck.

Just before the divorce, my ex secretly refinanced the land I had already paid for and kept the money. That meant I would now have to pay for the same land a second time. His good banker friend made it easy for him, and the banker's notary handled the paperwork. She also happened to be one of my ex-husband's girlfriends, a wealthy one, and the woman he was spending his nights with during the divorce. They later married. She told her out-of-town family that she had met him while playing Monopoly with their combined teenage children.

But that's another story… literally.

"Cutting vinyl siding with large tin snips is just like cutting fabric for a sewing pattern," I explained as we opened the boxes of siding panels. "We can all sew and quilt," I continued, "and siding is similar."

A neighbor and his wife stopped by and showed us how to stagger each panel in layers. After we finished one full side, we had to stop and build corner boards for each end of the house.

Aunt Bernice's visit came to an end. I thanked her for helping us and for handing up the materials while we worked on ladders. Now, it was just Mother and me.

I placed two boards across the sawhorses. Nailing them together to form a corner wasn't a problem, but holding them in place before they slipped down was another story. They were heavy!

We took turns. One of us held the boards while the other nailed them to the house. Then we'd step back, proud of our work, only to see that the boards had slipped out of place while we nailed. Back up the ladders we went, fifteen feet in the air, pulling them off and starting again. After two failed attempts, Mother threatened to quit.

I looked at her quickly. We were both dripping with sweat, tired, and ready for a break. I laughed and told her she couldn't quit. I reminded her that if she did, she could only go home—and she had no other place to go! She couldn't drive, and besides, we were out in the woods, on the river, at the end of a dead-end road.

She laughed too, and we decided we were trying to make entirely too much progress in one afternoon. Before the week was over, we finished hanging all the corner boards. I boxed in the outside rafters, and through trial and error, we taught ourselves about remodeling. Every bit of progress encouraged us to tackle something new. We even did a little roofing before it was all over.

One day, when I was hanging vinyl siding at the top of a gable end, I had to borrow a neighbor's ladder because ours wasn't tall enough. For two days I worked up there. People driving by would smile and wave, and I'd smile back.

On the third morning, my neighbor, Mr. Clyde, ambled over. He was eighty years old, sweet as could be, with tobacco juice stains on his chin and clean overalls. He had lived in Karnack, Texas, for years and I always called him my supervisor.

"I don't want to tell you your business, but people are watching you on that ladder," he said solemnly, squinting up at me.

"I noticed cars going by," I told him.

"Well," he said slowly, grinning, "you have that ladder upside down."

"What?" I was shocked.

"The feet on the ladder don't go on the house. They go on the ground," he announced.

I laughed. "Do you mean you've sat on your porch and watched me for two days and never said a word?"

He spit, smiled, and said, "Well, I'm telling you now." Then he walked off.

Mother and I glanced at each other as he called out "Okay!" and we all three burst into laughter. I nearly fell off the ladder laughing.

After that, whenever I worked on the other side of the house, where he couldn't see me from his porch, he'd walk over to check. He worried about me using power saws. He knew I'd never done anything like this before.

It only took Mother and me one weekend to do the underpinning on the house. The hardest part was digging the trench underneath. We did have a helper for a while—a young teenager. He worked until he saw my niece, who was visiting from across the road. Suddenly, he was beside himself. He asked her to go bowling, went home to clean up, came back with flowers, and off they went. And just like that, I lost my helper.

After they left, I accidentally chopped my water line while cutting roots in the trench with an ax. Thankfully, my stepfather's toolbox had plumber's glue, tape, and fittings. A quick repair later, the water line and the underpinning were finished.

I hired an elderly man to hang an acoustical ceiling in the kitchen. The wiring still wasn't finished, but it was progress. After the carpenter completed the ceiling, I started on the kitchen walls, covering them with slat boards.

An elderly friend sold me her new hot water heater from a rental house that was being torn down. I also bought two old phone booth panels to hide it since it had to be installed in the kitchen. Mother and I carried that hot water heater to my car and then into the house. Another older gentleman installed it and ran new gas lines to the meter. Now I had a ceiling, gas, and hot water. Progress felt wonderful!

By this time, I'd grown comfortable with the power saw. I enclosed a window in the second room and turned the space into shelves for books. Then I built shelves for the kitchen, sanded and stained the hardwood floors, and even started painting. The kitchen became a soft blue-gray, and I displayed my can collection—fifteen years' worth—on the shelves. The middle room, over thirty years old, still had its original slat walls, which I painted white.

I'm still not finished with the last room. The windows aren't trimmed, and there's still no gas line in there, but we've come a long way.

When the weather turned beautiful, I stopped working inside. I couldn't help it—the fresh air was calling! Spring had arrived.

I laid out a driveway, shaping it with vinyl trim about two inches above the ground and filling it with white rock. It took only a weekend. Then I cleared out my beetle-infested pine trees, sold the pulpwood, burned the limbs, and planted new trees and flowers.

I added flowering quince shrubs, a rose bed, tulips, and chrysanthemums near the picnic area. Dogwood and redbud trees went by the riverbank, along with wildflowers. I planted a tulip magnolia, and a neighbor gave me plum and peach trees. Oak, cedar, dogwood, pine, and mimosa trees already grew on the property. White bridal wreath shrubs stood on each side of the driveway entrance.

Around the house, I planted azaleas bordered by a small white picket fence. Their hot pink blossoms looked beautiful against the light gray siding trimmed in white. On the other side of the house, I planted gardenias.

Now it truly looks like people live here. Driving through the woods and around the bend, my neighbors can hardly believe their eyes when my clean, remodeled home comes into view. The white rock driveway, the gray house, the picket fence, the blooming trees, and the bright azaleas—what a sight!

It had been such an eyesore before. Now, it feels like home. We've reached the point where it can all be enjoyed.

†□ †□ †□

Philippians 4:13 I can do all things through Christ Who strengthens me.

Moral of the story: When everything comes together and it all falls smoothly in place; Yehovah has His hand on it. It is truly a blessing!

The End

Chapter Twenty-Two

My Aunt Marie

My intension in writing this story is to show you how most nursing homes are only after the money, and do not watch over, or care for their patients as they should.

Aunt Marie was 105 years old when her daughter, Trudy, fell 4 ft off their back porch and had to have rods and screws inserted into her body. She had to learn how to walk again. She is using a walker now. My cousin and I are very close and keep in contact with each other weekly.

Trudy was Aunt Marie's only caregiver. They lived in Trudy's home for years and were hundreds of miles away from me. Until Trudy fell, Aunt Marie was fine. She quilted daily. She easily crawled under her bed to pull out boxes of sewing squares. She had organized each box with different color patterns.

The four of us talked often on the phone, as I was the only caregiver to my mom who was Aunt Marie's sister. My mom also lives with me in my home, and she is now 97 years old. Trudy and I are the same age, 76 years old, and grew up together. We both will be 77 in a few months.

When Trudy fell, she was sent by ambulance to the local hospital. (I'll refer to Aunt Marie as Marie to not confuse readers.) Trudy's daughter, who had her own family, was unable to care for Marie, and recalled a local nursing home owned by a couple from their church. It was wonderful and all the residents were well cared for. She contacted that nursing home and admitted Marie there. Unbeknownst to her, the couple had transferred ownership of the nursing home, which was now under new management.

Trudy remained in the hospital with ongoing surgeries. After 5 weeks of therapy, Trudy was in a wheelchair. Concerned about her mother's well-being, Trudy requested her retired friend Dennis to accompany her to the nursing home. He picked her up from the hospital and they went to the nursing home.

Marie had lost weight.

"Here, Mom, drink some water. Aren't you thirsty?" Trudy reached for the insulated container and almost dropped it.

"Yes, but it's too heavy. I can't pick it up. I told them to bring me water in a cup. I get so thirsty here, but they won't do it. They fill that thing up with ice and walk out." Marie shook her head in disgust.

Trudy looked at her mother's frail, small frame. "Well, Mom, I'll bring you a sippy cup. You know the kind little kids use? It has a handle on each side and it's small. It would be perfect for you."

"I don't care what it looks like. I think it would work." Marie grinned.

"Great! So how do you like it here?"

"Well, I want to go home as soon as you get better. I can wait until then."

Trudy smiled. "I am learning to walk, but it will take a while. I miss being home with you too. So, what activities do they have here? Are you doing any crafts here?"

"We must all remain in wheelchairs. No one can walk anywhere. I haven't heard of any activities."

"Well, that's odd. Why do they make you stay in a wheelchair?"

"I guess so we don't fall, and they are liable." Marie laughed.

Trudy shook her head. "So, how is the food?"

"Cold." Marie chuckled.

"No wonder you have lost weight. Have you seen many people working here? Do they have enough employees to deliver the food to the rooms, or do you go eat in a dining room?"

"Oh, we eat in our rooms. And the workers stand around talking at the nurse's station a lot. It's like no one is watching them. If I worked here, and did what they do, I'd be fired."

Trudy frowned. "That doesn't sound like the good reputation this place has."

Before she could say anything else, her friend Dennis interrupted. "I'm going to start coming by here every evening to check on you, Ms. Marie. If you need water or food, just let me know. And how about a cheeseburger right now?" He raised an eyebrow and smiled at her.

"Oh, I'd love that." She agreed.

"I'll be right back. Trudy, you want anything?"

"Yes, thank you. I'll take the same thing, and I'd like fries with mine, with bottled water, please."

"Me too, same thing." Marie added.

He soon returned and they all three ate cheeseburgers and fries. He passed out the bottled water, and they enjoyed a nice visit.

And so it began.

Dennis would stop by to check on Marie at the nursing home in the evenings and run by the hospital earlier to see how Trudy was progressing.

 Before entering the nursing home, Marie had a sore on her upper arm. Trudy had administered Neosporin ointment on it at night and left it dry during the day. It had shrunk and was almost gone. The nurses' aides, however, began bandaging it day and night at the nursing home. It grew. It wasn't getting any air for it. Soon, it became infected. They covered the bandage up by putting long sleeve shirts on Marie. When Dennis arrived, he believed she was receiving good care. However, the sore had become larger and deeper.

Marie complained that her arm hurt but was ignored. One evening, Dennis brought Trudy back to visit her mother, and Marie showed Trudy her arm.

"Oh, no! This is badly infected!" Trudy gasped. She pushed the button for the nurse's station. No one answered. "Wheel me down there, Dennis, I want to talk to them."

They left the room and hurried down the hallway only to find the nurses station empty. One nurse's aide exited a nearby room and approached Trudy and Dennis.

"May I help you?"

"Yes, the sore on my mother's arm is much worse. She needs antibiotics right away."

"Who is she?"

"Marie Aubacher."

"I'll look on her chart. She may be on them now." She went to the nurse's station with Dennis following pushing Trudy in the wheelchair. After a brief check on the computer, she glanced at Trudy. "No, the doctor hasn't prescribed her any antibiotics. I'll make a note to tell him your request."

"Thank you. She desperately needs the medicine."

Dennis and Trudy returned to visit Marie and left that evening.

The following day, Trudy called the nursing home and was told the doctor had ordered a 25 mg antibiotic for Marie to be given twice a day.

I happened to call Trudy that day and she told me about it. I was shocked.

"Trudy, that is not enough mgs. When I have an infection or my mother does, our doctor prescribes 4 pills a day of 500 mg each of antibiotics for 10 days. What that doctor is giving your mom is not near enough to fight that infection."

"Well, thanks for letting me know. I'll start watching to see what happens."

We got off the phone.

Two days later, Dennis and Trudy returned to the nursing home. As soon as they entered, a nurse rushed to Trudy with a handful of papers.

"You need to sign these papers about your mother."

"What is this about?" Trudy frowned.

"Oh, we need to get her social security checks. And does she have a life insurance policy? Or a burial plot paid for?"

"I don't think that's any of your business. I do know she is on Medicare and Medicaid. That should be enough money for you."

"You need to follow me and talk to our manager and sign these papers."

"No," Trudy huffed, "I'm not following you anywhere and I'm not signing anything."

The employee left in a hurry, and Dennis shook his head at Trudy.

"That wasn't very professional. Signing papers in a hallway? No copies for you to keep? Trudy, don't ever sign anything here."

"I'm not."

They finished their visit with Marie and left again.

They returned two days later. Another employee quickly approached Trudy demanding she sign paperwork concerning her mother. It was an almost identical confrontation.

Trudy's voice rose loudly. "Look, I did not sign her in. I was at Memorial Hospital when she arrived here. I am still at the hospital. I cannot walk. They are letting me out to visit Mom, and I am not responsible for her. She is responsible for herself. Now leave me alone."

Dennis and Trudy decided to visit after the nursing home office was closed at five o'clock.

198

This became their new routine.

And the nursing home staff began a new routine towards Trudy.

They began calling Trudy on her home phone demanding two thousand dollars for keeping Marie at their nursing home.

Trudy refused.

Harassment continued. They stated Trudy was responsible for her mother.

Trudy denied that it was her responsibility.

One employee threatened to put Marie on a gurney and drop her off in Trudy's front yard if they didn't receive payment.

Trudy's stress level was making her sick. She knew she couldn't take care of her mother, as she still couldn't walk, and she hated leaving her mom in the nursing home. She did find out the doctor continued with Marie on the antibiotics.

The next week Trudy went to the bank to get her mother's social security check, and it was not there. She and her mother had a joint checking account. Trudy's own social security check had not been deposited either.

Trudy went to the social security office and no one there could explain what happened.

The next month the same thing happened. No checks. She called the local social security office again. They would refer her to someone else then keep her in the automated menu without talking to anyone.

Trudy went back to the social security office. She was informed to stop harassing them about the checks. It was out of their hands, and if she didn't stop it, she would no longer receive her widow's benefits.

DEI hire employees? I believe so. It is a small local office, and yes, the local hospital is a small hospital in the same town. DEI employee friends working in the same town? Sharing information? Anything is

possible…and for those of you who don't know what DEI stands for; it is Diversity, Equity, and Inclusion. DEI hires are not skilled at the job they have.

Trudy and her mother had each lost 2 months of social security checks. Late that night, she received a call that Marie had taken a turn for the worse. She was sent by ambulance from the nursing home to the hospital. Trudy and Dennis hurried to the E.R. where Marie was being examined.

Trudy was alarmed that Marie could not talk. She could not move her arms.

The doctor had Trudy leave the room so he could examine Marie. When he completed his exam, he had Trudy return. He stated that Marie had been diagnosed with sepsis. Then he showed her pictures of Marie's arms. That original small sore Trudy remembered on Marie's arm had grown to include her entire arm down to her wrist. Both arms. Trudy turned her head so her mother couldn't see the tears flowing down her face. Trudy could see exposed veins, bones, and what was left of muscles.

"They did this to her, the nursing home." Trudy told the doctor.

"She must be in a lot of pain. I'm administering morphine for her comfort. If she recovers, she'll lose both arms and be unable to speak.

Trudy remembered I had told her months earlier that patients who are given morphine immediately have their horrific pain eased, but it also shuts their organs down. Usually, this is what Hospice does.

Trudy began talking to her and praying out loud while Marie blinked her eyes at Trudy and obviously tried to communicate. Marie was alert. Trudy held her hand and softly sang a gospel hymn to her.

A nurse motioned for Trudy to follow her to the door. "We can take her downstairs to the Hospice floor, if you'd like." The nurse stated.

"No, it would scare her. She'd just be laying there with strange nurses sitting around the room waiting for her to die. At least here in the hospital room, she knows the doctor is trying to help her."

Trudy returned to her mother's bedside and tenderly brushed her hand across her mother's forehead. Marie started blinking rapidly.
"I love you, mother, and Jesus Christ loves you too."

"We must take her to surgery now. You must go." One of the two nurses coldly announced to Trudy.

"No, just a few more minutes, please." Trudy looked at Marie and Marie was blinking fast at her. Trudy bent close to Marie and told her again how very much she loved her, and how much God loved her.

Instantly, a nurse yelled, "We're taking her to surgery." They pushed the poles with medication running to Marie's veins and literally ran down the hall as fast as they could go pushing Marie's hospital bed. In all the sudden loud chaos and running Marie past people standing against the walls, Marie passed away.

We believe the excitement displayed by the nurses running with her bed was too scary for Marie. It was too much for her.

Trudy crumbled.

"You took her from me. You took that moment we had together." She cried.

Later, after the funeral, Trudy was still harassed from the nursing home. She finally bought a cordless telephone with an answering machine.

After the life insurance company paid for the funeral, they sent a check for the amount left of $300.00 and made the check out to Marie. Trudy called them. She could not cash the check. They insisted Trudy get each sibling's social security number and have them sign a release form and they would divide the $300. equally with the siblings. Trudy told them to forget it.

Finally, the death certificates arrived. It stated Trudy died and had Trudy's social security number.

Trudy called the funeral home who had no explanation for the mistakes.

She took the death certificates to the social security office and informed them that she was alive. They refused to return her back month's checks. She was told her checks went to the nursing home. Trudy went to the nursing home, and someone in the office showed her a consent form with what was a forged signature stating Trudy's name and social security number.

Trudy demanded to know who forged her name and how did they get her social security number.

An argument ensued and Trudy left.

She contacted an attorney who had been a friend of hers for many years. He gave her legal advice, but she didn't care about suing for money, and she doesn't like confrontation. All she wants is for her mother's death not to be in vain. She seeks assurance that similar incidents do not occur to others at a nursing home. She wants a registered complaint against that nursing home to be available to the public.

The attorney is talking to her now.

Trudy is convinced if she had not fallen from her back porch, her mother would still be alive. She does know that Marie is in the arms of Jesus now.

So, how is she doing? Her physical therapy has progressed with her using a walker instead of a wheelchair. She is back home. She continues to avoid entering her mother's bedroom.

Trudy finally received the correct death certificates. Aunt Marie died of sepsis. And Trudy's social security checks began once again by direct deposit to Trudy's checking account, but she was never reimbursed for the months for didn't receive a check.

†☐ †☐ †☐

Proverbs 1:19 So are the ways of everyone who is greedy of gain; which takes away the life of the owners thereof.

Matthew 6:14-15 For if you forgive men their trespasses, your Heavenly Father will also forgive you; 15: But if you forgive not men their trespasses, neither will your Father forgive your trespasses.

Moral of the story: We don't know why bad things sometimes happen to good people. It's not for us to understand. We have to forgive, turn it over to Yehovah, and keep praying.

The End

Chapter Twenty-Three

Time to Mow

(I did not change the names in this story. This is about my Uncle Tex and my Aunt Betty. Both passed away several years ago.)

Tall, lanky weeds brushed against my legs as I hurried through my front lawn toward the mailbox, glancing around with a sigh.
"So much for today," I said aloud. "Time to mow."

My plans for picking out new garden plants in town would have to wait.

I gathered a handful of mail and sorted through it as I walked back. One envelope stood out from the rest.
"Thief River Falls, Minnesota. Well, who could this be from?" I tore open the end and pulled out a letter. My eyes widened. "My Uncle Tex!"

He was my late father's only brother. While he often phoned, I had never received a letter from him before. I knew he lived close to Canada. He told me he and his two married sons often went ice fishing together and had recently enjoyed a trip to Alaska.

I read the short letter and felt thrilled. He wrote that he and Aunt Betty were coming to Texas on a business trip and would stop by to see me in a few weeks. I smiled and shook my head. "How nice of them to come."

I had told him on a phone call how much I loved planting flowers, shrubs, fruit trees, and vegetables on my property. He mentioned that he couldn't wait to see everything in bloom. Spring was here, and everything was budding out. It used to be my favorite season—until the Bahia grass took over my lawn.

Grass? That's not a good word for it. It grows taller and taller until you cut it, then crowds out all the other grass you've planted. The tall weeds are loaded with tiny black seeds, ready to spread everywhere. And of course, chiggers love tall weeds.

I went inside and put the mowing problem out of my mind. I grabbed a bottle of liquid soap, spread the sudsy film over my legs, and waited before rinsing it off. That removes any chiggers that might have hitched a ride. You can't see them, but they'll leave big red whelps that itch constantly. I always paint over them with clear nail polish—it kills them because they can't breathe.

Still, mowing came right back to mind. I had mowed only five days ago, and already the weeds were shooting up again. If you mow, you know!

I sighed again and checked my calendar for any plans while Uncle Tex and Aunt Betty would be here. Nothing. I did notice it would be during high humidity season. No problem. He grew up in Texas and was used to the heat. Aunt Betty had visited often and knew locals stayed inside when it got bad.

I had just enough time to get things ready before they arrived. Excited, I thought about what they'd enjoy. He would love fishing off my deck, I was sure of it. Fishing is great here. I could fry chicken, make deviled eggs and potato salad, and have a lazy picnic on the patio with iced tea. I'd show them my rock garden, grape vines, berries, and fruit trees. They both loved antiques, so I'd take them to a few local shops and show them around Caddo Lake. I couldn't wait!

I raked leaves around the flower beds and rearranged the porch furniture and potted plants. The house was clean. I'd decluttered that winter, so there wasn't much to do. By the time the day came, I was ready.

They drove in mid-morning. I ran out to meet them, and we hugged tightly. Smiles all around.

"Everything looks great," Uncle Tex said, glancing around. "All the flowers, the hibiscus, the bridal wreath, the forsythia—it's beautiful. Peaceful. You're blessed. God must be smiling down on you. Your dad would have been proud."

Aunt Betty nodded. "We all are."

"Thank you," I said, smiling through happy tears.

We sat on the patio while he watched boats go by. "I didn't realize the river was right in your backyard," he said. "You know how I love to fish."

"Oh yes, I do," I laughed.

Then his tone softened. "I know you thought we'd be here for a few days, but unfortunately, we can't."

"Oh?" I said, surprised. "But you drove all this way."

"Things change fast when you get our age," he said. "We've both had some health problems come up and need to get back to our doctors in Minnesota."

"I'm so sorry. I had so many plans to entertain you."

"That's all right," he said kindly. "At least we got to see your place. You've done well here."

"Give us a quick tour," Aunt Betty added. "Then we need to make Hot Springs before dark. We promised ourselves a bath in the mineral waters there. These old bones need it."

We walked through the house and into the backyard. He turned to her and said, "You know, Betty, it would look perfect right here."

"Yes, it would," she replied, smiling.

"What are you two talking about?" I asked.

"I'll be right back," he said, heading into the house.

Aunt Betty grinned. "We have a surprise for you."

"You didn't have to do that," I said, smiling back.

Uncle Tex returned carrying a long box. "Found something we thought was special for you," he said. "You were always sending packages to your dad when he was in the VA hospital. He told me every time you did. He called them his care packages."

I smiled softly. "The last one I sent was full of peppermint candy. He said his stomach hurt. He was still in a wheelchair then, recovering from a procedure on his legs. The doctors later found cancer in his stomach. It was so sudden."

"Yes, it was," Uncle Tex said. "Took us all by surprise."

He opened the box. "Hold it while I pull this out. It's heavy."

I held the box as he lifted out something wrapped in thick cellophane. When I tore it open, I gasped. A round pewter top with cherub angels glistened in the sunlight, with long silver wind chimes hanging beneath it—some nearly three feet long. The design was intricate and graceful, like lacework.

"Oh my, I've never seen anything so beautiful," I said in awe.

He grinned. "You're an angel, so what better way to remind you of that than a wind chime of angels?"

I hugged them both, tears filling my eyes. "This is so thoughtful. I'm overwhelmed."

"We're getting older," he said softly, "and we wanted you to have something to remember us by. And for all you did for your dad."

"This will always be special to me. Thank you both so much."

He nodded, and they got back in the car. As he rolled down the window, he said, "Hey, I saw those weeds in your neighbors' yards—you must have that Bahia grass too. Let me tell you how to handle it."

I laughed. "How'd you know?"

"I used to live here, remember? Get a weed eater. Cut the Bahia grass down to the dirt once a week. Don't let it seed. And don't get a battery one—they don't last. Get an electric one with a long extension cord. Buy a big roll of plastic string and refill your own spools. Saves a lot of money."

"Thank you. I'll try that."

"It'll work," he said with a wink, and they drove away.

They both passed later that year. He didn't realize it, but he taught me something that day. Change often begins inside ourselves. I can smile now when I think about mowing. With that weed eater, the chore became an achievable challenge.

My cherub wind chimes still hang under my porch, and when I hear them, I remember his words about the flowers and the birds singing. It reminds me of one of my favorite gospel hymns, *In the Garden.*

"In the Garden" (1912)
Written by Charles Austin Miles

1. I come to the garden alone,
   While the dew is still on the roses.
   And the voice I hear, falling on my ear,
   The Son of God discloses.

Chorus:
And He walks with me, and He talks with me,
And He tells me I am His own.
And the joy we share as we tarry there
None other has ever known.

2. He speaks and the sound of His voice
   Is so sweet the birds hush their singing
   And the melody that He gave to me
   Within my heart is singing.

Repeat Chorus

3. I'd stay in the Garden with Him
   'Tho the night around me is falling
   But He bids me go, through the voice of woe,
   His voice to me is calling

Repeat Chorus.

†☐ †☐ †☐

Moral of the story: Enjoy your friends and relatives while they are still here. We never know when someone may pass away.

The End

Chapter Twenty-Four

Joe Palmer

Joe Palmer consistently provided his undivided attention during conversations. Those crinkle lines at the corner of his eyes, and that little side smile with a cocked eyebrow…could have you wrapped around his finger instantly. Yet, he continued to be humble and genuine. Good looking? Yes…he easily could have been a model for Sports Magazine. Great personality.

His sincerity established a personable relationship with others, as he showed care and interest.

And he was new to our area.

And lonely.

And recently divorced with a special needs daughter.

He had moved to our town because his parents lived here. It meant a lot to him for his daughter to be raised with Christian values. He got a job and purchased a truck. It was red. Soon, you would notice that red truck zipping along everywhere. In the country, in town, at the grocery store, at school, typical days with an 8 to 5 job that kept Joe busy.

He and his fourteen-year-old daughter, Betsy, had a strong bond with each looking after the other. Joe made regular trips with Betsy to the movies, the library, or simply to go eat ice cream.

And he loved playing a game of pool and found a place nearby to enjoy. He joined the relaxed camaraderie of the local group, despite not knowing many people here. Unfortunately, he encountered some of the town's less reputable individuals, which could happen in any town.

However, appearances can be deceptive, and Joe was under the impression that this was merely an amicable group.

He first met Monica playing a game of pool.

And so it began.

She was attracted to him and said all the right words. Flirted often, and playfully. It wasn't long before all Joe talked about was Monica.

Finally, he informed his parents, Max and Nora Palmer, about the young woman he had encountered.

"Her name is Monica, and she can't take her eyes off me. I've never laughed so much in years."

"Son, you're not talking about Monica Ratcliff, are you?"

"Why, yes. Do you know her?" Joe glanced at his mother wide-eyed.

"I know of her. Joe, she is not for you. She is not a trustworthy individual; she appears to be attempting to deceive you. And she is a gold-digger; she is after what she can get from anyone."

"Mom, you can't be talking about the same girl I know." He laughed.

"Oh yes I am."

"Does she know you own land nearby?" His dad inquired.

"Ahh, yes, I think I did mention it. She was excited about having horses there."

"And did she happen to mention she's been married?" His Dad continued.

"Yes, as a matter of fact, she did. They are divorced and her ex-husband moved overseas with their son."

His Mom shook her head. "Joe, it's not gossip. It's common knowledge she poured boiling water on her husband and he and his child left for their safety. Then they got their divorce. She was horrible. Cunning too and could lie through that sweet smile on her face. Stay away from her. She is bad news."

211

"That's hard to believe, Mom. Sounds like vicious gossip to me. She isn't like that at all."

"It's true son, and your mom and I don't gossip. You know that...let me ask you something. What does Betsy think of Monica?"

"Oh, they haven't met yet."

"I hope they don't. I hope you discover her true nature before they meet." His Mom blurted.

Joe shrugged. "You two shouldn't worry so much." He told them and hurried out the door. He was completely taken in by her.

Over the next two months he couldn't understand why his daughter and his girlfriend did not get along. He decided Betsy was simply jealous of him being with someone else. Betsy insisted that Monica would snicker at her behind Joes back, and smirk when Betsy wasn't allowed to go with them out to eat, or even just for a ride in the truck.

Yet, Joe continued to make excuses for Monica.

After the third month, Joe announced to his parents that he'd really fallen for Monica and planned on asking her to marry him. He was confident that Monica and Betsy would build a positive relationship, though it might require some time.

Were his parents shocked? Yes!

However, Joe maintained that Monica was his ideal partner, and they subsequently married.

They moved into an apartment and Joe bought a washing machine and dryer. Monica promptly quit her job. She began driving him to work and keeping the truck all day. She would take Betsy to school, pick her up at the end of the day, and later get Joe from his job.

It wasn't long before Betsy and Monica were arguing daily.

The couple had only been married for two weeks at this time.

"Joe, I can't take your daughter any longer. She must leave." Monica yelled with a glaring look towards Betsy.

"What?" Joe gasped. He stared at Monica wide-eyed. "She is my daughter. I would never do that," he yelled back.

They argued until Betsy blurted "Stop. Take me to Granny's house."

Joe frowned and quietly said, "Maybe they were right." He glanced at Betsy and grabbed the truck keys from Monica, "Come on, Betsy, let's go to Granny's." He gave Monica a stern look before he and Betsy departed.

His anger continued as he tried to sort things out.

Betsy starred out the side window and finally blurted, "she doesn't like me, Dad. She never has."

"Well, we'll see about that." He tried to assure his daughter.

Soon, he recounted the event at his parents' house.

Joe quietly added, "maybe you two were right."

Nora frowned and bit her bottom lip. Max raised his eyebrows and then suggested Betsy stay with them.

"No. That's my daughter. She goes where I go."

Max sighed. "Son, let her stay until things cool off at your home. We'll take Betsy to school. She doesn't need to hear arguing."

"I don't know, Dad. That would be postponing it. They both need to live with me."

Nora interrupted. "It will give you time to figure out what to do. This is intended to be a temporary arrangement."

He ran his hand through his hair and groaned. "Okay, I need to talk to Monica. Betsy knows how I feel. I'll always be her dad."

He hugged his daughter. "I'll be back to bring you some clothes for a few days."

She nodded and Joe left.

Monica started yelling as soon as he arrived. He took some of Betsy's school and everyday clothes, then left.

He arrived at his parents' house and found them peacefully enjoying ice cream on the front porch. Joe smiled as he set the pile of clothes in a nearby chair. "Maybe that's what I need to calm me down, some ice-cream." He laughed.

"I'll get you some." His mom grinned.

"No, I must finish this talk with Monica, thanks though."

He rushed to his truck and departed. Arguing began as soon as he arrived.

Neighbors later recalled they heard Monica and Joe yelling at each other all night. The following day, Joe left in his truck and went to a nearby clinic. He told the doctor what was happening and that he needed something to calm his nerves. The doctor prescribed a prescription of very low dosage to merely calm him and keep him from becoming anxious about the Monica/Betsy situation. The doctor said it was neither a drug nor habit-forming, and okay to drive while taking a pill. Joe expressed his gratitude and proceeded to a pharmacy to have the prescription filled.

Next, he went to bring Betsy home. He told his parents he would inform Monica to cease the conflict regarding his daughter or leave. They approved the plan.

Joe and Betsy returned to a quiet apartment. He found Monica in the back yard sitting in a lawn chair; obviously intoxicated. She glared at him while her shoulders rose and fell in heavy breathing. Her eyes were half open.

Neither spoke as Joe returned inside the house.

He called his parents.

"Could you come and get Betsy? Monica is drunk, and I need to sober her up. This is not a good time for Betsy to be here."

"We'll be right there." His dad stated.

Soon, Betsy left with his parents.

He assured them everything would be okay.

The following morning Nora called Joe to check on the situation.

No answer.

She assumed they were sleeping late and decided to call again in thirty minutes.

It was Max's birthday, and she began getting ingredients out to bake him a cake.

After getting the cake in the oven, she called again.

Still no answer.

Max was working. He couldn't go check on them. She wouldn't worry him but would go check on them herself.

As soon as the cake was done, she and Betsy took off for Joe and Monica's apartment. Upon arrival, she saw Joe's truck parked in the front yard.

She and Betsy got out of her vehicle and approached the truck.

In the front seat, lay Joe's cellphone, and a string of pills were scattered on the floorboard of his truck. The open pill bottle of his new prescription lay half full on the seat.

No Joe. Nora and Betsy glanced at each other.

"That doesn't look right, Granny."

"No, it's not right. Betsy, it looks "staged' to me. Like someone placed everything where we see it."

"Sounds like Monica."

Nora nodded and made her way to the house. It was unlocked.

They called out but no one answered. They entered and found no one home.

Nora grabbed her cellphone from her pocket and called the Sheriff's Department to report suspicious activity and a missing person.

They left and drove down the road in search of Joe. Sometimes he went for a morning walk before going to work.

As they drove through the neighborhood, they spotted two men working on their car.

Nora knew them both; it was a small town.

Nora rolled her window down and called out to them. "Hey, have either of you seen Joe this morning?"

"Yeah. We offered help when we saw him walking. We didn't know if his truck broke down or what. He shook his head and said, "No, I'm just blowing off steam." Everyone knows how he and Monica argue, so we didn't interfere. He kept on walking down the road."

"Thanks," Nora told them and continued driving.

She and Betsy couldn't find him.

They turned around and drove slowly over the same long, winding road four or five times.

No Joe.

Upon turning back, they observed a group of individuals near the edge of the same road they had traversed repeatedly.

The people were looking at something on the soft bed of monkey grass in someone's yard.

Nora and Betsy both screamed.

It was Joe. He was lying in blood. His position that he lay in clearly showed he was deceased.

They rushed out of her vehicle to him, wading through about fifty people staring at him.

"Can't you stop gawking at him? Can you at least give him the respect of covering him up?" Nora screamed as she started shaking uncontrollably.

"This is a crime scene. Stop tramping around him!" She pleaded.

The woman who owned the house where Joe lay in her yard, cried. "I will go get a sheet."

She instantly returned and she and Nora covered him up as both sobbed loudly.

Someone must have reported it, as the Sheriff's car and the coroner both arrived at the same time.

Nora noticed that Joe's red bandana was missing from around his neck. He always wore it with his cowboy hat. His cowboy hat was missing also. She saw horrible scratch marks around his neck and a fingernail was gone on his right hand.

He must have fought someone viciously.

After the body was removed, Nora saw a woman's gold necklace, broken, and laying near the road where Joe had laid.

The Sheriff told her it could have been laying there for weeks.

"No, not being gold. Someone must have killed him and dumped him out of their car." She insisted.

"We will investigate." He assured her, and they all left.

Nora and Betsy were the last to leave and were completely traumatized. She called Max, crying, and told him about Joe.

He and his buddy came to get them.

Both men were crying when they arrived. His buddy drove Nora's vehicle back to her and Max's home.

It was horrible for all of them.

Max never celebrated another birthday, as that is the same day that Joe was killed.

Betsy was fourteen and lost her father.

And Nora kept reliving it to everyone she saw. She would tell everyone that Joe and Monica were only married for three weeks. She had to have medication to stop crying. No one could eat or sleep.

Days went by. Then about two weeks later, the Sherif arrived at Max and Nora's house. They saw him enter their driveway and both met him at the front door.
"Max, Nora; since Joe's passing has been such a shock, I wanted to personally tell you what we have discovered about the case."

Max rubbed the back of his neck. "Please come in and take a seat." Max motioned towards the living room. Nora's eyes were puffy and red. She remained silent as they were all seated.

The Sheriff cleared his throat and proceeded.

"After reviewing all of the evidence, we have closed the case and ruled it a suicide."

"Suicide!" Nora and Max both jumped to their feet.

"Joe had a ten-dollar bill wadded up in his hand. We don't know what that was about, but there were horrible scratches around his throat. I'll try and be as gentle as possible, but when someone overdoses…they can't breathe. It is common for them to claw at their throat trying to get a gasp of air…"

"No, no, no! Joe would never commit suicide." Nora's voice rose shrilly. "He loved his daughter too much to put her through that!"

"Joe had problems." The Sheriff stated.

"Joe wasn't perfect, but he didn't have problems." Nora fumed.

Max yelled then. "How do you know if Joe had problems? You never even knew Joe!"

The Sheriff continued. "We completed our investigation…"

"And who is your lead detective?" Max interrupted.

"A man who is a great asset to our department. George Ramano."

With nostrils flaring, Nora raced across the room and stood face to face in front of the Sheriff. Her chest rose rapidly but she managed not to raise her voice. "That is a conflict of interest. He and his wife are friends with Monica's brother and his wife. Both couples go out to eat every week. So that is where you heard stories about Joe having problems? No sir, that isn't right. And I know George has had no training in crime scenes or investigating anything." Tears flowed down her face as she stepped back from the officer. "I'll say it again, sir. That is a conflict of interest for George to make a clear decision in this case when he overhears what Monica tells her relatives. He assumes entirely too much."

"I stand by my decision."

They stared in shock at the Sheriff, until Max motioned at the front door.

"I'll see you to the door, sir."

"Thank you. If you hear of anything else, please don't hesitate to contact me."

Max nodded and closed the door behind him.

He turned to Nora and embraced her. Finally, pulling slightly away from her, he opened his mouth, but no words formed. He gave her a slow, disbelieving head shake.

"She killed him or had him killed." Nora choked out the words with a quivering voice.

"I know. I'm just thankful Betsy spent the night with us, or she may have been killed too." Max flinched as the door opened, and Betsy walked in.

"I saw the Sheriff's car leave. Is everything okay?"

"No. I'm glad you were out with your dog. We'll talk later. It was upsetting. I can't talk anymore right now," Nora's gaze bounced from Betsy to Max.

219

He grabbed the remote and turned the TV on. The three of them sat silently staring at it, each obviously lost in their own thoughts.

They were still seated, staring at the TV thirty minutes later when Nora's phone rang.

The Caller I D. displayed "Monica."

Nora hurried to put the call on speaker phone.

"Hello?" Nora's stomach knotted up instantly.

"We threw all of Joe's and Betsy's things out of the apartment. It's all on the curb." Monica laughed and sounded drunk. "And, hey, don't be in a hurry if you think it will get rained on. Me and my pool buddies peed all over everything, so it's wet already." She squealed with laughter and hung up the phone.

Nora clenched her teeth. "I can't take any more of this."

Max called the Sheriff.

In telling the Sheriff what had just transpired, he also told him that he and Nora wanted the truck back. Joe had it before he and Monica were married and they did not want to see Monica driving it all over town again.

The Sheriff agreed.

"Max, tell Nora I think Monica did it, but I just don't have enough evidence."

"I will, and thanks."

They later had the Sheriff take papers to Monica to sign so they could have Joe cremated. Legally, Monica was his wife, and they couldn't do anything without her signature. She told the Sheriff she was not burying him after Joe's body was sent to two different funeral homes still in a body bag. Nora, Max, and Betsy were furious with Monica. Finally, his ashes were buried and prayed over in the local cemetery.

The death certificate arrived soon after that.

It stated Joe's death was by suicide.

Nora and Max went to the doctor who prescribed the pills to Joe earlier. He told her if Joe had taken the entire bottle of pills, it would never have killed him. They were very mild, and not an opioid. Not a drug at all.

Nora looked at Max wide eyed, "I smell a rat."

"So do I." He assured her.

The following day, the copy of the autopsy report arrived in the mail.

Nora had requested an autopsy.

It stated the only medicine in Joe's body was a small amount of the prescription the doctor prescribed to calm him. It also showed several large bruises to his head, inconsistent with merely falling onto a thick, soft bed of money grass. It appeared strangulation marks were around his neck but that was dismissed because of all the claw marks also around his neck. A fingernail was missing. It went on and on.

They examined the rest of the report, which claimed it was death by suicide.

So, in this small town, it was told to officials that Joe had "problems" …but I've never heard of an autopsy report for a suicide that had twelve, detailed, full pages.

Nora would read it so often that her own doctor told her she should get rid of it. It was destroying her. Max talked to her about what this was doing to her physically. It was making her sick.

She finally agreed to let her doctor shred all twelve pages.

Some of the local people told Monica she needed to leave town and not return. Noone trusted her, and they all thought she killed Joe, or had him killed. For a time, they discussed who had a car with a large enough trunk that would hold Joe's body until it was rolled out into that yard. It was clear that Nora and Betsy drove past the spot several times that morning and it wasn't there until later.

Monica took the washing machine and dryer and left town.

Max, Nora, and Betsy continue to have a hard time with Joe being gone. After several years… they are still convinced Joe was killed. As a Christian, you forgive others so God will forgive you.

It was needed in each of their lives to forgive the killer. There was too much bitterness to carry inside, eating away at them and their emotions daily. They did forgive.

And the entire town still says it was not a suicide; he was killed. R.I.P. Joe.

†☐ †☐ †☐

Mark 11: 25-26 And when you stand praying; forgive, if you have ought against any: that your Father also which is in Heaven may forgive you your trespasses, but if you do not forgive, neither will your Father which is in Heaven forgive your trespasses.

Psalms 86: 5 For You, Lord, are good, and ready to forgive; and plenteous in mercy unto all them who call upon You.

Moral of the story: Don't fantasize about a situation being better than it appears. You never know where it may lead.

The End

Chapter Twenty-Five

The Renter

My head shot up from the pillow as I rolled toward the side of the bed closest to the window. Straining to listen for whatever noise had awakened me, I shivered in the cool air from the ceiling fan.

Pitch black in the room, I waved my arm until I felt the little chain and pulled it three times to stop the fan. The noise came again.

"I know I heard something."

A glance at the clock showed 1:15 a.m.

"Might as well get up," I mumbled. "There it goes again. Sounds like a door slamming."

I slid my bare feet across the floor, stepped on a shoe, and managed not to fall. Feeling my way to the window, I gripped the wooden blinds and twisted the rod. Moonlight flooded the room. I unlocked the window and raised it just an inch.

Outside, all was quiet. The crickets and frogs sang their usual summer chorus. Then, movement across the street caught my eye. My renter, Wade, was pushing his car out of the driveway. Once it reached the street, he started the engine without turning on the headlights and quickly drove away.

"Hmm."

The sudden ring of the telephone made me jump. I hurried to answer.

"Hello?"

"Lynn, did you see that?"

"Mother? What are you doing up?"

"I forgot to take my hearing aid out," she said. "All kinds of noises are waking me."

"Wade's decision to go for a ride woke me up too," I said, stifling a yawn.

"Do you think he's up to something?"

"No, ma'am. Maybe a girlfriend called and wanted to meet him somewhere."

"Oh no, Lynn, she broke up with him."

"Mother! How do you know that?"

"He seemed sort of down the other day, so I took him a plate of fried chicken with mashed potatoes, gravy, and corn on the cob. Poor thing looked thin to me."

I sighed. "I thought we weren't going to be overly friendly with the renters anymore. The last ones took advantage of our kindness, remember? We said we'd keep it strictly business this time."

"Lynn, he looked so sad. I couldn't help it. He was all alone over there."

"I guess we shouldn't live so close to my rent house," I said. "Maybe it should be across town instead of across the street."

"Well, from my house I can see the end of his place, the carport, and the patio. He's hard to miss."

"I know. From my window, I can see the entire front of his house. Not much privacy for him."

"Doesn't seem like he's been here long," Mother said.

"Wade's lived there over a year. Time's gone by fast, hasn't it?"

"Yes, and he's been helpful."

"Helpful?"

"I asked him to scoot my couch across the living room one day, and he was happy to do it. He even suggested a better spot for my television, and before I knew it, he'd rearranged the whole room. I was impressed. He has a flair for decorating."

"I thought you hired someone from the classifieds to do that," I said, my voice rising as I walked into the kitchen with the cordless phone.

"I can't afford that. You know I'm on a fixed income."

"Mom, I could've helped you if you'd just told me."

"Lynn, it worked out fine. Wade enjoys my home-cooked meals. He even changes my light bulbs when they go out. He said I have no business climbing ladders at my age."

I sighed. "I didn't realize how much time you spent with Wade while I'm at work."

"You work long hours, Lynn, and have enough to keep up with."

"We're supposed to be a team," I reminded her. "We're completely on our own out here."

"I wouldn't trade living here for anything," she said. "We watch out for each other, and we do it well."

"I agree," I said, taking a sip of tea. Then, faint barking caught my attention. "It's late. We need to get back to sleep."

"You're right. I'll read a few more pages in my book and call it a night."

I started toward my bedroom, but the sudden roar of an engine made me stop. I set my glass down and peered through the blinds. Headlights shone toward my house before suddenly cutting off.

"Mom," I whispered into the phone. "Look out your window. Can you see what's going on?"

"I can," she said quietly. "Wade just pulled back into his driveway, and there's a truck with him pulling a long flatbed trailer."

"I see them now. They both got out and ran inside. Did you see that?"

"Yes, Lynn, I have a good view from my kitchen."

"I've never seen that truck before."

"I don't like this," she said. "Something doesn't feel right. Let's stay up a while and watch."

"Oh, we will," I replied.

"Look," she said. "Someone just ran to the truck and threw armloads of things inside. It looks like clothes on hangers."

"Oh no, Mom. Surely not."

We both watched in disbelief. Wade carried his computer to the trailer while the other man spread a blanket out for him to set it on.

"Lynn, he's sneaking out in the middle of the night."

A rush of heat went through me. My heart pounded in my ears.

"Lynn," Mother said urgently. "There goes the queen-size bed, mattress and all. They're loading it onto the trailer. You need to go over there now. He owes you rent."

"I'm not going over there," I said firmly. "And it's not one month's rent he owes, it's six weeks."

"You need that money," she said. "That house was your retirement investment."

"Let him go," I said quietly. "He's had a hard time. Remember, he just replaced his transmission and tires."

"Lynn, the taxes and insurance still have to be paid."

"I know," I said with a yawn. "I get paid at the end of the week. We'll be fine."

"Why does he owe six weeks rent?" she pressed.

"We talked," I said. "He told me he'd made some bad choices and just needed a little time to get caught up. As a Christian, I couldn't turn him away. I prayed for him and gave him two more weeks."

"Excuse me," Mother said pointedly. "I thought we agreed not to get too friendly with renters."

"I know, but I saw a good person in a hard spot. That's not the same as being used."

"Lynn, we both liked him," she said softly.

"Yes," I sighed, turning back to the window. "But now look at him. He's running back and forth like someone on a cop show. He just darted to the trailer with a laundry basket. This breaks my heart."

"There goes his microwave and a few more boxes," she said.

We both sat in silence as Wade and his friend finished loading the trailer and car. Engines roared to life, and moments later both vehicles disappeared down the road.

"Lynn," Mother said quietly, "he's gone."

"Fine," I said with a tired sigh. "We'll clean the house tomorrow. It wasn't in bad shape anyway."

"You can put the 'For Rent' sign back up."

"Yes," I said, yawning again, "but Mom, we've got to stop getting too close to them."

"Good idea," she said brightly. "We can work on the ad in the morning."

"That'll work," I said, smiling despite my exhaustion.

Her voice perked up. "I can't wait. It should run in this weekend's paper."

"Goodnight, Lynn."

"Goodnight, Mom."

†❑ †❑ †❑

227

Job 28: 28 (New Living Translation) And this is what He says to all humanity: The fear of the LORD is true wisdom; to forsake evil is true understanding.

Psalm 111: 10 Fear of the LORD is the foundation of true wisdom. All who obey his commandments will grow in wisdom.

Moral of the story: You cannot mix business with friends; it seldom works out.

The End

Chapter Twenty-Six

Olga

It started with a Venezuelan flag placed beside a county road in a small, rural Texas town. Word spread fast. ABC News from Shreveport, La. arrived to interview, film, and investigate.

A group of over 200 illegals had turned off the county road onto a dirt road marked by the flag to a destination deep in the woods. They gathered to an area not seen from either road.

Locals were fearful to complain due to retaliation.

Except for one.

He acknowledged his neighbors refused to be interviewed on television and indeed were afraid of the illegals. He stated he was a U.S. Veteran and would gladly speak about the situation.

Loud music flooded an area with a radius of about ten miles. It would hurt your ears. And it was a weird, screechy, horribly loud noise; no rhythm to it at all. Nothing an American would refer to as music, but they claimed they did. It was blasted from the illegals gathering place all day and all night for the entire weekend.

Locals decided as loud as it was, they could be involved in weapons training, and no one would hear the gunfire. A perfect cover. And yes, it was that loud.

The veteran lived within that ten-mile radius. He said he couldn't understand how the illegals could have such loud "music" when we can't. Not that he wanted loud music, it was just the principal of it.

The news reporter asked the same question to the county Sheriff.

"Our hands are tied." He explained. "Homeland Security won't help us. And they are on private property, so they don't need a permit. The owner of the property is a Venezuelan. I had to get an interpreter to speak to him on the phone. He recently bought the property. They are all from Dallas. I asked him if he needed us to patrol the area and he said no, they have their own security. He claimed they were just getting together to listen to music."

The Sheriff then stated that a similar group was also "enjoying music" in the western part of the county that same weekend, but that was a group of over 500 illegals, also from Dallas. And also, in a remote country setting.

Nothing else was mentioned, but I personally was glad the TV station checked into it. None of us locals believed the story of them merely enjoying music. And it would be a stretch of imagination to refer to it as any type of music.

I realized for the group to have their own security that they must be armed with guns.

Great! Now we have armed illegals in our county!

How alarming!

Shortly after that, the same television station gave details of two young boys in Louisiana that were eight and ten years old, who were raped by Venezuelan gang members. Those poor children! Brutally raped by men! Then a thirteen-year-old girl was kidnapped and raped in the same town by an illegal man from Honduras. Robberies by illegals were also on the rise.

Another encounter with them happened in a Texas town near our small town. An elderly woman was pulling out of a grocery store parking lot, only to be rammed into by an illegal driving a truck. The police were called. The illegal had no driving license, no insurance, and never even got a ticket. The policeman told the elderly lady that he was sorry but there is nothing they can do to the illegals. So, there she was… an elderly lady on a fixed income with a wrecked car. The illegal was free to go!

I had heard enough. I had no regard for any illegal.

I immediately assessed my situation. I live in a remote area. Yes, I have guns to protect myself, but I needed something else. Something that would alert me to danger.

I needed a German Shepherd dog.

And I needed one right away!

I prayed about it. I scanned animal shelters for what was available to adopt. I read about the breed. I recalled my stepfather had a German Shepherd dog years ago, and it was the absolute best dog I had ever been acquainted with.

I was more determined to find just the right one for me. I kept praying.

Suddenly, there it was!

I was scrolling through Facebook and came across a German Shepherd that needed a forever home. A local volunteer group rescued animals in a different nearby town and arranged for them to be fostered or permanently housed. They were a reputable group. They also send puppies and kittens through another organization up north to be adopted in that area.

The dog had been abandoned after the owners moved to another town. This was a two-year-old German Shepherd, female, and beautiful! I left a private message on their page with my phone number, and that yes, I was interested in the dog.

Again, I prayed about it.

Frances, the woman who found the dog, called me back right away. We arranged to meet in the parking lot of the local Sheriff's Department since we were unfamiliar with each other.

In twenty minutes, I would meet the potential new member of my family! Excitement mounted!

I pulled into the parking lot and parked my car under a shade tree. I had my 97-year-old mother with me. I was her caregiver. She sat in the front passenger seat anxious to see the new dog. I had a 9-year-old yorkie, who barely weighed 4 lbs. that was home in her kennel. I knew I'd have to keep them separated as the weight difference alone would become a safety issue…weather the two dogs got along or not.

I was ready.

We patiently waited for five minutes until the woman's vehicle arrived and parked beside my car. Her adult daughter, Amy, was with her. She and I both exited our vehicles and greeted each other. I went to the back window of her car and peeped at the dog.

The dog greeted me with a deep, ferrous growl and even deeper bark.

"That's exactly what I wanted." I told Frances. "I want this dog."

I told her I lived in a remote area and needed not only a good guard dog but a great companion as well. We agreed this dog needed me as much as I needed her. It was a win, win situation for both of us!

They were kind to offer to follow me to my house, since we weren't sure how the dog would treat my frail mother. It worked out well.

Frances helped me bring the extra-large kennel from storage into my house. She brought a blanket for it and I supplied several toys. The dog was curious and wasn't barking. I patted and baby talked the dog, and it seemed happy to meet me. Tail wagged. Still on a leash, Amy brought the dog into the house, and it went straight into the kennel.

Everything fell in place. I got my German Shepherd in April, 2025.

Satisfied we would be okay, Frances and Amy left. They assured me if I ever needed their help to call them. And if I did change my mind about keeping the dog, they wanted it back. I agreed.

We did fine together.

I decided since my family was of German descent, I especially needed to give this female German Shepherd dog a German female name. I selected one from one of my many aunts; Olga.

She instantly came to her name and let me change out her collar to a larger one. Within a week, though, she pulled out of her collar while scrunching down low in the grass and pouncing on crickets. She and I both froze! I went to her and walked her back to the cyclone fenced, concrete patio area, and we both went inside, and I shut the gate. Wow! That was a close call. She could have run off! It surprised her as much as it did me!

I called one of my sons and he recommended a sturdy harness for Olga. He even looked it up and sent the link to me to order it from Amazon. I thanked him and placed the order.

She was afraid of it. I gave her a treat and let her smell it.

Nope. Not going to happen.

I put the collar back on her and held a tight leash so she couldn't pull out of it. She had been super about doing her business outside on the grass! No problem there! I was determined to get this arrangement to work and get the harness on her.

The following day, I walked up to her and gently placed my hand over her eyes as I baby talked her and scooted the harness over her head. She looked at me in amazement and stood still while I snapped it in place.

 No problem! Now I can slip the harness over her head while locking the snaps in place on both sides to secure the harness. Sometimes she will twist around to try and see what I am doing to her, and I tell her to be still. She stops moving around. As soon as I am done, I walk away, and she races to the door to go outside.

She doesn't object to my brushing her hair. I do this every other day, as she is shedding her winter coat now. I walk her on a leash three times a day, and yes, she pulled on the leash at first wearing a collar but doesn't with the harness.

I did call Frances and Amy for help. I needed to take Olga in for her shots and didn't dare put her in the car with my mom. And I had no one to stay with Mom while I went to the vet with Olga.

They were so gracious and kind! Frances drove with Amy to my house, put Olga in their car and took off to the veterinary clinic. I had made arrangements at the clinic beforehand to pay for the shots. The ladies would not accept any money for helping me, so I autographed my latest book for them and surprised them with that.

They later returned with Olga, her rabies tag and papers stating what shots she had with a zero balance.

However, it did not go well at the clinic.

Olga did not like the veterinary doctor.

He had the ladies put a muzzle on Olga and he went into the waiting room to give the shots…while the two ladies held Olga. He said he would not check her for worms due to how she would not stop trying to attack him. He also said he wouldn't give her shots again. I don't know how I'll get her shots done next year! If Frances and Amy still live nearby, I may have to contact them again!

I was so surprised. But Olga did go berserk once when my sister peeked her head around the doorway to look into the room at Olga…who was in her kennel at that time. Olga barked, growled and her hair stood up on her back and her tail when she saw my sister. She even tried to bust out of her kennel! She reminded me of a bull bucking in its stall at a rodeo…trying to buck the guy off it's back.

That was the first time she saw my sister, and no, my sister hasn't been back. She lives in another state, and we don't get to visit often. So, it wasn't that the doctor was a man. She did my sister the same way.

Yet, to this day she is sweet as can be with me.

Mom can be at the table eating and I'll be taking Olga outside. She will walk behind Mom's chair, wagging her tail and stop to lick Mom's hand as she goes by. No problem, but she is so big she could knock Mom over

234

playing. I still keep her away from my little Yorkie, Tinkerbell, for the same reason.

Since this Texas heat is becoming hotter and hotter, I got Olga a kid's 36-inch plastic swimming pool. I keep it on the patio in the enclosed cyclone fenced area. She loves it! She will run into it and splash water, jump out, run around the patio in a circle and do it all over again. Happy dog! And she wears herself out! I also throw a cube of ice onto the concrete floor in the patio area, and Olga chases it, batting it with her paws. She gets so excited and finally lays down holding the cube of ice with her paws and licks it as it melts! I get another one after it has completely melted, and the race is on again batting at it and chasing it across the concrete! Great fun for her, and great exercise too!

She did suddenly bark ferociously the other day…so much that I had to stop and see what she was barking at. It could have been someone on the back deck. I entered the room and glanced at the windows; no one was there. She continued. I followed her gaze to something moving on the floor. It was a spider. I stepped on it with my tennis shoe and gave Olga a treat. This is her territory! And she was guarding it!

I do enjoy her as much as she enjoys me. I have my morning coffee on the patio while she checks out the area from inside the fence. Sometimes she spots a squirrel, a cat, a stray dog, or a neighbor. She gets her guard dog mode going and can scare the socks off anyone. I let her bark.

Of course, I have her food and water set out there, along with toys. When she is ready to do her business, she goes and stands at the gate. I put her leash on her and take her out on the grass. She potties in one area and poops in a different area. I make over her, and she gets so excited. She does love to look for crickets and grasshoppers in the grass. She'll ponce onto the ground and put those big paws out as if bracing herself, then searches the ground for a bug, and eats it.

Then we return to the patio, and I throw toys at her. She'll catch one and we play tug-of-war. It is so relaxing to spend time with her. She weighs about 85 pounds now.

She is such a blessing. I thank God for her. And she was completely free! I can't imagine her not being in my home and not being part of my family. She can't either! ☺

† † †

Ephesians 5:20 Giving thanks always for all things unto God and the Father in the name of our Lord Jesus Christ.

Moral of the story: When you pray, don't be afraid to ask Yehovah for something you need, no matter how insignificant it may sound. I prayed for a German Shepherd dog, and He gave me one for free! And one that's house broke, and a great guard dog! She is such a welcomed, fun companion! To Yehovah be the glory!

The End

Chapter Twenty-Seven

When Help is Needed

I was third in line, stopped at a red light in Longview, Texas and the last car in the line. Suddenly the rear end of my car was hit as an elderly woman drove full force directly into it. I gasped as the impact to me and Mom, who was my passenger in the front seat…shot our bodies straight into the ceiling. My body turned crookedly as the impact flew me up in the air banging into the ceiling. Mom remained upright as she hit the ceiling. After checking on Mom, I got out of the car. The front of the elderly woman's car was smashed into the shape of an Indian teepee. The back of my car was horribly caved in and impossible to open the back door. The elderly woman was seated in the driver's seat, crying. She looked into my eyes and pitifully said "my son will never let me drive again!" I grimaced and scanned the inside of her car.

And there it was. Her cellphone. Laying on the passenger seat next to her. No, it wasn't lying on the floorboard from the impact of the wreck. She had to have been talking on it and didn't even see the cars stopped at the red light. That is why she continued crying so hard.

 A policeman came. A report was made. No, she didn't get a ticket. I couldn't prove she was actually talking on her cellphone when the wreck happened. I did get an attorney, and I sued. The money the court awarded me didn't go very far. My attorney got 40% of the total amount, my car was repaired, and most of the remaining money went to The Spine Institute of Tyler, Texas. I needed many treatments and injections for my back.

 Yes, I badly needed help! And yes, I prayed about it! Tyler was a two-hour drive away from my town, and that was just one way there. It was another two-hour drive back home. I was so very thankful when my oldest son, Mike , called to say he'd take me to my appointments there. Mike was such a big blessing! It would be a long process to complete all that they would do for me. I was so relieved! And yes, I gave God the glory that Mike was available to help! And he did help even though I became nauseated after the anesthesia. I held my face away from Mike inside his truck and threw up into a hospital bag for the entire two-hour drive back home. I think he had to lower the window for fresh air. And yet, he kept taking me back for more treatments knowing I'd get sick again. Now that's what I call helping someone! And that's also what I call love! They did many injections at different places on my spine, and finally they burnt the nerve endings on the left side of my spine…and six weeks later burnt the nerve endings on the right side. And I never had to return! Praise God!

Years later, I again needed help badly! I was about to list my home and property for sale when I decided to hire an estate sale company to help me. I thought it would be no problem. Wrong! I knew the owners of the first company I contacted. They came out and looked at what I had. My 30x40 shop was completely full! There was hardly any room to walk around everything that was stored inside. It was not all mine. Some belonged to my mother and had been there since she moved in with me years ago. Some left by my ex-husband that he didn't want to take. Mine, and other family members' belongings, and years of my own collected memorabilia, also farm implements, a boat and trailer, a new car motor, etc. Then there was the "Man Cave" …full of tools, machines, and gardening and fishing equipment, gallons of paint, and lumber. And the upstairs of my home was full of stuff, as well as the attic. Antique blue Carnival glass pieces that filled three hutches, Jim Shore statues, antique cookbooks, quilts, an extensive antique salt and pepper collection, antique can collection, paintings, rugs, etc.

They continued quietly looking at all of it, glancing at each other often. "Do you have a restroom at the shop?" The man asked.

"No, I don't." I answered, surprised at that question.

"Is the shop air conditioned?"

"No, it's not." I slowly replied.

"Well, we have to have a restroom available for our customers."

 "Oh, I wasn't aware of that. They are more than welcome to use the restroom at the house next door to the shop."

The woman smiled. "This is too far out in the country for our customers, anyway. We won't be able to do your sale."

I was shocked! Mom's Dementia and Alzheimer's had become so much worse that I could no longer leave her alone...for her own safety. There was no way I could de-clutter everything much less haul it off and take care of her at the same time. I handed them a stack of framed pictures of vehicles my ex-husband didn't take when he moved out and gave them to the couple. It was pictures of their relatives' cars from many years ago. They thanked me and assured me they'd see that their relative got them. I thanked them for taking time to come out. They left as quietly as they had arrived. I was so disappointed, but I called another company.

 It was no longer in business. The next one I called only worked in the Longview, Texas area. And finally, I called the last one. The company that was no longer in business recommended her. She was close to me in a nearby town. She agreed to come out and look at what I had. She was friendly but told me that no, she couldn't do the sale. She explained that she'd show the items online, and customers would text her if they wanted to buy a certain item. She could not get a signal on my property. She was sorry, but it was impossible. She left. And there weren't any more companies here to have my estate sale.

So, yes, I badly needed help! And yes, once again, I prayed about it! I was so surprised at this outcome of no estate sale that I talked to everyone about it. This was mindboggling to me. I recalled all of the estate sales I'd gone to as a customer held by the very companies that turned me down! I made a mental note not to attend any of their estate sales again. They no longer needed my business. And most of them had estate sales that had been way out in the country. And I recall signs taped to the bathroom door of the house the sale was at that stated, "Keep Out." Maybe it was too much work. Maybe because some of them knew my ex-husband from over twenty years ago...and not the man he was now. I don't know. I do know that if God would have had His hand in

239

it, everything would have fallen into place and went smoothly. By it not happening, He was protecting me from something. I give Him the glory for watching out for me!

And that afternoon, my phone rang. It was my youngest son, Jeff Brannon. "Mom, Miranda and I talked it over, and we can come help you get ready to sell your place." "Hallelujah!" I yelled. I instantly pictured Jeff and his wife, Miranda, being here, and what I would cook... "But wait...are you sure? That's a long way to drive here!" I blurted. "It's okay, Mom. I just finished a job, and we can do this!! Three days drive to Texas from West Virginia will be like going on a vacation. We'll be just fine, and besides we want to help." I was overwhelmed with gratitude! "Well, you don't know how much this means to me! I am so thankful!" "Glad to do it! We'll see you in a few days. Love you!" "Okay! Love you too!"

And they came, even brought their dog Kinsley, and stayed working for nearly an entire month. (Kinsley and I bonded, and I enjoyed her immensely!) Jeff and Miranda sorted through everything. Piles were made of what to keep, what to haul off to the dump, and what to take to Goodwill. Except for a desk and two filing cabinets that could stay, they emptied everything from upstairs at my house, and they emptied the attic as well. They emptied the "Man Cave" building and removed some furniture from one of the two houses I rented out. One of the two I'd sell furnished. One day after they'd drug a lot of stuff out of the shop and onto the concrete driveway, a man stopped and talked with Jeff. He was just passing through the area and was here from Georgia to help his mother and stepfather move. He was looking for a job. Jeff told him we needed help removing a lot of this stuff, but instead of paying him money; would he consider bartering? And bartering for a metal Jon boat and its trailer? The guy was excited and agreed. He returned with his mother and stepfather, a truck, and a long bed trailer. They all worked for days, going to the dump, and going to Goodwill. We gave them a lot to keep for themselves as well. It was a good deal for everyone! Jeff and Miranda continued sorting through boxes and helping to load the trailer when it returned empty. We all stayed busy and made great progress. After three and a half weeks, they had to return home to West Virginia. Very little was left in the shop. The boxes I wanted to take with me when I did sell my place and move took up less than 1/4 th of the shop. All nicely stacked on shelves. Jeff and Miranda outdid themselves! Everything was even swept clean!

It was such a big blessing to have Jeff and Miranda helping me! Once again, that's what I call helping, and that's what I call love! I could never sell my place until all of that was removed! The guy told Jeff he'd come back to get the boat and trailer the following day. All the work was done! Jeff, Miranda, and Kinsley left. I thoroughly enjoyed our time spent with each other! Wonderful family time; our talks together, cooking together, and working together! I give God the glory for everything! I signed the boat title over to the guy the next day. They pulled it out of the woods, and they too were gone. I gave away 3/4ths of everything. No, I didn't make one penny from an estate sale. But God provided! It all fell in place, smoothly! Everything was cleared out and ready to list with a realtor!

Notice how God works? He had one son from West Virginia come to Texas to help his mother, and another son…a total stranger…from Georgia come to Texas to his own mother to help her. Coincidence? Not hardly! Yeshua placed both sons in each other's path, at the same time, in the same town, and at the same place…for the benefit of all! Praise Yeshua! Hallelujah!

And what happens when someone needs help and doesn't get it? What happens when it appears like their family member's greed takes over where love should be? I saw it happen to a young girl, and it almost destroyed her life. In those years, most schools had a Special Education class for slow learners. Today, Special Education students are no longer separated from mainstream students. They are all blended together in the same classroom.

One little girl attended school her entire 12 years in a Special Ed. classroom. She was quiet and well behaved. The teacher was given two aids to help with the group of students. Each day, the little girl was given a coloring book and crayons. She was left alone after that. She colored out of the lines often. Eventually, her coloring improved. She colored beautifully! And unknown to the teacher, or the teacher's aide employed

As soon as Iris turned eighteen and graduated, she moved in with her grandmother. Mildred drove Iris to the MHMR learning center (Mental Health and Mental Retardation; now called Texas Department of State Health Services or DSHS.) in a nearby town five days a week and paid for private tutoring for Iris. It wasn't long until Iris could read a regular watch and tell you the exact time. And this was not a digital watch! Progress continued. And she could read…she'd been listening to instructions for years! Within the year, Iris passed her driving test and was issued a driver's license in the State of Texas. Mildred bought her a brand-new car and paid for Iris to have her own home. She had a "New House" shower by church members and friends of the community. Iris was so appreciative and no, she was not bitter at her father. She also has a job as cashier at a store.

Sometimes we recognize situations that are unjust and legally, we cannot interfere. But we can pray! I give Yeshua the glory for having Mildred there to help Iris as soon as she turned eighteen and was no longer in her father's control. Mildred could have become sick and frail and not able to help Iris. But, no…that was not God's plan. His timing is different than our timing. He knew Mildred's heart, and he knew Iris's heart. Everything fell in place! Turn your problem over to God and let Him handle it. And don't take the problem back! Help is just a prayer away from happening!

†☐ †☐ †☐

Proverbs 3:5 New Living Translation: Trust in the Lord with all your heart; do not depend on your own understanding. Psalms 55: 22 New Living Translation: Give your burdens to the Lord, and He will take care of you. He will not permit the godly to slip and fall.

The moral of the story: Keep praying! Never give up! Trust in Yehovah!

The End

Chapter Twenty-Eight

Don Lewis

The song isn't as popular now, but it does get airtime on the local radio stations occasionally. It always reminds me of Don Lewis. The song is "Wasted Days and Wasted Nights" by Freddy Fender. Some of the lyrics mentioned how someone left him and the singer does a terrific job singing the lyrics with raw emotion. I learned, later, it was one of Don's favorite songs.

I had heard of Don Lewis but wouldn't know him if I saw him. Our paths never crossed until one day when I happened to travel down a busy highway heading into town…and something caught my eye. I was still on the outskirts of town, near a tiny used car lot on one side of the highway and a liquor store across from it on the other side.

One of the cars…and it was one parked close to the busy highway…was moving up and down.

In was moving in rhythm.

Nothing attached to it. No one near it.

It was amazing! And no, I wasn't seeing things in shadows. This was in broad open daylight.

I stopped at the red light and circled back. It was still moving.

Finally, I dismissed the entire episode. I had plans for the day and watching a car wasn't one of them. As I passed by the vehicle again, on my way back into town, I gasped out loud.

A long legged, lanky boy climbed out of the back seat holding onto a girl's arm. They stood on the pavement and straightened their clothes…glancing around sheepishly.

Yes, the car had stopped moving.

And that was my first encounter…or should I say, unencounter… with Don Lewis.

What nerve!

I was later told it was his car lot, and he was tall, long legged, and had a lanky frame.

Our paths continued not to cross. We were worlds apart, and I never met him in person.

I did hear about him often. I was told he came from a poor but hard-working family.

Pearl, an older woman in my church, had been asking members if they could recommend a handyman to do some much-needed maintenance at her home.

Someone mentioned Don Lewis, and that he lived here in our town. Another said he did work for them and did a good job and charged a reasonable price. He lived with his mother and helped her as she was in bad health. He could be reached there.

She later contacted him, and he worked for her for months. He mowed her lawn often that summer, painted her house, fixed a leak on her sewer line, cleaned her gutters, and killed fire ant mounds.

And they became friends. He told her he'd lost the car lot and was relying on his handyman work to survive. He also shared how his mother didn't have long to live, and he and his girlfriend were both helping her.

Pearl invited them to church, but he turned her down. They discussed the Bible often, though, and she did lead Don Lewis in prayer to accept Jesus Christ as his Lord and Savior.

He finally completed the work she needed done and began working for others in the community. She spoke highly of him to everyone and sent business his way.

Months later, one morning…early…our small town was flooded with sirens and sheriff deputy cars. Red and blue lights were flashing, as many vehicles surrounded several houses and officers ran with weapons drawn to apprehend their perpetrators.

And one was Don Lewis.

Several people were arrested for making and distributing drugs: methamphetamines to be exact.

Each received prison time and Don Lewis was sent to one in Alabama.

He began writing letters to his mother and to Pearl. He claimed he did it for the money to help his mother.

Within a year, he developed cancer, and his mother passed away.

He was about forty years old, and a broken person with no hope.

His own family had nothing to do with him.

Pearl encouraged him to pray and continued helping him through prayer.

He was told he now had stage four cancer and didn't have long to live. He was released early from prison. He asked for a bus ticket to our small town in Texas. They sent him as close as they could with the funds they had for a bus ticket. He was still over a hundred miles away when he got off the bus. He contacted Pearl.

She spoke to the congregation about his dilemma, and they decided to take up a collection of money to help him return here. Pearl wired him the money, and she picked him up at the bus station in town when he arrived here. He stayed at Pearl's home and began planning for his funeral.

He wanted to give his body to science for research. He contacted a teaching hospital in a nearby city, and Pearl drove him there to fill out the paperwork.

They would not transport the body for free though.

Once again, Pearl took up a collection, and our church paid the hospital to get him when the time came. They also paid for a funeral home to have a memorial for him at our church with a rented casket.

How sad, but a burden was lifted from him, and he was thankful for what the church did for him.

He attended our church and rededicated himself to Jesus Christ.

He soon passed away, and the memorial was announced for the following week.

His casket was at the front of the church surrounded by flowers. Pictures of him were displayed by many of his friends.

The pews of the church continued filling up until all seats were taken.

Even his family were there, the very ones who wouldn't have anything to do with him.

The pastor began the service and said a prayer. He then informed everyone how proud he was to have met Don, and that Don had prayed, repented, and accepted Jesus Christ as his Lord and Savior.

As he finished talking about the deceased, he glanced across the rows of people and spoke. "Don was married before, and I'm sorry, but I don't know who his ex-wife is. I'd like for you to come to view him first, before the public is invited."

Everyone gasped as seven women stood and made their way to the front of the church.

The pastor looked at everyone still seated and cleared his throat. "Don asked me to play, Rock of Ages, a gospel song that he and his mother loved, and we played that earlier. Now, we'll play his other request, a song that also has a lot of meaning in it for him."

He nodded at the music director.

And there, in that little Baptist church, Freddy Fender's song, "Wasted Days and Wasted Nights" played softly as tears flowed down the faces of his seven ex-wives…and many in the congregation.

John 8: 1-12 New Living Translation

Jesus returned to the Mount of Olives, but early the next morning he was back again at the Temple. A crowd soon gathered, and he sat down and taught them. As he was speaking, the teachers of religious law and the Pharisees brought a woman who had been in the act of adultery. They put her in front of the crowd. "Teacher," they said to Jesus, "this woman was caught in the act of adultery. The law of Moses says to stone her: What do you say?" They were trying to trap him into saying something they could use against him, but Jesus stooped down and wrote in the dust with his finger. They kept demanding an answer, so he stood up again and said; "All right, but let the one who has never sinned throw the first stone!" Then he stooped down again and wrote in the dust. When the accusers heard this, they slipped away one by one, beginning with the oldest, until only Jesus was left in the middle of the crowd with the woman. Then Jesus stood up again and said to the woman, "Where are your accusers? Didn't even one of them condemn you?" "No, Lord," she said. And Jesus said, "Neither do I. Go and sin no more." Jesus spoke to the people once more and said, "I am the light of the world. If you follow me you won't have to walk in darkness, because you will have the light that leads to life."

† † †

1 Peter 5: 6-11 So humble yourselves under the mighty power of God, and at the right time he will lift you up in honor. Give all your worries and cares to God, for he cares for you. Stay alert! Watch out for your great enemy, the devil. He prowls around like a roaring lion, looking for someone to devour. Stand firm against him, and be strong in your faith. Remember that your family of believers all over the world is going through the same kind of suffering you are. In his kindness God called you to share in his eternal glory by means of Christ Jesus. So after you

248

have suffered a little while, he will restore, support, and strengthen you, and he will place you on a firm foundation. "All power to him forever! Amen.

Moral of the story: Wasted days can become redeemed nights when we turn back to the Light.

The End

Chapter Twenty-Nine

Bonus Section

Fiction Short Stories

Many of my readers wanted me to include some of my fiction stories. I gladly agreed. I also included a few award-winning ones. This will be the first time to publish them as a collection, but it does not include everything! Enjoy!

1. The Shoe Fit the Wrong Sister

Greasy wisps of stringy hair caressed the hollow cheeks of Cinderella's gangly stepsister. At six foot four, she stood erect and giggled.

The sisters gathered outside the hamlet to try on the glass slipper.

Dressed in a dusty rose gown, stepsister #2 weighed in at over four hundred pounds. A new permanent had burnt her hair, leaving a tight, fuzzy brown covering upon her head. She grinned and displayed three missing teeth: two at the top and one at the bottom.

Shoved aside earlier, long-legged and attractive, Cinderella, remained hidden behind the skirts of her ugly stepsisters.

All eyes were on the Prince. He approached in a carriage pulled by a pair of gorgeous horses, muscular with shiny coats the color of midnight, and contrasting snow-white hair cascading over their hooves to a fourth of the way up to their knees. Coughing, he placed the back of his hand against his mouth. "Do three sisters live here, or is it four?"

His question hung in the air, and no one answered.

A quick leap and he disembarked. He scanned the growing crowd of women and carried a glass slipper upon a burgundy pillow. Heavy blends of perfume assaulted his nostrils, and he sneezed.

The woman dressed in dusty rose sauntered towards the Prince, and spicy aroma followed. She held her petticoats with one hand and tried to slip her foot into the slipper. After several futile attempts, she grimaced and ambled away.

He spotted Cinderella, wearing brown homespun attire, and she glanced at him in the same instant. Eye contact held briefly until the tall stepsister pushed Cinderella away from the Prince.

"Let me try." She rudely demanded while shoving others aside. The crowd fell back as she made her way closer to the Prince. Her foot went inside the slipper, and it fit perfectly.

Wide-eyed, the Prince turned pale as the tall sister and the entire crowd gasped out loud together.

"No, oh no. I haven't had my turn." Cinderella whimpered and scurried to the Prince,

"Too late." The tall sister yelled, and people milling around took up the chant. The noise grew in volume. "Too late. Too late."

Horses reared up on their back legs at the loud commotion. They threw their mouths open in an even louder whinny.

Cinderella grasped the slipper, noticed the glare of her stepsister, and tried it on.

No, the glass slipper didn't fit Cinderella's foot.

A low hush fell over the crowd as she returned the slipper back to the Prince. The moment was quickly interrupted by another woman.

"I'm a stepsister, let me try too." A woman pranced about, flinging her green skirts to and fro.

A chorus of "So am I. I'm also a stepsister," could be heard from women scattered throughout the crowd.

"Enough. All of you, back off." The Prince ordered.

He looked up at the stepsister who towered above him and narrowed his eyes at her. "Your foot fit the slipper. You will be my Princess: however, I do not remember dancing with anyone as tall as you."

Cinderella stepped forward. "It was I who was your dancing partner. My feet are swollen today, and I cannot wear the slipper." She hung her head in obvious sorrow.

"I must stand by my word. I had said whose foot fits the slipper will be my Princess. So be it."

He motioned for the taller girl, and she hurried to stand by his side. "I will display you to all as an example of keeping my word."

He quickly turned to Cinderella, grabbed her rough hands and examined her calluses. "Your hard work has paid off, Cinderella. I will give all of my horses to you as a new business venture."

He pivoted to the crowd. "Here ye, hear ye. Be it known as of this hour; Cinderella is the owner of the magnificent, Budweiser Clydesdales."

Cinderella clapped her hands together and jumped up and down, squealing with laughter.

A loud cheer sailed forth and he reached to hold the hand of his potential Princess. He helped her into the carriage, and they drove off amid all the shouts and applause.

The End

2. Escape

Light as a feather, she took a step off the concrete walkway. Mindful of possible discovery, her eyes glanced in all directions. *Great. No one is here. I can finally do this.*

Sheer excitement dared her to walk further, her heart raced from a sudden adrenalin rush, like she hadn't experienced in years.

Gusts of wind blew a salty sea smell into her nostrils. Gulls scurried about; their loud screeches increased in volume at her approach. She threw her head back while a strong breeze overcame her. It whipped her hair about with a sudden icy chill that only the fall winds could bring.

Proud and still, she stood, absorbed in the bounty of rewards the Gulf Coast offered, until her senses filled. A few steps closer to the powerful white caps of water swirling in the sand, and her desire to return to the ocean was satisfied. Seaweed littered the area – a stringy mass of goop to avoid. Precarious, she caught her balance after a stumble on a large, hidden shell protruding from the sand. A flex of muscles and a generous arch of her back helped to loosen her old aching joints.

Startled by the intrusion of others, her body jerked. Voices floated down concrete stairs, distending a bluff onto the beach. Her ears strained, she opened her eyes wide and tried not to panic.

They're close, whoever it is. I have to hide. Can't let them find me.

A quick scan across the area did offer relief.

Hmm, yes, perfect.

In a hurry, she eased herself down onto the sand behind a cluster of enormous rocks. Weary, she remained silent.

~

"Jack, come on, let's wiggle our toes in the sand."

"It's cold out here, "he blurted. And crossed his arms over his chest.

"Adventure calls, "she yelled into the wind. Undeterred, she slipped off her shoes and skipped across the water, while waves swept over her ankles.

"We didn't even bring a towel, Sherry. You'll be a muddy mess."

"I *won't* waste our solitude here." She gave a mischievous grin.

Jack grabbed her into his arms, as he spoke in a deliberate deep voice, "frankly, Scarlett, I don't give a …*hoot*…about wasting this beach, *either.*"

"Oh Rhett, that was *not* how it went in the movie." Sherry gave her best southern accent, followed by infectious laughter.

He swung her around, laughed, and looked her right in the eye. "Alright, we can stay, but let's find someplace to sit down, out of this cold wind."

Jack whistled a merry tune while they strolled along.

"Happy?"

"Yes, my de-ah," his new southern drawl kicked in, "I bask in the exhilarated elements of our favorite rendezvous."

Sherry threw her arms up in the air, "Enough, Mr. Twain, I can't take anymore."

"Okay," he grinned. "Remember those huge rocks?"

"Do I ever."

Arm in arm they continued, until the distance between themselves and the rocks disappeared. Jack helped her sit, first, before he sprawled out. Careful to position both their backs against the natural windbreak, each stretched their legs out on the sand. Sherry leaned her head onto his shoulder, as they sat close together.

"I'm glad you insisted we make this trip, especially after the summer season is over. I treasure this privacy."

"So do I Jack. Galveston has many fond memories for me. I used to walk across the top of the sea wall when I was younger. We camped out here a lot in those days."

"Your childhood and mine are different as night and day. I think because I grew up in the north with all the ice and snow, I can't get enough of this coast." He took a deep breath of fresh air and glanced upward. Sea gulls flew in with their piercing calls, landed for a brief moment, only to fly further inland. Another flock of shorebirds, the smaller sandpipers, scattered about the edge of the water on tiny legs.

Sherry sat upright. "I've always loved being born and raised in Houston with Galveston nearby. As a child, I'd play games with my cousins on this beach. Wow, those days were full of excited activities and laughter, and noise." She paused. "Mom had sixteen brothers and sisters, and everyone was married and had kids. At least four or five of the families would spend the weekend here during good weather. We'd sing around a huge bonfire at night, while the men cooked on their portable grills. Later I was amazed when my uncles wore hip-waders and would simply walk out into the ocean, stand still and fish."

"I think it's against the law to have bonfires or camp out here, now." Jack replied.

"It is, and I noticed the signs warning not to fish off the jetties or even stand on them."

"What's the jetties?"

"See that row of boulders coming out from the shore and going straight out to sea for nearly a mile? That is just one of the jetties, and we used to climb all over them. It was not so perilous, if you watched the tide. When the tide was in, waves splash water across the top of the rocks, and the green algae that grows there, become slimy and wet. No one can move without sliding, which could prove fatal. Tides out, the wind dries the algae, and you can walk to the end of the jetties. The top surface is jagged and rough, though, you have to be careful where you step," Sherry recalled, "but the fishing and the view are so worth it."

256

"I can see why they put warning signs up." "

"My dad used to bring fresh oysters, still in their shells, home from Galveston. He would have a huge croaker sack full, and shuck them in our garage. I was about eight years old when he taught me how to eat then raw. He was sitting on a stool in the garage, shucking oysters from their shells when he first handed me one. I swallowed the whole oyster, and it came right back up completely whole. He laughed and said I had to chew it up. Later, we'd dip them in a horseradish concoction to enjoy raw with crackers, and Mom refused to join us. Times have really changed. Now, you can't make me eat oysters, they are not for me. Yes, this place brings back a lot of good memories," she jabbered.

From the other side of the rocks, a low moan clearly sounded as a majestic cold wind thrust down upon the beach.

Sherry refrained her reminiscing and froze. "Did you hear something?"

"No, only the wind."

"It was not *the wind*."

"Okay. *Miss Imagination*. It was a shipwrecked *sailor in distress,* hanging onto a plank, eighty feet out at sea, *shouting* for help."

She frowned and turned to squarely face Jack, balled her fist, and promptly hit him on his arm.

"Babe, I couldn't resist." He grabbed and kissed her, before she realized what he was going to do.

Tide began rolling in, and a massive gust of wind covered them from head to toe, with a mist of salty seawater.

"Yuck," Sherry sputtered as she stood up, and attempted to wipe her face.

Jack raised his lanky self-up and grinned at Sherry. He lightly caressed his hand across her cheek. "My, can you ever *talk*, girl." He smoothed the windblown hair back from her face and held her in his arms.

257

Disturbed by hearing a long groan, Sherry eased away. *I know what I heard but I'm not going to tell him.* "And you sure can *whistle.* What was that tune, while ago?" Sherry stood aloof.

"Two bottles of beer on the wall, two bottles of beer, take one away…"

Sherry interrupted. "I've heard of it. We did something else where I grew up, the name song."

"What in the world are you talking about? What is the *name* song?"

"Use my name, Sherry. It would go like this; Sherry, Sherry, boe berry, boe nana, fana, fo ferry-Sherry!"

"Man, what a song." Jack sighed and looked away.

"Listen to this, we'll sing it with your name," Sherry rattled on.

"No, I don't want to hear it."

"Oh, Jack. It would be fun to sing with you, come on."

He kicked sand into the air with his shoe and danced his fingers across her arm. Raising eyebrows in obvious expectation, he lightly kissed her on the forehead. "We are all alone," he mumbled into her ear.

"Stop it, Jack, big difference between animal instinct and real love. Someday I'll be married, and it *will* be special."

Jack cocked his head to the side and spoke slowly. "You are *not* loose with your affections, like the other girls I have dated."

Her response was halted by another moan. "I hear it again. Jack, something is on the other side of the rocks."

"Well, come on, let's check it out."

Sherry beat him around to the other side. "Oh," she gasped, as a head rose up, and gave her a pleading look. "Oh, Jack," Sherry whimpered, and a bark could be heard along the beach.

"What?" He said behind her.

"Jack, it's a cocker spaniel, with auburn hair, and…no collar." She gingerly picked up the dog and wrapped it in her arms.

Jack took the dog from her and circled his other arm around Sherry's waist. Distant sounds of wind chimes tingled in the breeze, and beckoned them up to the souvenir shops, nearby.

"If we hurry, we can make the ferry to Port Bolivar."

He smiled at Sherry and tightened his grip on the dog as she wagged her tail.

The End

3. Mothers Blind Date

"Don't smirk your mouth." I told my mother.

She cut her eyes and gave me a warning look. I'm divorced and forty years old, she's widowed and sixty years old.

After months of her stubbornness, and my preparations, she was going on her first date in thirty years. She was finally eager to go out.

The fact that it was an arranged date is what bothered her. A girlfriend of mine knew the man. She and I decided he and my mother would do just fine. His name is Harold and her name is Fran.

Harold was supposed to call her at five o'clock today. They were supposed to plan a dinner date, after talking on the phone. This was the plan.

Mother walked outside at a quarter to five. I stood by the phone and winked at her through the glass patio doors. I'd been teasing her and knew she had to get away from me for a while.

"You're making me nervous." She laughed.

I had been assured by my girlfriend that Harold was a gentleman. He was recently divorced and had a nice smile. He also owned a racing car. Mother and I had been discussing Harold all day.

The phone began ringing abruptly. It was straight up five o'clock.

Mother hurried in and grabbed the phone.

"Hello." Mother said a bit cautiously.

"Hello." Some man answered back quickly. "Is this Dan?"

"No, this is Fran."

"Oh well, I'm sorry." He apologized. "I was calling Dan."

"Oh well, I'm Fran." Mom was clearly disappointed as they hung up the phone.

"That was sure strange." She began telling me about the phone call, when the phone rang again.

It was my girlfriend.

Harold had just called her. He said he would have to wait until Friday evening to meet my mother. He had to leave and take his racing car to an out of state race. He wanted my girlfriend to explain that to Mom. He said it would be better to meet her at her house, on Friday evening, than over the phone.

Fine. No problem.

Mom was actually relieved. The date was still on.

I left and went home, promising not to tease her anymore about the Friday date. I was determined not to interfere. It was her life. I left her alone for a few days.

It was Friday evening when Mother finally called me.

"Aren't you coming over?" She asked rather smartly.

"Sure, I want to meet him too. I'll be there in a few minutes."

I drove over in record setting time. Walking inside, I noticed that Mom really looked great. She was simply glowing. I sat at her table and told her I was proud of her calmness.

She grinned.

We heard a car driving up, then footsteps on the sidewalk. It had to be Harold walking to the front door. We'd never seen this man before.

Mom opened the door as he approached.

"Hi!" He grinned at Mom.

"Hi!" She answered him and smiled.

"I hope you're Fran." He glanced at her and raised his eyebrows.

"Yes. Are you Harold?"

"Yes ma'am." His southern drawl came out in full force.

They both laughed, and Mom had him come inside.

That's when he handed her the flowers he had hidden behind his back.

"I wasn't expecting anything like this!" Mom's voice rose with excitement.

"Read the card!" Harold exclaimed.

Mom opened the card.

"To Dan…" Mom read it out loud and looked at him questioningly.

"Men get nervous too." Harold nodded.

They both gazed at each other and smiled.

I slipped out the back door and left them alone.

They were going to be just fine.

The End

4. Not Interested

"Cordell." A deep voice boomed.

The sound of his name bellowed through the café. Cordell turned on the swivel stool.

"What's up?" The older man continued approaching him. His bald head glistened.

"Mr. Warren." Cordell stood, and they hugged each other. The older man towered over Cordell's muscular frame.

"Look at you." Mr. Warren stepped back, cocked his head to the side, and scanned the younger man. "What's with the beard?"

"It's growing." Cordell gave a half-smile and motioned toward the stools. "Lunch is on me. Glad you could make it."

Mr. Warren nodded, opening the menu. After ordering the lunch specials, he glanced at the young man again. "Heard some talk...you divorced Ovella."

"Yes, sir."

"Hear me out. She was a flighty thing. All fluff, and all about herself. Guess you know that now."

"I know it well...and I should have trusted your judgement...not my hormones."

"Sometimes no one can tell anyone anything. They have to experience it firsthand for themselves."

"Oh, it was an experience. I did everything for her." Cordell's voice cracked. He raised his head and squinted at his older friend. Hot rays of Texas sunshine flooded the counter. "It was never enough, though." Moisture beaded on his upper lip. He drank from his glass of iced tea and cut into his chicken fried steak.

"I'm here for you, man. You may have graduated high school three years ago, but I'll always be your mentor." The older man spoke in an easygoing manner. He mixed gravy into his mashed potatoes and waved his fork at Cordell. "Tell me about it."

Cordell's shoulders slumped. He glanced at the other customers who were talking to each other. "Ovella," He paused, lowered his voice, and made eye contact with his mentor. "...couldn't cook. I'd buy something and bring it home. I heard one lie after another. She'd say she didn't feel good. I didn't know she stayed up all night and slept all day. She wouldn't wash dishes or clothes, wouldn't pick up after herself...she always had an excuse. After I washed or cleaned, she'd get out of bed and act sleepy saying she felt better. Then on weekends, she'd go out with her friends with no problem."

"Cordell, there is an old saying for your marriage."

"What?"

"That's too much buck for a little sugar."

"Hey, that's it. I tried so hard to please her...and for what? She never did anything for me."

The older man gently bit his lip. Leaning forward, he looked straight at Cordell. "Ever consider it was your will to have Ovella, and not God's will?"

"What are you talking about?"

"Had it been God's will for you to be with Ovella, she would have been a blessing, not a lesson."

"Wow. What a powerful statement, Mr. Warren."

"Same principal applies to your money, and your budget. Is it something you want, or something you need? Chances are if you overspend on something you want, you'll end up needing something important, and you can't afford it. You are either broke by then, or your credit rating is holding you back."

264

Cordell nodded.

"Hear me out, Cordell. I pray for guidance, and God's will in my life. It is as important to me as it is the choice to live a good life or an evil one. I'm glad you didn't join Ovella in her way of life."

"I appreciate you, Mr. Warren, and I intend to pray as you do."

"Wonderful. Thank the Lord, and I'm happy Ovella is behind you now. There is more to a woman than a pretty face."

"No more women for me. I'm done."

"I wouldn't go that far, Cordell."

"Nope, not interested."

"See the waitress taking drinks to the corner table? Her face glows when she talks to those people. Seems genuine, and friendly."

"Because she doesn't know anything about them. Give her time, and she'll be manipulating."

Mr. Warren flashed Cordell a wide grin. "Easy on assuming, now. They aren't all like that."

"Maybe, but I'm still not interested."

"Here she comes, behave."

"Sir, may I get you anything else? Would you care for dessert?"

"No thank you, we are done. I'll take both tickets."

She scribbled on the order pad and handed Cordell two slips of paper. "Hope you enjoyed the meal."

"It was delicious." Mr. Warren beamed.

She smiled and hurried to the other end of the counter.

"So…what did you think about the waitress while she was here?" He pivoted to face Cordell.

265

"I wondered if I'd ever find a bag of rotten potatoes gooey on her kitchen floor…"

"Shame on you."

"I found that on mine and Ovella's kitchen floor, scooted against the wall."

"Not everyone is nasty. Most are clean."

Cordell rose and veered toward the cashier. Mr. Warren followed as Cordell paid for the meal. Meandering through the crowded café, Cordell opened the exit door. The outside heat engulfed them.

"Mr. Warren, thanks for meeting me here today."

"My pleasure."

"Let's do this again, same time same place next week."

"Cordell, I'll look forward to it."

They strolled in opposite directions to their vehicles when the door of the café flew open. The waitress raced toward Cordell.

"Sir, you left your phone on the counter."

Recognizing his phone that she waved high in the air, he stopped.

"Why, thank you." He gave her his full attention noticing her warm, caring eyes. "Thank you very much."

Her skin flushed as she slipped the phone into his hand and hurried back inside.

He sprinted to his car and drove off with a glance at the café. He smiled to himself as the waitress lingered on his mind.

The End

5. For Sale

Soap suds rose from under the lid of the churning machine as clothes washed in the perm-a-press cycle. Globs of bubbles slid down the sides of the washer and on the paws of Captain LeRoy, a two-year-old Yorkshire Terrier dog. Dancing about in the slippery mess, long flowing hair clung to his body, and he quickly rolled over and over, obviously happy to enjoy the moment.

Unaware of the chaos in the laundry room, his owner, Wendi Spencer, addressed a potential buyer at her front door.

Quick to size up the woman, Wendi considered her a no-nonsense person and decided to carry the conversation toward the common ground she would claim they both shared.

"Mrs. Luvenia Bernstein, please come into my home. I'm glad you came anyway for this appointment, even though my realtor had to cancel at the last minute."

"Thank you. I didn't want to postpone the appointment."

"Well, I delight in offering my home to you. And as my realtor said, 'It has a place for everything, and everything in its place.' No doubt today's tour will demonstrate how suitable it truly can be."

A smile flashed across Mrs. Bernstein's wrinkled face. She stepped inside the somber foyer and looked at the wainscoting halfway up the walls. Her hand ran over the polished molding, and she paused to examine the detailed woodcarving. Raising her eyebrows, she merely nodded her head and held it high. "Please continue, Ms. Spencer. Lead the way."

Wendi heard a faint sound like something gurgled, and her confidence came to an abrupt halt. She stepped gingerly, and at the nearest room, held the door open for her guest.

"This is the living room. Notice double paned windows-an absolute must for weather related efficiency. The fireplace has an insert that is safe and controls the room temperature."

"I am grateful this is such a pleasant fall afternoon. May I open the metals doors of the insert and peek inside the fireplace?" Mrs. Bernstein turned to glance at Wendi as she spoke.

"Of course. Here, let me help you." Wendi forged ahead and bent down to release the doors from their locked position.

Mrs. Bernstein approached and rested her knees upon the hearth. She opened the insert doors and gazes up into the bowels of the fireplace chimney. "Not even one crack. Very impressive."

"Let me show you the kitchen, Mrs. Bernstein. I think any woman would treasure the space and storage it has."

Further down the hallway, the kitchen resembled the pride of any small restaurant, plus twice the features. Wendi drew Mrs. Bernstein's attention to the various shelves and drawers hidden from plain sight.

"Oh my! Ms. Spencer, I thought that was part of a wall, and at eye level-how handy. Just push, turn the wall, and there are the utensils. I feel like I'm in a James Bond spy movie." She chuckled and pushed the wall again in complete amazement.

"Let me assure you, Mrs. Bernstein, I have spent many an hour here in creative bliss." Wendi relaxed and quit trying to sell the house.

"Obviously a lot of thought and gadgets were planned into this room, Ms. Spencer, quite a find." She grinned at the owner.

They toyed with more items the kitchen had, each one a pleasant bonus, until Mrs. Bernstein burst out with questions.

"So, who was the genius? I have never seen anything like this. Who planned the marvelous kitchen with such skill? It is remarkable, Ms. Spencer."

"Oh, I mentioned a few ideas to the builder, and he sort of jumped in with both feet." Wendi slid onto a nearby stool at the counter, and Mrs. Bernstein grabbed one and joined her. "I would relish my time in this environment. I can't possibly imagine ever leaving."

Wendi gulped. And tried to forget the same feelings she experienced when she originally bought the property.

"Wait until you see the rest of the house, and the landscaped back lawn has a privacy fence. There are several perfect areas to enjoy nature, read, or simply unwind after a hectic day."

"Sounds inviting." Mrs. Bernstein propped her elbow on the counter and rested her chin in the cradle of her open hand. "If I may be blunt, Ms. Spencer, tell me why you want to leave? Why is it for sale?"

Wendi chuckled. "Oh, I am all thumbs at maintenance, and I do the tasks anyway. The older I get, I realize how time consuming it can be, as well as the physical strength involved."

"What about your husband?"

"There is no husband."

"I'm sorry, Ms. Spencer, but surely you can find a solution. Can't you hire someone reliable to help?"

"Not on my fixed income. When they see my house, each worker I have used goes up on the price. What about you, Mrs. Bernstein? Why are you looking to purchase a home?"

"My so-called friends."

"Ouch, that sounds like a painful situation." Wendi grimaced.

"Well, I've had the same friends for years. I keep thinking they will change, but they are self-centered and treat me as an afterthought. I never should have rented in the same apartment complex as they did. They constantly try to outdo one another. I refuse to live like that and certainly don't want to get caught up in their drama."

"Not a happy camper, then?"

"Oh, no. I only hear from them when they need my help or want to brag about something."

"What a shame, Mrs. Bernstein. An apartment should have been the ideal living arrangement. Just a thought of being able to come and go without maintenance responsibilities appeals to me."

"Oh, does it now?"

"Yes, ma'am, and please, call me Wendi."

"Very well, Wendi, and I would prefer being called Venny instead of ma'am. You know, you would miss the peace and quiet available here."

"Hmm, hadn't thought about the alternative. Might not be so promising to leave here, after all."

"Might want to reconsider, and I might be persuaded to rent a bedroom from you. Of course, I would need one with a private bathroom."

"Mrs. Bernstein...I mean Venny. I could give you kitchen and laundry privileges, and extra rooms for storage." Wendi jumped off the stool.

"Wendi, I'm sure we can work out an agreeable rent amount. I will give references, and we can have a legal contract drawn up to sign." Venny watched a lop-sided grin appear on the younger face and got off her stool. She stood erect in front of Wendi.

"That is wonderful, Venny. Would you consider a thousand a month for rent?"

"Consider it? Oh, Wendi, we have a deal!"

Venny followed Wendi to the opposite end of the hallway. As Wendi opened the door, a strong gust of wind blew over a hundred leaves into the hall, whirling the brilliant autumn shades of red, orange, and yellow high into the air.

Both women struggled for a moment at the bombardment while leaves scattered about. The wind quickly left as fast as it had arrived. Tangled leaves poked from their hair, and some were still falling to the floor. In that same instant, Captain LeRoy appeared out of nowhere and raced down the hallway towards Wendi and Venny.

A sight to behold, his wet, gooey body slid through the leaves, and he landed on top of the laces of Venny's black S. A. S. shoes.

Venny looked down at him and gasped out loud. "Well, if you aren't a hoot." She glanced from the wet animal to Wendi. "I didn't know you have a dog."

"I didn't know you could tell it is a dog!" Wendi shot an amused look at Venny, and held a wiggly Captain LeRoy with both hands, keeping him at arm's length.

"His tongue comes out so fast. Is he trying to lick us?" Venny pondered out loud.

"Yes, he is." Wendi chuckled and laughter exploded from both women.

"He looks pitiful." Venny managed to say between laughing.

"Are you still positive you want to live here?" Wendi asked Venny.

"Oh my, yes, I wouldn't want to live anywhere else." Returning the smile, she leaned toward LeRoy and accepted a lick.

The End

6. The Song That Changed Everything

Her scissors clipped across his face as she combed and studied the white, bushy eyebrows. "Be still, you big baby." Rosie shook her head at Rubin and leaned towards him.

"Handsome baby, you mean, and I've sat in this chair long enough." Rubin squirmed in an attempt to stand. Rosie lunged and playfully pushed him back.

"My, aren't you something?" He laughed.

"I think I am. I can cut hair with the best of them." She grinned and poked him in the ribs.

Rubin pulled her to himself in one swift motion and rubbed his shaggy mop of eyebrows over her cheek.

"Ewww. That's it; those wild hairs have to go!" She cut fast and hair fell over his nose, down his neck, and on the kitchen floor.

Rubin sputtered, and Rosie quickly glanced at him.

"Close your mouth, I'm nearly done." A few well-placed snips, and she finished. "There, good as new." She smiled at her husband and dusted loose hairs off of him with a hand towel.

"I can get up now?"

"Yes, you can get up now."

He stood and stretched his arms and yawned. "My show starts in five minutes. I have a surprise for you today." Rubin turned the radio on and beamed.

Rosie listened as the theme song played, 'The Golden Oldies Hour.' She poured them both a glass of iced tea, and Rubin set a deck of cards on the table.

"Your deal."

She shuffled cards and passed them out to play a game of Skip-Bo. "I am grateful the station manager lets you tape your program ahead of time. We can enjoy it together." She paused. "You go first."

He nodded and gathered his cards. The taped program began, and his voice boomed from the radio. "And a special treat for Rosie, here is a song meant for the two of us."

She increased the volume. The smooth melody and a clear, rich voice blended as the words to her favorite song, 'We've Only Just Begun' sailed out into the kitchen.

"Oh, Rubin, it's Karen and Richard Carpenter! I love hearing them sing!" She reached and squeezed his hand.

"I remembered you did. I wanted to do something special. You've been working so hard on the night shift at the hospital, lately."

"Yes, I have." Rosie sighed.

"How much longer will you be on nights?"

Rosie frowned. "They are short-handed at the E.R. with qualified surgical nurses. I might be there another month."

"Well, I don't see how you do it." Rubin patted her shoulder. "Let's finish this game." He yawned.

An hour later, Rubin went to bed, and Rosie dressed for work. She pulled her salt and pepper hair into a bun, applied lipstick, and grabbed her purse. A brisk walk in the night air invigorated her, and she hummed the tune she'd heard earlier. "And when the evening comes, we smile...yes...we've only just begun."

She arrived at the hospital and when the automatic doors swung open, she was instantly struck by the silence.

How unusual for the E.R. to be this quiet.

She put her purse in a locker and approached a co-worker, Gwendolyn.

"I can't think of anything else I'd rather do." She smiled at the older woman.

Rosie smiled back, "You know, I've been wanting a friend I had something in common with. Who would ever think it would be Rubin?"

Celeria quickly hugged and released her.

Rosie turned to face Gwendolyn. "I'll be right back."

She pivoted towards Celeria. "Let's pray about it."

Celeria nodded as they held hands together.

"Heavenly Father, guide us as we confront Rubin. We do forgive him as you forgive us. And I pray for your peace and comfort to see us through. In the precious, Holy name of Jesus Christ, we pray, Amen." Rosie smiled at her new friend.

"Amen." Celeria smiled back.

"Ready?"

"Ready."

They both grabbed their packages and walked with determination out of the hospital in silence, but more ready than even they could possibly know.

The End

7. Cattle Rustlers?

"Twila, how much longer to that Pit Bar-B-Q place?" Kathy turned to her daughter and asked as she drove through the unfamiliar, dark countryside.

"About fifteen miles to Marshall, Mom. It's called Bodacious Bar-B-Q and it's so good! My favorite though is nearby in Jefferson; Riverport Barbeque- but it's closed at night...and thanks for being the driver. This pregnancy gets me nauseous at the worse possible moments."

"No problem, dear. It was worth the drive to Karnack to hear the gospel concert at First Baptist." She smiled to herself at being the official driver in Northeast Texas for her daughter. Born and raised in New York, this entire area was all new to Kathy. She wasn't used to either the piney woods, or the wide-open spaces. Twila had met a Texan while at college. Two years ago, she married him and became Mrs. Wayne Sherman. Of course, she couldn't wait to move and claim Marshall, Texas as her new home.

"Call your dad and ask how the sick horse is he's nursing."

"Ha, that is funny. It's possible that dad, being Wayne's helper, might need more help than the horse." Twila laughed again as she referred to her dad. "I know they're both in the barn, but I can't call Dad or Wayne. I forgot to charge my cellphone."

"Mine is in my suitcase," Kathy informed her daughter. "It's hard to get in a routine when we're only here for a visit."

"That's okay, Mom, sounds like it might need charging too."

Kathy could not answer, because at that moment, they were both startled by a horrific explosion. The tremendous "Ka-Boom" was so loud, it shattered their thoughts and senses. As she fought to control the unmanageable vehicle, Kathy could hear her heartbeat penetrate into her ears. The car slid across both lanes of the road as she gave thanks to the

Lord that no other traffic was around her. The tires screeched when she turned the wheel in a desperate attempt to right the car.

"I think we've been shot!" She screamed at her daughter.

Twila held on to the seat and dashboard, while her head seemed to spin. The car continued out of control. They briefly distinguished a different sound; a cur-plunk, cur-plunk noise that had a rhythm to it.

"We had a tire blow out!" Twila screamed back at her mother, just as the car raced front-end first, straight into the woods and came to an abrupt stop.

For a few seconds, they sat still; too weary to move.

With shaky hands they unlatched their seatbelts. Kathy got out of the car and stood on limp legs that felt like Jello. She discovered her door was the only exit available. Twila's side of the car was deep in heavy brush. She reached to pull Twila across the front seat, as gentle as possible, and with Twila scooting, she managed to get her out.

They stood beside the car for a while, as they tried to inhale and exhale in a slow manner to calm down.

"Are you alright?" Kathy asked her daughter.

Twila nodded to confirm yes.

"Half of the car is stuck in knee-deep red clay and underbrush." Kathy observed out loud as she scanned the wooded area. "Thank the Lord we didn't hit a tree. Do you think you can walk back to the road?"

"Yes, I don't trust myself to talk though, I might start to cry." She gave a shaky smile.

"Then we'll stand here and cry together until we're strong enough to walk." Kathy tried to laugh, and they hugged each other.

"Okay, Miss Sunshine, lead the way." Twila grinned.

Kathy stumbled on fallen tree branches and fell as her right shoe got tangled into vines. She held her hands out to brace herself and felt the damp mixture of grimy dirt and crumbled leaves stick to her hands, and arms. It covered her clothes. Her pants tore where her knee got scrapped. Twila tugged at her mother until she got her up and brushed the matted hair away from Kathy's face.

"Oh, I'm going to be sore in the morning." Kathy groaned, as she stood erect and rubbed her knees and arms.

"You can soak in a hot tub later tonight, Mom, aromatherapy is on the way." Twila assured her.

"Great, thanks. I wish we had more on the way, though, like a car. I'd gladly flag down anything. I am so ready to get back to your house." She sighed.

"Me too. At least it's a moon-lit night." Twila jabbered, glancing around. The sound of approaching motors instantly had them walking near the road in record time.

"Wait. That sounds like motorcycles. We must hide in the woods." Kathy demanded.

"No, we need their help. Let's walk faster before they've come and gone."

Kathy ran back into the brush. "Twila, girl, you are big and pregnant. They will make fun of you. Now, get over here and hide." She demanded.

"Okay, but only for you. Mom, there are a lot of good people who ride bikes. It is the people who pull out in front of them that are dangerous. The bikers will do anything to help you if they know you have a need."

"Well, I don't want to gamble if this group happens to be the good ones or the bad ones. I've enough to worry about in case they are the drugged up, mean bikers."

Kathy and Twila remained motionless and well-hidden as twelve motorcycle riders drove by. She let her breath out as they all drove out of sight.

Exhausted, with much care in each step they took, once again they walked to the quiet road.

The silence was broken as thousands of cicadas, crickets, and tree frogs made as much noise as fast as possible, and the distant sounds of coyote's howling grew closer. A low growl emitted near her made Twila jump.

"Did you hear that?" She whispered.

"It was me; it was my stomach." Kathy admitted.

"Mother," Twila's voice had more anger in it then simply being concerned, "How long have you been on that diet?"

"The diet is okay; I am trying to eat smaller portions to shrink my stomach."

"Fair enough. Wait. Listen, do you hear that?"

A bawling sound began coming towards them from the woods. Instinct prevailed, and they ran down the road.

It followed. Bawling all the way.

Kathy glanced over her shoulder and grabbed her daughter's arm.

"It's a little calf."

Twila stopped and Kathy waited. As the calf came within her range, Twila chased it and yelled, "I don't want it to get run over."

Kathy was able to reach one of the legs as it hobbled along, bawling louder. Twila encircled her arms around the calf and both women held on. Slobber flew from its mouth, and they were drenched as the terrified animal rubbed against them trying to free itself. "Let's carry him to the car and stick him in the trunk until we can get help." Twila demanded.

They did.

He was all safe and secure until the distant howling of coyotes came closer.

"I don't do coyotes." Kathy told Twila. She shivered at the mere thought of them.

More coyotes howled at random times as they continued to approach.

Both women scooted back into the car, now with a bawling calf in the trunk.

Kathy remembered to make noise to scare off an attacker and tried the ignition. While the car wasn't going anywhere, she could play the radio, and this she did. With loud music playing and lights flashing, the gruesome coyotes remained in the shadows.

Two deputies, out on patrol, noticed the lights that flashed deep in the woods. They slowed down on Highway 43, and upon hearing the loud ruckus, stopped to investigate. As the deputies approached with caution, Kathy turned off the loud radio. Relived and thankful help had arrived, the two women crawled out of the car.

As the deputies' flashlights shown upon the dirty women, they saw that even the women's hair was entangled with dirt and leaves.

The calf bawling in the trunk didn't help matters either.

"Cattle rustling is a serious offense." One deputy told Kathy.

She assured him their intension was to help the calf and proceeded to discuss the coyotes and explained their night. He inquired whether they were alright or if they required medical assistance. She assured him that they were fine. He called a Game Warden to get the calf and got a wrecker for the car.

The other deputy asked if there was someone they could call to come and get them, or if there was some place they could take them.

"If we could call my husband and my son-in-law they'd come after us." Kathy blurted.

"Let's do it then." The first deputy smiled.

"Mother," Twila grinned, "Just think, you can go back to New York and tell them you almost got arrested for cattle rustling."

"Please, dear, that's not funny." She took a deep breath and sighed.

The End

OTHER BOOKS BY THIS AUTHOR:

The Running Forward Series:

Book One: **Sin, Secrets, and Salvation** (a powerful faith and family saga; awarded 1st place in Religious Fiction 2013 by The Texas Association of Authors.)

Book Two: **River Town** (the saga continues; awarded 1st place in religious Fiction 2014 by The Texas Association of Authors.)

Book Three: **Hidden Creek** (completes the saga; awarded 1st place in Religious Fiction 2015 by The Texas Association of Authors.)

Lillie, A Motherless Child (inspiring life of this author's mother, born in 1928 and raised during the depression in Texas with 16 siblings. Her own mother died when Lillie was a young child; awarded 1st place in Biography 2016 by The Texas Association of Authors.)

The American Neighborhood Series:

Book One: **Eyes of a Neighbor** (introduction of the main residents in the Heights: an older, historical area of Houston, Texas. Kate; a Hurricane Katrina survivor from Louisiana, also Ethan and Becky Meyers from Kansas. All residents become entangled in a murder mystery. Suspense, intrigue, inspiration and romance intertwine beginning this series.)

Book Two: **Heart of a Neighbor** (Hurricane Harvey forms in the Gulf of Mexico. Size and speed are increasing. Can Kate convince her neighbors to evacuate? Who goes? Who remains, and what happens to them? Will Richard want to know Jesus as his Savior? Heartwarming. Church family bonding.)

Book Three: **Mind of a Neighbor** (Trust builds as a few neighbors leave the disaster of Hurricane Harvey together. Faith is tested as they relocate to Kansas. Locals stir up sinister rumors that develop into unexpected trouble. Gossip abounds. Can Ethan and Kate obtain God's peace that passes all understanding? Can Kate forgive an entire town? Whose faith will remain true and who is the neighbor with the evil mind? This book concludes the series.)

forgive an entire town? Whose faith will remain true and who is the neighbor with the evil mind? This book concludes the series.)

A Word From The Publisher

When you finish a book that speaks to your heart, your response matters more than you might think. Reviews are not just feedback; they are a way to share truth, encourage the author, and help others discover what you have found.

Online stores like Amazon use reviews and ratings to decide which books to recommend. The more readers engage, the more visibility a message receives. It is not about popularity; it is about reach. Every time you leave a review, you help the Word go farther than algorithms alone ever could.

If this book encouraged you, taught you something new, or helped you draw closer to Yehovah, please consider taking a moment to share that. Your honest review, even a few simple sentences, can lead someone else to find the same truth that touched your life.

Thank you for being part of this mission to awaken hearts, strengthen faith, and point people back to the fullness of who Yeshua is. Your voice carries farther than you realize.

How to Leave a Review on Amazon

1. Go to Amazon.com and sign in.

2. Search for the book title (for example: *Tales of Texas*).

3. Click on the book cover or title to open the product page.

4. Scroll down until you see Customer Reviews.

5. Click Write a Customer Review.

6. Choose a star rating, then share a few sentences about what you learned or enjoyed.

7. Click Submit and that's it.

   It only takes a minute, but it makes a lasting impact.

Thank you for reading, for sharing, and for helping this message reach others who are searching for truth.

Thank you for being a READER!

_____